The Second Generation

Critical Perspectives on Asian Pacific Americans Series

Books in the series will educate and inform readers in the academy, in Asian American communities, and the general public regarding Asian Pacific American experiences. They examine key social, economic, psychological, cultural, and political issues. Theoretically innovative, engaging, comparative, and multidisciplinary, these books reflect the contemporary issues that are of critical importance to understanding and empowering Asian Pacific Americans.

Series Titles Include

Diana Ting Liu Wu, *Asian Pacific Americans in the Workplace* (1997)

Juanita Tamayo Lott, *Asian Americans: From Racial Category to Multiple Identities* (1997)

Jun Xing, *Asian America through the Lens: History, Representations, and Identity* (1998)

Pyong Gap Min and Rose Kim, editors, *Struggle for Ethnic Identity: Narratives by Asian American Professionals* (1999)

Wendy Ho, *In Her Mother's House: The Politics of Asian American Mother Daughter Writing* (2000)

Deborah Woo, *Glass Ceilings and Asian Americans: The New Face of Workplace Barriers* (2000)

Patricia Wong Hall and Victor M. Hwang, editors, *Anti-Asian Violence in North America: Asian American and Asian Canadian Reflections on Hate, Healing, and Resistance* (2001)

Pyong Gap Min and Jung Ha Kim, editors, *Religions in Asian America: Building Faith Communities* (2002)

Pyong Gap Min, editor, *The Second Generation: Ethnic Identity among Asian Americans* (2002)

Submission Guidelines

Prospective authors of single or coauthored books and editors of anthologies should submit a letter of introduction, the manuscript or a four- to ten-page proposal, a book outline, and a curriculum vitae to:

Critical Perspectives on Asian Pacific Americans Series
AltaMira Press
1630 North Main Street, #367
Walnut Creek, CA 94596

The Second Generation

Ethnic Identity among Asian Americans

EDITED BY

PYONG GAP MIN

ALTAMIRA
PRESS

A Division of Rowman & Littlefield Publishers, Inc.
Walnut Creek • Lanham • New York • Oxford

ALTAMIRA PRESS
A Division of Rowman & Littlefield Publishers, Inc.
1630 North Main Street, #367
Walnut Creek, CA 94596
www.altamirapress.com

Rowman & Littlefield Publishers, Inc.
4720 Boston Way
Lanham, MD 20706

12 Hid's Copse Road
Cumnor Hill, Oxford OX2 9JJ, England

British Library Cataloguing in Publication Information Available

Library of Congress Cataloging-in-Publication Data

Min, Pyong Gap, 1942–
    The second generation : ethnic identity among Asian Americans / Pyong Gap Min.
        p. cm.—(Critical perspectives on Asian Pacific Americans series)
    Includes bibliographical references (p.) and index.
    ISBN 0-7591-0175-2 (alk. paper)—ISBN 0-7591-0176-0 (pbk. : alk. paper).
        1. Asian Americans—Ethnic identity. 2. United States—Ethnic relations. I. Title. II. Series.

E184.O6 M57 2001
305.895073—dc21

2001022783

Printed in the United States of America

♾™ The paper used in this publication meets the minimum requirements of American National Standard for Information Sciences—Permanence of Paper for Printed Library Materials, ANSI/NISO Z39.48-1992.

CONTENTS

CONTENTS

ACKNOWLEDGMENTS

Russell Leong, editor of *Amerasia Journal*, agreed with me on the importance of having a special issue of the journal focusing on ethnic identity among second-generation Asian Americans, and invited me to serve as a guest coeditor for the issue. Four of the chapters in this book were selected from articles published in this special issue of *Amerasia Journal* (Spring 1999). I wish to thank Russell for giving me an opportunity to collect papers on ethnic identity among second-generation Asian Americans for that issue and for allowing me to republish four of the articles in this book. Kyeyoung Park also served as a guest coeditor for the special issue, and I would like to thank her for her input on the articles.

Three other chapters were originally published in *Identities* (chapter 1), *Ethnic and Racial Studies* (chapter 6), and *Qualitative Sociology* (chapter 8), respectively. I wish to thank each of these journals for permission to republish the articles as chapters in this book. I would also like to acknowledge that Anna Dessipiris and Michelle Legere, students at Queens College, typed and edited various chapters of this book. My thanks also go to Mitch Allen and Rosalie Robertson, editors at *AltaMira Press*, for enthusiastically supporting this book project and efficiently coordinating with me, and to Terry Fischer, production editor at Rowman & Littlefield, for expediting the book's publication.

Finally, I cannot hide my heartfelt thanks to Young Oak for spending time reviewing the galleys and for her loving support and encouragement during my research.

INTRODUCTION

Pyong Gap Min

The Asian immigration to the United States started after the California Gold Rush in 1848 when cheap labor for mining and railroad construction was needed in California and other parts of the West Coast. In the next three decades, about 225,000 Chinese immigrated to the United States, mostly to the West Coast. Yet, the Chinese Exclusion Act of 1882 ended the earlier Chinese immigration, and the ensuing rampant racial violence against Chinese workers in California pushed many of them back to China. After the Chinese were legally barred from entry into the United States, plantation and farm workers in Hawaii and California began to bring in other Asian workers. About 450,000 more Asian workers came as legal immigrants to Hawaii, California, and other West Coast states between 1882 and 1924. Although most of them were Japanese, they also included Filipinos, Koreans, and Indians. But laws passed in the early twentieth century barred the legal immigration of Asians to the United States for about forty years.

The abolition in 1943 of the Chinese Exclusion Act and other measures taken during and after World War II helped a significant number of Chinese to immigrate to the United States. Furthermore, the McCarran-Walter Act of 1952 relaxed immigration restrictions on Asians and made Asian immigrants eligible for citizenship. In addition, the U.S. government's military and political involvement in several Asian countries to contain communism in the 1950s and 1960s resulted in the immigration of many Asian women to the United States as wives of U.S. servicemen.

Nevertheless, there was no mass migration of Asians to the United States in the nineteenth and the first half of the twentieth

1

centuries, comparable to the mass migration of Europeans at the turn of the twentieth century. It was the abolition in 1965 of the forty-year-old Asian Exclusion Act that ignited a mass influx of Asian immigrants to the United States. Between 1965 and 2000, more than twenty-eight million immigrants entered the United States, with an overwhelming majority of them (more than 85 percent) hailing from non-European countries. Approximately 25 percent of the post-1965 immigrants—seven million—originated from Asian countries. They include a large number of highly educated professional immigrants in the 1960s and early 1970s, the later mainly family reunification immigrants, and approximately one million Indochina refugees. Close political, military, and economic connections between the United States and several Asian countries in the latter half of the twentieth century, along with the liberalized immigration law, have led to a mass migration of Asians to the United States.

The influx of Asian immigrants over the past three decades has expanded the Asian American population in the United States, from less than 1.5 million in 1970 to about eleven million in 2000. It has also led to its diversity; in addition to the Chinese, Japanese, and Filipino groups with sizable populations in the early twentieth century, Koreans, Indians, and Vietnamese have emerged as major Asian groups. Immigrants from Pakistan, Bangladesh, Cambodia, Laos, and Thailand are gaining recognition as new Asian groups. Immigrants of Chinese and Indian ancestries from Asian, African, and Caribbean countries have remigrated to the United States, contributing to the internal diversity within each of the two Asian ethnic groups.

While the earlier Asian immigrants were heavily concentrated in California, Hawaii, and other West Coast states, post-1965 immigrants are more widely dispersed throughout the United States. Still, approximately 40 percent of Asian Americans are concentrated in California, with more than 30 percent settled in Los Angeles and San Francisco—the two major destinations of the turn-of-the-century Asian immigrants. Yet various Asian immigrant communities have been established in New York, Chicago, Washington, Dallas, Houston, Atlanta, and other smaller cities. While Asian Americans in each of these cities have been affected by the local economy, school system, politics, culture, and other areas of life, they have also influenced the latter in the host city.

The Importance of Ethnic Identity among Second-Generation Asian Americans

Until the mid-1980s, research had exclusively focused on first-generation immigrants, with almost no attention to the second generation. However, research on the "new second generation"[1] has gained increasing momentum since the late 1980s,[2] when second-generation children of post-1965 immigrants composed a significant portion of the student body in many high schools, colleges, and universities throughout the United States. Significantly, second-generation Asian Americans have received more scholarly attention than second-generation Latinos or Caribbean blacks. As is clear from the titles of the books listed in the above note, most books on the new second generation focus on second-generation Asian Americans. This is due mainly to the fact that many 1.5-generation (defined as those children who were born in their parental countries and immigrated at early ages, usually 12 or before) and second-generation Asian American academics specialize in Asian American studies, in response to the expansion of Asian American studies programs that have mushroomed in colleges and universities since the early 1980s.[3]

School performance, socioeconomic adjustment, and ethnicity are probably the most significant topics pertaining to the experiences of the new second generation. Interestingly enough, while the mainstream sociologists fascinated with the new second generation have focused on school performance and/or socioeconomic adjustment,[4] scholars of Asian ancestry interested in second-generation Asian Americans have done research mainly on their ethnic identity. Not only most books[5] but also most articles[6] on second-generation Asian Americans have examined the ethnicity issue directly or indirectly.

This has much to do with the specialization of many second-generation Asian American academics in Asian American studies. Younger Asian American academics in Asian American studies and various social science disciplines seem to show great interest in the issue of second-generation Asian Americans' ethnic identity probably because they themselves have gone through inner conflicts over their ethnic identity.[7] Also, they may prefer the topic of ethnic identity to other topics because of their proclivity toward ethnographic research. While many

3

Asian immigrant scholars in social science use quantitative techniques for research on Asian Americans, most second-generation Asian Americans, especially women, seem to feel more comfortable with ethnographic research than with any survey research technique. Ethnographic research is ideal for examining the second generation's ethnic identity, whereas survey research is often needed for investigating their school performance or socioeconomic adaptation. In fact, all studies focusing on ethnic identity included in this book, with the exception of one coauthored by this editor, are based on ethnographic research.

As noted above, four monographs and a dozen journal articles focusing on ethnic identity among second-generation Asian Americans have been published. To date there is no book that puts together several studies of ethnic identity among second-generation Asian Americans for different ethnic groups. Such a book would be immensely helpful to many academics who conduct research on the topic. Several second-generation Asian American doctoral students have contacted me for references on ethnic identity among Asian Americans for their dissertations. Whenever they have contacted me, I have felt frustrated with my inability to single out one or a few books offering a comprehensive coverage of Asian American identity issues. In fact, this personal experience has led me to start this edited book project. This book would also be very useful to the instructors who teach various courses related to ethnic identity among Asian Americans and other minority groups. As American cities have become more and more ethnically diversified during recent years, the college courses related to immigration and ethnicity have greatly increased.

An Anthology of Eight Empirical Studies

This book intends to meet the need by putting together eight empirical studies, each of which covers Asian Americans' ethnic or pan-ethnic identity. Four of the studies (chapters 1, 2, 4, and 5) were selected from the articles included in the 1999 special issue of *Amerasia Journal*, for which I served as a co–guest editor. Three studies (chapters 6, 7, and 8) were respectively published in *Identity* (1994), *Ethnic and Racial Studies* (2000), and *Qualitative Sociol-*

ogy (1999), while the remaining one (chapter 3) is a new study prepared for this book.

Chapters 1 to 4 respectively examine ethnic identity or ethnic attachment among second-generation Filipino, Vietnamese, Indian, and Korean Americans. As such, these chapters compose the backbone of the book. Chapter 5 is unique because it looks at the Filipino American gang as the site for ethnic identity construction. As the author argues, "in the Filipino American community, gangs have played a significant role in the formation of a youth culture and provide a rare, albeit 'deviant' vehicle for ethnic identity construction."

While chapters 1 through 5 examine ethnic attachment or ethnic identity among second-generation Asian Americans for four groups—Filipino, Vietnamese, Indian, or Korean—separately, chapter 6 covers ethnic and racial identities of Asian Americans as a whole based on fifteen personal narratives. Chapter 7 discusses second-generation Chinese and Korean Americans' different notions of "Asian American" during college years based on their tape-recorded personal interviews. Although the notion of "Asian American" as a basis for affiliation and political identity is popular in the pan-Asian literature, this chapter shows that second-generation Chinese and Korean informants accepted it more as a signifier of community based on shared culture and history.

Chapter 8 differs from the previous chapters in that it focuses on ethnic and racial identities among third- and fourth-generation Chinese and Japanese Americans. I have included this chapter because it gives clues to what will happen to the children and grandchildren of today's second-generation Asian Americans. Cultural heritage has been an important source of ethnicity for second-generation Asian Americans covered in the previous chapters. By contrast, the societal perception of them as "foreigners," as different from "Americans," has been the major source of ethnicity for third- and fourth-generation Chinese and Japanese Americans in this chapter. No matter what levels of acculturation and intergenerational mobility they achieve, the children and grandchildren of today's second-generation Asian Americans may continue to encounter rejection and treatment as less-than-full American citizens. Thus, unlike multigeneration white ethnics and similar to other racial minority groups, they are likely to hold ethnic and racial identities.

Theoretical Perspectives on Ethnicity

The Primordial Perspective

The primordial perspective emphasizes premigrant, primordial ties associated with physical affinity, a common language, a common religion, and other cultural and historical commonalities as the basis of ethnicity.[8] It considers ethnicity an extension of a premodern social bond, such as kin and tribal ties, based on commonalities in physical and cultural characteristics and common historical experiences associated with the place of origin. People have a natural inclination to seek out others who share ancestry, physical affinity, language, and/or religion. This primordial bond, which is more emotional than rational, is the central element of ethnicity. Members of an ethnic group, like class-based interest groups, often participate in collective actions to protect their economic and political interests. However, ethnic collective actions differ from class-based actions in that the former "combine an interest with an effective tie."[9]

Ethnicity differs from race, class, and gender in that it is mainly characterized by cultural distinctions—language, dress, food, holidays, customs, values, and beliefs. As Richard Alba points outs, "ethnic groups generally define their uniqueness in regard to other ethnic groups largely through the medium of culture."[10] As the central component of ethnicity, language has the strongest effect on integrating members into a particular ethnic group.[11] Yet language is also the first element of the immigrant culture to disappear. In Alba's survey study conducted in the late 1980s, only 16 percent of his native-born white respondents reported that "they actively use a mother tongue, either as a language for conversation or as an ethnic garnish when speaking English."[12] Ethnic foods and holidays are much easier to maintain over generations than language. Research shows that even intermarriage does not do much to hinder the preservation of ethnic cuisine.[13]

In general, religion has stronger effects on ethnicity than any other element of the home-country culture. Religious groups can use their religion to preserve their ethnicity in two basically different ways. First, religion helps members of an immigrant/ethnic group to maintain ethnicity because regular participation in a religious congregation facilitates both ethnic social interactions and ethnic cultural retention.[14] Second, religion helps them to preserve their ethnicity because religious values and rituals are often inseparably tied to their ethnic values, customs, holidays, food, and dress.[15] Amish and Jewish groups have been more successful in retaining their cultural traditions through religion mainly because their religious values and rituals compose the core elements of their ethnic cultural traditions. The close connection between the nativity of religion and ethnic solidarity is supported by the persistence of ethno-religious conflicts and movements all over the world.[16]

There is no question that primordial ties based on a common language, religion, physical characteristics, and history associated with their home country are the major sources of their ethnicity for Asian immigrants. The question is to what extent these primordial ties contribute to ethnic identity among second-generation Asian Americans. Despite the tendency among Asian American scholars to downplay their importance,[17] I consider primordial ties, especially their parents' home country and its culture, of great significance for second-generation Asian Americans' ethnicity. Ethnic culture is important for ethnic identity among the second generation mainly because the latter have no choice but to live with it in an immigrant home in their formative years. As Sharmila Rudrappa points out in connection with the Indian immigrant family in chapter 3, the immigrant family in the United States becomes a repository of ethnic culture and provides an anchoring for minority identities.

As I have tried to clarify elsewhere,[18] contemporary immigrants, including Asian immigrants, have advantages over turn-of-the-century white immigrant groups for transmitting their ethnic culture to their children because of technology-based transnational ties and multicultural policy. Of course, members of the second generation selectively pick and choose some elements of ethnic culture and reject others, while revising many cultural elements. Nevertheless, it is impossible to deny that the culture of their parents' home country has a powerful influence on formation of their ethnic identity.

Empirical studies based on ethnographic research, including those included in this book, reveal that the parental home country and its culture have strong influence on identity formation among second-generation Asian Americans. Personal narratives by fifteen Asian American professionals analyzed in chapter 6 show that 1.5- and second-generation Asian Americans hold ethnic identity largely based on ethnic culture practiced at home in their early years as their primary identity, while many also have moderate levels of pan-Asian and Third World (person of color) identities.[19] Overall, the narratives show that their immigrant parents, with the exception of the Filipino,[20] made efforts to teach their children the home language and ethnic culture. Most of twelve 1.5- and second-generation essayists visited their parental home country at least once, while three of them spent one or more years there learning the mother tongue and ethnic culture. In fact, results of a survey of second-generation Korean adolescents conducted in New York in 1988 and 1989 presented in chapter 4 of this book show that 80 percent of the respondents visited their home country once or more and that 20 percent visited it twice or more. Few children of the turn-of-the-century immigrants from Europe are likely to have visited their parental home country. This partly supports my point made in the above paragraph that contemporary immigrants have advantages over the earlier white immigrants in transmitting their culture to their children.

The above-mentioned personal narratives also show that second-generation Asian American professionals, as expected, accept some ethnic cultural elements as positive, but challenge others. The contributors generally consider work ethic, emphasis on children's education, and respect for adults as positive elements of their ethnic culture while all female contributors are very critical of patriarchal traditions and gender stereotypes associated with their ethnic culture. Chapter 2 by Hung Thai also reveals that in young adulthood second-generation Vietnamese Americans increasingly accepted a collectivist ideology, as reflected in their family lives and coethnic friendships, as a cultural marker with which to separate themselves from non-Vietnamese people.

The Structural (Mobilizationist) Perspective

If premigrant primordial ties associated with the home country are its only sources, ethnicity will wither away with people's progressive acculturation to American society over generations. Yet African Americans still have strong racial and ethnic identities, although they have lived in the United States for several generations and have lost most of their African cultural reper-toire. Patterns of postmigrant adjustment to the host society—es-pecially levels of residential and occupational segregation and experience with prejudice and discrimination—have effects on the development of a particular group's ethnicity as well.[21] For highly acculturated multigeneration white ethnics who are ac-cepted as authentic Americans, ethnic identity is a matter of per-sonal choice to meet their psychological need to belong to a com-munity.[22] However, for members of racial minority groups in the United States, no matter how acculturated they are, ethnicity is imposed on them by societal expectations.

African Americans in particular have endured more severe forms of prejudice and discrimination than other minority groups in the United States. Their ethnic and racial identities have been generated almost entirely by structural factors—their settlement in inner-city slums, their concentration in low-paying occupations, and their experiences with racial prejudice and dis-crimination. As a result, although they have lived in the United States for many generations, African Americans have strong eth-nic and racial identities. Ronald Taylor uses the term *ethnogene-sis* to refer to African American ethnicity generated by the struc-tural conditions under which most African Americans have struggled for survival in American cities in the twentieth cen-tury.[23]

Asian immigrants in the nineteenth and early twentieth cen-turies encountered many legal barriers and racial violence.[24] Al-though Asian Americans are now treated far more favorably than they were fifty years ago, as people of color they still en-counter moderate levels of prejudice and discrimination. De-spite the prevalence of the positive image of Asian Americans,[25] many Americans still tend to view them, regardless of the level of acculturation to American society and generation, as "for-eigners" or "aliens" who cannot be fully assimilated. As dis-cussed in chapters 6 and 7, second-generation Asian Americans are often embarrassed by such remarks as "What country are you from?" or "Go back to your country."[26] Today, most third- and fourth-generation Asian Americans, like multigeneration white Americans, are thoroughly acculturated to American soci-ety, far removed from their Asian cultural heritage. Yet, as per-sonal interviews in chapter 8 reveal, these multigeneration Asian ethnics are forced to accept their ethnic and racial identities by societal expectations. The children and grandchildren of contemporary second-generation Asian Americans are likely to live in a far more multicultural and socially favorable environment than today's third- and fourth-generation Asian Americans. Nevertheless, they are expected to encounter moderate levels of rejection because of their color, which will be the major source of their ethnic and racial identities.

As shown in chapter 6 of this volume and other publications,[27] most second-generation Asian Americans, like most other second-generation Americans, accept a "hyphenated" American (such as Chinese American or Filipino American) identity as their primary identity. But they also hold a moderate level of pan-Asian identity. Structural factors are more important for pan-Asian identity than for ethnic identity. Government agencies, including Bureau of the Census, and schools tabulate Asian Americans together for administrative and statistical purposes. This racial lumping by government agencies and schools contributes to pan-Asian coalitions and solidarity. Many white and black Americans have difficulty differentiating different Asian ethnic groups, often referring to Vietnamese and Koreans as "Chinese" or "Japanese." Thus, Asian Americans have often been physically attacked by white or black Americans who mistook them for members of other Asian ethnic groups. This kind of random racial violence against Asian Americans is another source of pan-Asian unity.

Finally, the need for various Asian ethnic groups to coordinate activities to protect their common political, economic, and social service interests is another source of pan-Asian solidarity. Individual Asian ethnic groups in most American cities, with the exception of Japanese in Hawaii, are too small in number to influence even local politics. Yet, the Asian American population in many West Coast cities and in New York City is large enough to influence city politics through a pan-Asian coalition. Thus, in Monterey Park, California, and many other cities, two or more Asian ethnic groups have formed coalitions to get Asian American candidates elected for mayor or the city council.[28]

As discussed in chapter 7, pan-Asian identity and consciousness are strong especially in college campuses with a large number of Asian American students. Since minority students developed the Third World movement on some West Coast campuses in the late 1960s, college campuses have become the main arena for debates on racial equality and multiculturalism.[29] Asian American students have steadily increased in both the number and the proportion in colleges and universities during recent years, composing 20 percent or more in many prestigious private colleges and public universities. These campuses have developed a critical mass of U.S.-born Asian American students who are conscious of their common destiny as "Asian Americans" in a white-dominant society. Their contact with many Asian American students of different ethnic backgrounds and their participation in various Asian American organizations heighten their racial identity as Asian American. As a result of a continuous increase in the proportion of Asian American students and pressure from Asian American students, a number of colleges and universities have established Asian American and/or Asian area studies programs since the early 1980s. The institutionalization of Asian American and Asian studies programs, in turn, further facilitates a pan-Asian identity and solidarity among Asian American students.

The Social Construction Perspective

The social construction perspective on ethnicity considers ethnicity, not as fixed, but as fluid and dynamic, socially constructed in people's concrete social interactions with others.[30] As reviewed above, societal expectations and structural barriers have a powerful influence on the formation of ethnic and racial identities on the part of minority groups in the United States as well as in other societies. However, members of minority groups do not passively accept an ethnic label given by members of the dominant group. As social actors, they actively try to negotiate ethnic and racial identities in social interactions with others, resisting negative categorizations and presenting an identity they consider positive or advantageous to them in a particular situation. In their social interactions with whites, second-generation Jamaican college students may present themselves as Caribbean or Jamaican by emphasizing their ethnic heritage and resist the categorization of them as black.[31]

In the social construction perspective, people have multiple identities and they selectively use a particular identity in a

11

particular situation and use another one in another situation. A second-generation Muslim Indian woman is likely to emphasize her Muslim identity in her interaction with Muslims of other national backgrounds. But she may emphasize her Indian national background when she attends an Indian club meeting. As shown in chapter 4, we can list a few or several ethnic identity labels and ask the respondents to choose one of them.[32] However, because of the multiplicity of ethnic identities this kind of survey research, although useful for understanding the overall picture, can distort the complexity of ethnic identity. Ethnographic research that involves tape-recorded personal interviews is effective for capturing the multiplicity of ethnic and racial identities. It is therefore not accidental that all studies included in this book, with the exception of the one on Korean high school students in chapter 4, are based on ethnographic data (either tape-recorded personal interviews or personal narratives).

The social construction perspective also pays special attention to the changes in one's ethnic identity over time. As well documented in several chapters of this book (see chapters 1, 2, 3, and 6) and other studies, during childhood second-generation Asian Americans are under strong pressure to conform to white Americans. Second-generation Asian American children who live in a white middle-class neighborhood are likely to "try to be white" and "act white," rejecting their ethnic culture and making friends mainly with white students. During this period, they suffer from negative self-image and so-called internalized racism, the replication of racist prototypes within one's own mind. But, as they grow older (in adolescence or at least in young adulthood), they realize that they cannot dismiss their cultural and physical differences from white Americans. Thus, they increasingly accept their ethnic and racial identities, showing more interest in their ethnic culture and interacting more with their coethnic and Asian American friends. As they accept their ethnic and racial identities, they become more confident about themselves and more proud of their ethnic and racial backgrounds. To capture these changes in ethnicity over different stages of life, we need to conduct ethnographic research.

Not only structural factors discussed above, but also ethnic culture has bearing on the social construction perspective of ethnicity. But social constructionists do not consider "ethnic cultural traditions" as given, fixed, inherited, or vertically transmitted over generations. As discussed in several chapters of this book, they rather view ethnic cultural traditions or "Asian American cultural traditions" as revisions of inherited cultural traditions and inventions of new traditions in Asian immigrants' and their children's active interactions with the host society. Thus, Asian immigrants and their descendants are in the process of making ethnic and Asian American cultural traditions, and the process produces their ethnic and racial identities. As Lisa Lowe puts it: "The making of Asian American culture includes practices that are partly inherited, partly modified, as well as partly invented; Asian American culture also includes the practices that emerge in relation to the dominant representations that deny or subordinate Asian or Asian American cultures as 'others.' "[33] Since social constructionists interpret ethnic culture as created in the mediation between immigrants' and their descendants' transplanted culture and structural conditions in their host society, they do not make as clear a distinction between "primordial" and "structural" sources of ethnicity as I have done in this introduction.

Notes

1. Researchers have referred to 1.5- and second-generation children of post-1965 immigrants as the "new second generation" in comparison to the second generation of the turn-of-the-century white immigrants. See Alejandro Portes and Min Zhou, "The New Second Generation: Segmented Assimilation and Its Variants among Post-1965 Immigrant Youth," *Annals of the American Academy of Political and Social Science*, 530 (November 1993): 74–98. Strictly speaking, we should refer to U.S.-born children of immigrants as the second generation and to those children who were born in their parental countries and immigrated at early ages (usually 12 or before) as the 1.5 generation. However, researchers have used the second generation in a broad sense to include both the 1.5 and second generations. In this chapter, I also use the second generation or the new second generation to include both groups.

2. For theoretical discussions of the adaptation of the new second generation, see Herbert Gans, "Second Generation Decline: Scenarios for the Economic and Ethnic Futures of the Post-1965 American Immigrants,"

Ethnic and Racial Studies, 15 (1992): 173–92; Alejandro Portes, *The New Second Generation* (New York: Russell Sage, 1996); Portes and Zhou, "The New Second Generation." For empirical studies on the new second generation, see Margaret Gibson, *Accommodation without Assimilation: Sikh Immigrants in an American High School* (Ithaca: Cornell University Press, 1989); Stacey Lee, *Unraveling the "Model Minority Stereotype": Listening to Asian American Youth* (New York: Teachers College Press, 1996); Pyong Gap Min and Rose Kim, eds., *Struggle for Ethnic Identity: Narratives by Asian American Professionals* (Walnut Creek, Calif.: AltaMira, 1999); Carola and Marcelo M. Suárez-Orozco, *Transformations: Immigration, Family Life, and Achievement Motivation among Latino Adolescents* (Stanford: Stanford University Press, 1995); Ruben Rumbaut and Wayne Cornelius, eds., *California's Immigrant Children: Theory, Research, and Implications for Educational Policy* (San Diego: Center for U.S.-Mexican Studies, California State University, 1995); Mary Waters, *Black Identities: West Indian Immigrant Dreams and American Realities* (New York: Russell Sage, 1999); Min Zhou and Carl Bankston III, *Growing Up American: How Vietnamese Children Adapt to Life in the United States* (New York: Russell Sage, 1998).

3. According to *Directory of Asian American Studies Programs* compiled by the Asian American Studies Program at Cornell University, thirty-seven colleges and universities had Asian American studies programs in 1998. Because more universities, such as Columbia, University of Texas at Austin, and Northwestern University, have established Asian American studies programs since 1998, at least fifty higher educational institutions should have Asian American studies programs as of summer 2000. Moreover, many other colleges and universities offer one or more Asian American courses. In the 1990s, many schools on the West Coast expanded the already established Asian American programs while many schools on the East Coast and in the Midwest created new programs. The creation and expansion of Asian American programs have helped many 1.5- and second-generation Asian Americans to find academic jobs in Asian American studies.

4. See Gans, "Second Generation Decline," 173–92; Portes, *The New Second Generation*; Portes and Zhou, "The New Second Generation," 74–98; Rumbaut and Cornelius, *California's Immigrant Children: Theory, Research, and Implications for Educational Policy*.

5. Gibson, *Accommodation without Assimilation*; Lee, *Unraveling the "Model Minority Stereotype"*; Min and Kim, *Struggle for Ethnic Identity*; Zhou and Bankston, *Growing Up American*.

6. In addition to several articles included in the Spring 1999 special issue of *Amerasia Journal*, the following journal articles examine ethnic

identity among second-generation Asian Americans: Yen Le Espiritu's chapter in this book, originally published in *Identity*, 1 (1994): 249–73; Nazli Kibria, "The Construction of 'Asian American': Reflections on Intermarriage and Ethnic Identity among Second-Generation Chinese and Korean Americans," *Ethnic and Racial Studies*, 20 (1997): 523–44; the book coedited by Min and Kim, *Struggle for Ethnic Identity*, 1999; the chapter by Min and Kim, "Formation of Ethnic and Racial Identities: Narratives by Young Asian-American Professionals," originally published in *Ethnic and Racial Studies*, 23 (2000): 735–60.

7. As the title of the book suggests, most personal narratives included in *Struggle for Ethnic Identity*, edited by Min and Kim, reveal that 1.5- and second-generation Asian American professionals experienced conflicts over their ethnic and racial identities.

8. Harold Abramson, *Ethnic Diversity in Catholic America* (New York: Wiley, 1973); Milton Gordon, *Assimilation in American Life: The Role of Race, Religion, and National Origin* (New York: Oxford University Press, 1964); Andrew Greeley, *Ethnicity in the United States: A Preliminary Reconnaissance* (New York: Wiley, 1974); Harold Issacs, *Idols of the Tribe* (New York: Harper and Row, 1975); Nash Manning, *The Cauldron of Ethnicity in the Modern World* (Chicago: University of Chicago Press, 1989); Pierre L. van den Berghe, *The Ethnic Phenomenon* (New York: Elsevier, 1981).

9. Daniel Bell, "Ethnicity and Social Change," in *Ethnicity: Theory and Experience*, ed. Nathan Glazer and Daniel Moynihan (Cambridge, Mass.: Harvard University Press, 1975), 169

10. Richard Alba, *Ethnic Identity: Transformation of White America* (New Haven: Yale University Press, 1990), 76.

11. Gillian Stevens, "Nativity, Intermarriage and Mother Tongue Shift," *American Sociological Review*, 50 (1985): 74–83.

12. Alba, *Ethnic Identity*, 94. Mary Waters's interviews with third- and fourth-generation white Catholic ethnics also showed that only four out of sixty-three informants were fluent in their mother tongue. See Mary Waters, *Ethnic Options: Choosing Identities in America* (Berkeley: University of California Press, 1990), 116.

13. Alba, *Ethnic Identity*, 91.

14. Timothy Smith, "Religion and Ethnicity in America." *American Historical Review* 83 (1978): 1155–85; Stephen Warner, "The Place of the Congregation in the American Religious Configuration," in *The Congregation in American Life*, vol.2, ed. J. P. Wind and J. W. Lewis (Chicago: University of Chicago Press, 1994), 24–99.

15. Smith, "Religion and Ethnicity in America."

16. For an overview of ethnoreligious conflicts, see Milton Yinger, *Ethnicity: Source of Strength? Source of Conflict?* (Albany: SUNY Press, 1994), 270–300.

17. See Yen Le Espiritu, *Asian American Women and Men: Labor, Laws, and Love* (Thousand Oaks, Calif.: Sage, 1997); Lisa Lowe, *Immigrant Acts: On Asian American Cultural Politics* (Durham: Duke University Press, 1996).

18. Pyong Gap Min, "Contemporary Immigrants' Advantages over the Turn-of-the-Century Immigrants in Intergenerational Cultural Transmission," in *Mass Migration in the United States: Classical and Comtemporary Periods*, ed. Pyong Gap Min (Walnut Creek, Calif.: AltaMira Press, 2002). See also Douglas Massey, "The New Immigration and Ethnicity in the United States," *Population and Development Review*, 21, 631–52.

19. Min and Kim, *Struggle for Ethnic Identity*; Min and Kim "Formation of Ethnic and Racial Identities."

20. The narratives written by three 1.5- and second-generation Filipino Americans indicate that their parents did not emphasize teaching their children the ethnic language and culture. This may be due to the legacy of cultural colonization on the part of Filipino professional immigrants. Interestingly enough, Espiritu's ethnographic research in chapter 1 of this book also shows that Filipino professional immigrants did not pay great attention to teaching their children ethnic culture.

21. Leo Despres, *Ethnicity and Resource Competition in Plural Societies* (The Hague: Mouton Publishers, 1975); Susan Olzak and Joane Nagel, ed., *Competitive Ethnic Relations* (New York: Academic Press, 1986); William Yancy, Eugene Ericksen, and Richard Juliani, "Emergent Ethnicity: A Review and Reformulation," *American Sociological Review*, 76 (1976): 391–403.

22. Waters, *Ethnic Options*. See also Gans, "Second Generation Decline," 173–92.

23. Ronald Taylor, "The Black Ethnicity and Persistence of Ethnogenesis," *American Journal of Sociology*, 84 (1979): 1401–24.

24. See Sucheng Chan, *Asian Americans: An Interpretive History* (Boston: Twayne, 1991); Ronald Takaki, *Strangers from a Different Shore: A History of Asian Americans* (Boston: Little, Brown, 1989); Bill Ong Hing, *Making and Remaking Asian America through Immigration Policy, 1850–1990* (Stanford, Calif.: Stanford University Press, 1993).

25. For an extended discussion of changes from the negative to the positive image of Asian Americans, see Won Moo Hurh and Kwang Chung Kim, "The 'Success' Image of Asian Americans: Its Validity, and Its Practical and Theoretical Implications," *Ethnic and Racial Studies*, 12 (1989): 512–37.

26. See Min and Kim, *Struggle for Ethnic Identity*; Min and Kim "Formation of Ethnic and Racial Identities."

27. See Ruben Rumbaut, "The Crucible Within: Ethnic Identity, Self-

Esteem, and Segmented Assimilation among Children of Immigrants,"
International Migration Review, 28 (1994): 748–94.

28. See Yen Le Espiritu, *Asian American Panethnicity: Bridging Institutions and Identities* (Philadelphia: Temple University Press, 1992), 63–64; Leland Saito, *Race and Politics: Asian Americans, Latinos, and Whites in a Los Angeles Suburb* (Urbana,: University of Illinois Press, 1998); William Wei, *The Asian American Movement* (Philadelphia: Temple University Press, 1993), Chapter 8.

29. Russell Endo and William Wei, "On the Development of Asian American Studies," in *Reflections on Shattered Windows: Promises and Prospects for Asian American Studies*, ed. Gary Okihiro, Shirley Hune, Arthur Hansen, and John Liu (Pullman: Washington State University, 1988), 5–15; Glenn Omatsu, "The 'Four Prisons' and the Movement of Liberation: Asian American Activism from the 1960s to the 1990s," in *Contemporary Asian America: A Multidisciplinary Reader*, ed. Min Zhou and James Gatewood (New York: New York University Press, 2000), 80–112.

30. Stephen Cornell and Douglas Hartman, *Making Identities in a Changing World* (Thousand Oaks, Calif.: Sage, 1998); Ruth Frankenberg, *White Women, Race Matters: The Social Construction of Whiteness* (Minneapolis: University of Minnesota Press, 1993); Kibria, "The Construction of 'Asian American'"; Lowe, *Immigrant Acts*; Sanford Lyman and William Douglass, "Ethnicity: Strategies of Collective and Individual Impression Management," *Social Research*, 40 (1973): 344–65; Joane Nagel, "Constructing Ethnicity: Creating and Recreating Identity and Culture," *Social Problems*, 41 (1994): 152–76; Waters, *Ethnic Options*.

31. Waters, *Black Identities*, Chapter 3.

32. See Alejandro Portes and Dag McLeod, "What Shall I Call Myself?: Hispanic Identity Formation in the Second Generation," *Ethnic and Racial Studies*, 19 (1996): 523–46; Rumbaut, "The Crucible Within"

33. Lowe, *Immigrant Acts*, 65.

CHAPTER ONE

THE INTERSECTION OF RACE, ETHNICITY, AND CLASS: THE MULTIPLE IDENTITIES OF SECOND-GENERATION FILIPINOS

Yen Le Espiritu

This chapter examines the construction of identities among the children of professional immigrants from the Philippines. Since the 1960s, the Philippines has sent the largest number of occupational immigrants to the United States, the majority of whom migrated as professionals and other highly trained individuals.[1] Because of a recurring shortage of medical personnel in the United States, a large number were health practitioners.[2] Like other professional immigrants, highly trained Filipinos are dispersed among and within metropolitan regions and thus seldom form tightly knit ethnic communities.[3] For example, an analysis of the settlement patterns of Filipino professionals in midwestern metropolitan areas indicated that because of "their ability to speak English and their good educational backgrounds," these immigrants did not "settle in any particular area in such overwhelming numbers as to constitute a distinct concentration."[4] This is not to say that Filipino suburbanites are wholly isolated from other Filipinos. Although they may not live in immigrant neighborhoods, these Filipinos actively maintain social ties with friends and kin through membership in various professional and alumni organizations and through family get-togethers both in the United States and in the Philippines.

However, as I argue below, from the perspective of the second generation, these "ethnic events" are periodic, brief, and disconnected from their otherwise white-dominated environment. Given the absence of strong ethnic networks that reinforce the culture of origin on a *daily* basis, how do these children "imagine" their ethnicity, and how does their race complicate the process of ethnic construction?

Filipinos also present a theoretically interesting case because of the socialization to U.S. culture in the Philippines. Coming from a former U.S. colony, Filipinos have long been exposed to U.S. lifestyles, cultural practices, consumption patterns, so much so that before the Filipino gets to the United States "she, her body, and sensibility—has been prepared by the thoroughly Americanized culture of the homeland."[5] According to Pomeroy,[6] this colonial mentality is one of the major catalysts behind the contemporary "brain drain" of educated, highly trained Filipinos to the United States. Because these Filipinos are professionals, acculturated, and dark-skinned, their experience, and specifically that of their children, provides an interesting case study of the intersection of class, ethnicity, and race in contemporary U.S. society.

"Filipinos: Forgotten Asian Americans"[7]

Despite the long history of immigration and settlement of Filipinos in the United States and their long emergence as the second largest immigrant group to the United States as well as the second largest Asian American group, very little sound research has been published about either their history or their contemporary life.[8] As San Juan[9] maintains, the existing studies on the historical development of the Filipino community in the United States "have been sketchy, superficial, and flawed in their methodology and philosophical assumptions." Lamenting the neglect of Filipino Americans in the literature on U.S. immigration, ethnicity, and communities, others have declared that Filipinos are the "forgotten Asian Americans,"[10] that "not much is known about them,"[11] and that there is "no history. No published literature. No nothing." [12] However, most scholars and writers stop short of asking why this is the case. In a rare analysis, Campomanes argues that the institutional invisibility of the Philippines and Filipino Americans is connected to the historical amnesia of the U.S. colonization of the Philippines and to the general self-erasure of U.S. imperialism.[13] Employing a cultural perspective, Cruz further asserts that the academic neglect of Filipinos stems from the erroneous assumption that the Philippines lacks an "authentic" indigenous culture.[14] This perspective echoes Renato Rosaldo's observation that most anthropologists had ignored the Philippines because they regarded it as "too westernized" with "no culture" of its own.[15]

Moreover, the available literature on Filipinos in the United States focuses almost exclusively on the social, political, and economic adaptation of the immigrant population both in the continental United States[16] and in Hawaii.[17] In part, the paucity of research on the second-generation Filipinos reflects the small size of this population: Only 30 percent of Filipinos in the United States today are U.S. born.[18] Also, that generation—the children of the post-1965 immigrants—is still mainly composed of children and adolescents.[19] This demographic imbalance is not accidental but stems from immigration policies that were shaped historically by race and nativist movements in the United States.[20]

Race, Ethnicity, and Class in the United States

Developed to explain generational change among European immigrants, the assimilationist school predicts that with each succeeding generation, U.S. ethnic groups will improve their economic status and become progressively more similar to the "majority culture."[21] The myth of class mobility is an important component of this model. As a "melting pot," the United States promises mobility and success based on individual motivation and effort.[22] It is not that assimilation has not occurred. On the contrary, the economic success of the descendants of European immigrants has been dubbed "The Ethnic Miracle."[23] In 1980, the once large socioeconomic gaps and cultural gaps between white groups had all but disappeared; at the same time, intermarriage among white ethnic groups had increased.[24] The problem is that assimilationists ignored racial divisions—the "European–non-European distinction [that] remains a central division in this society."[25]

In the 1960s, reacting primarily to minority demands for empowerment, cultural pluralists maintained that cultural differentiation divides the U.S. populace into separate but *equivalent* "ethnic groups," each with its own history, culture, and political interests.[26] This approach had little to say about race—or more specifically, about the problem of racial inequality. The pluralist ideal of an equality of heritages ignores U.S. institutional practices that racialize and homogenize people of color as Asians, Latinos, or blacks, thus preventing them from fully identifying as unhyphenated Americans or as ethnic Americans in a pluralist society.[27] Pointing to the dangers of generalizing from the Euro-American experience, recent scholarship calls attention to "racial categorization," the process whereby a more powerful group seeks to dominate another, and, in so doing, imposes upon these people a racial categorical identity that is defined by reference to their inherent differences from or inferiority to the dominant group.[28] As Williams reminds us, "Not all individuals have equal power to fix the coordinates of self-other identity formation. Nor are individuals equally empowered to opt out of the labeling process, to become the invisible against which others' visibility is measured." [29]

For Asians in the United States, the very term "Asian American" arose out of the racist discourse that constructs Asians as a homogeneous group.[30] Seen by the dominant culture as "nonwhite" but not black, Asian Americans simultaneously are celebrated as America's "model minority" and condemned as the unwanted "Yellow Hordes."[31] While blatant exclusion of and legal discrimination against Asian Americans are largely matters of the past, Asian Americans continue to encounter many barriers that prevent them from participating fully in the economic, social, and political institutions of the United States.[32] As an example, although many Asian American groups exceed the average native white population's educational attainment,[33] their returns from education remain consistently lower than those for white Americans.[34] More important, while economic mobility enables white ethnic groups to become "unhyphenated whites,"[35] it does not lead to "the complete acceptance of Asians as Americans."[36] In an essay on Asian Americans, Rose concludes, "No matter how adaptive in values and aspirations, no matter how similar to whites in thoughts and actions, Asian Americans cannot be members of the majority."[37] Given the persistence of cultural racism and nativism in U.S. society, Asian Americans have challenged both the assimilationist and pluralist models by mobilizing at *multiple* levels to force outsiders to be more responsive to their grievances and agendas. [38]

The historical construction of race is so firmly entrenched within the structures of inequality of the United States that incoming populations are forced to "develop self-identifications, if not broader collective action, in accordance with categories and related behavior that are not of their own making."[39] Because they are dark-skinned immigrants from Asia, Filipinos, irrespective of their class status and their familiarity with U.S. culture, are defined as Asian American and face the attendant consequences of being a "nonwhite." The racialization of immigrants of color—in this case, Filipinos—ignores internal class differentiation. Class differentiation is important because members of the same immigrant population who experience different degrees of upward mobility tend to develop different common values and patterns of behavior.[40] Historically, ethnic groups that have remained on the economic margin, and thus have been more insulated from assimilating forces, have been relatively more successful at preserving their ethnic distinctiveness than those who have experienced widespread economic mobility.[41] This is so because the structural conditions of middle-class suburbia reduce ties to the original ethnic culture and increase associations with people from outside the ethnic group.[42] As a result, for the middle-class descendants of European immigrants, "symbolic ethnicity " is all that is left.[43] Abstracting ethnic symbols from the older ethnic culture, these later generation ethnic groups look for easy and intermittent ways to express their ethnic identity, for ways that do not require rigorous practice of ethnic culture or active participation in ethnic organizations.[44] But how much can we generalize from the experience of these white ethnic groups to the experiences of the largely non-European immigrants arriving since 1965? In other words, will social mobility similarly lead to symbolic ethnicity for the children of immigrants of color who live in middle-class suburbs?

Because of their racial status, ethnic origin, and class background, the children of Filipino professional immigrants provide an interesting case study of the intersection of race, ethnicity, and class in contemporary society. As people of color, they have to confront simultaneously the political pressure for assimilation *and* the racism that signals to them that they will never be accepted. On the other hand, as children of middle-class, acculturated parents, they have grown up largely without assigned roles or groups that anchor ethnicity. The majority do not live in an ethnic neighborhood, attend school with other Filipino children, or belong to Filipino organizations. Thus, like later generation white ethnic groups, their ethnic behavior is largely symbolic, characterized by a nostalgic but unacquainted allegiance to an imagined past. However, there is a crucial difference; because Filipinos are dark skinned, their ethnic/racial role is ascriptive rather than voluntary, and thus their ethnicity often is politicized rather than just a leisure-time activity. The intersection of their race, class, and ethnicity means that these Filipinos simultaneously conform to the forces of acculturation and assimilation, challenge the U.S. model of multiculturalism, and construct a distinct new culture that is not simply an extension of the "original" or of the mainstream "American" culture.

Measuring Ethnic Identity

To understand ethnicity as a multilinear and varying process, one cannot rely solely on a sample survey or a decennial census that asks individuals for their ethnic affiliation. These data reveal neither the strength nor the extent of ethnic identification. More important, while these data capture the static moment, they can conceal social process—the continuous process whereby people define and redefine their ethnic identity. In an analysis of the 1980 census data on ethnic ancestry, Lieberson and Waters concluded, "The census question and the other indicators we use to test ancestry are not designed well enough to cope with the flux and changes occurring in American ethnic processes."[45] In order to understand if, when, and why ethnic changes occur, one needs to listen to people's own interpretations, definitions, and perceptions of their ethnic experiences; in other words, one needs to collect their life histories—the "truths" of their experiences.[46]

This methodology has an obvious limitation. Because most of what is ethnic about a person may be hidden from his or her consciousness,[47] interviews only identify behavior and characteristics that the individuals perceive as ethnic but may miss the ways in which ethnicity might unconsciously affect them. In other words, "Even if interviews did not find people acknowledging any ethnicity, it might, in fact, influence their lives."[48] This is partly so because the larger society's idealized images of "ethnic" culture as primordial, static, and foreign influence how individuals talk about their culture and identity.[49] For the most part, these mass images imply that ethnicity is an import from abroad rather than a product of domestic social conditions. The Filipino Americans that I interviewed imagined their "ethnic" culture to be that of the "original" culture—the languages, folk dances, music, and history of the Philippines—rather than that which has been forged out of their relationship to the U.S. dominant society. As a consequence, in talking about their ethnicity, they may dismiss the subtle interpersonal styles, child-rearing patterns, and mindsets that exist within their family cultures. As such, "Interviewing is not necessarily conclusive regarding the total effect of ethnicity on the respondents."[50] On the other hand, because ethnicity approximates "an object of cognitive orientation" for the second and later generations,[51] it is important to understand the manner in which these individuals imagine and construct their ethnicity—the meanings they attach to their ethnic background and the degree of importance they give to these meanings.

This project came out of my conversations with Filipino American students at the University of California, San Diego, who maintained that compared to other ethnic groups, Filipino Americans have been less diligent in transmitting their culture to the next generations. Regardless of its accuracy, this perception marks the beginning of their ethnic awareness and their recognition that ethnic experiences vary across groups. To understand their actual experiences as well as their visions of being Filipino in the United States, I asked them to tell me their life stories. Some of the storytellers were students in my classes; others were people that I had met in the context of research.[52] When I first approached them, most informed me that given their limited knowledge of Filipino culture (by which they often mean the culture of the Philippines), they might not be good subjects to interview. The prefatory comment signals their awareness of the tension between their own life stories and the "expected story"[53] that they, as Americans of Filipino ancestry, should be experts on the history and culture of their parents' country. When assured that I did not expect any particular biography, most were eager to share their stories (with sessions lasting three to four hours) and were keenly interested in my "diagnosis" of their ethnic experiences. I believe that my own immigrant background—I came to the United States from Vietnam at the age of twelve—and relative youth facilitated the interviews, because these storytellers did not view me as a disinterested outsider but as a fellow Asian American who shared some of their life processes. Indeed, I did not wish to be detached and often shared with those I interviewed my own struggles with identity issues. Besides minimizing the inequalities inherent in a "researcher-subject" relationship, my self-revelations often triggered long-forgotten memories and thus prompted more storytellings.

The following accounts come from my tape-recorded interviews with Filipinos who were in their twenties and thirties at the time of my field research in the summer and fall of 1992 in San Diego County. In 1990, there were close to 96,000 Filipinos in San Diego County. Although they comprised only 4 percent of the county's general population, they constituted close to 50 percent of the Asian American population in the county. While the evidence that informs my analysis comes from conversations with a large group of Filipino professional immigrants about their children and with the children themselves, in this chapter I develop my argument through an account that concentrates on the life stories of just three second-generation Filipino Americans. I hope in this way to show how the relationship between culture and power has been played out concretely in the details of people's daily lives. My intent here is not to present a comprehensive analysis of their life histories but rather to present some key stories that highlight their struggles to rework ideologies about their place in U.S. society. These stories show the deliberate courses of action that these individuals have taken to resist the system-level constraints that have impinged on their identity.

The Ethnic Experience of Immigrant Filipino Professionals

The historical and contemporary ties between the Philippines and the United States certainly frame the immigration histories of the three Filipino American storytellers in this chapter. Responding to the preference for highly educated labor in U.S. immigration legislation, between 1966 and 1976 close to one-third of all Filipinos admitted into the United States came through the third preference as professionals and other highly trained individuals.[54] Overrepresented among those leaving were Filipino nurses, many of whom had been recruited to fill the nursing shortage in the United States, particularly in inner-city hospitals in older metropolitan areas.[55] Armando Alvarez's mother, a Philippine-trained nurse, was among those recruited by a hospital in Flint, Michigan.[56] In 1971, when Armando was five years old, his family left Cebu City for Michigan but ended up settling in Los Angeles where Armando's mother found work at a local hospital. His father was less fortunate. A civil engineer with ten years' experience, he was unemployed for the first eight months before being hired as a draftsman. When Armando's father secured an entry-level engineering position in a nearby city, the family moved to a middle-class, all-white neighborhood. This environment had a strong influence on Armando's ethnic identity, "Being in an all-white environment when I was not white has, in a lot of ways, helped to retard my own sense of myself as a Filipino."

Born in 1968 in Manila, Ruby Partido came to the United States when she was ten months old. Her parents, also of professional background, settled initially in Alameda, California, to be near family and friends. A certified public accountant with five years' experience, Ruby's mother found work as a bookkeeper for the county government. Her father, an experienced merchant marine, could not find employment in his field. He worked first as a janitor and later as a supply clerk for the county government. When Ruby was eight years old, her parents bought a home in an "all-American middle-class suburb" in Northern California. It was there that Ruby began to "lose track of my culture and dialects."

Elaine Reyes's parents left Manila for San Diego in 1970 to escape the political repression of the Marcos regime. Her mother, an experienced certified public accountant, had to accept an entry-level accounting position at a local aerospace company. Her father, a computer programmer, found a job as a data entry operator. Both were the only Filipinos in their companies at the time. When Elaine was born in 1972, her parents moved to a suburban community in North San Diego where "All the people in the popular groups at school were white and blonde."

Before discussing the ethnic identification of the children of professional immigrants, we first need to examine briefly the experiences of the professionals themselves. The immigration experiences of Armando, Ruby, and Elaine's parents mirror those of other professional immigrants that I interviewed. As a result of strict licensing procedures, hiring preferences, and racial discrimination in the labor market, many Filipino professional immigrants have found themselves underemployed or misemployed.[57] Nonetheless, after several years of toiling at various entry-level positions and "pinching pennies," the majority were able to move to middle-class suburban neighborhoods where they were the lone Filipino family. When asked why they chose to purchase a home in that particular community, the majority cited the "reputation of the school district" and other quality-of-life issues such as "It is near the coast," "It is quiet," and "It is a safe area." For the most part, these Filipinos did not factor in ethnicity when choosing a neighborhood. In fact, several mentioned that "We don't want to live in a place that is all-Filipino because the neighborhood becomes cheaper when it is saturated with just one ethnicity." Others felt that given the racial composition of the United States, an ideal neighborhood would be a multicultural, multiracial one. As one physician, the father of five children, said, "I want my children to grow up not so much in an all-Filipino neighborhood as in a diversified environment. I think they will be more successful if they are more cosmopolitan in their thoughts and in their perspectives."

Although most Filipino professionals do not live near their compatriots, they maintain social ties with other Filipinos through membership in various professional, alumni, and political associations. Although ethnic identity is highlighted in these associations, there may not be much cultural behavior that differentiates these immigrants from their professional peers. In an analysis of Filipino nurses' associations, Ong and Azores conclude, "Although these associations are based on ethnic bonds, they are nonetheless colored by their particular class interests and concerns."[58] The relative class homogeneity of these associations suggests that these professionals limit their contact largely to Filipinos of the same background. As a surgeon commented,

I have very little contact with Filipinos from other classes because of the needs of my profession. My profession occupies a lot of my time. Then whatever time I have, I give to the Pilipino Medical Association. When I get invitations for dances, picnics, or other social functions, I universally turn them down. I just don't have the time for it. Whatever time I have on the weekends, I'd rather spend with my children. (Author's interview)

As suggested by this comment, professional immigrants, due to the demands of their professions and of being parents (both of which are linked to the particular stage of their life cycle), seldom attend the many picnics, beauty pageants, and town fiestas sponsored by the various regional and provincial associations.[59] In not doing so, they forgo the very cultural and family oriented events that incorporate the second generation. Thus, in their decisions, about where to live and which organizations to join, these immigrants inadvertently provide their children with few ethnic networks and activities that reinforce the culture of origin.

The majority of professional immigrants do not teach their children any of the Filipino languages. A journalist refused to teach his children Tagalog because, "I want my children to know that they are American. I want them to learn English, to be very, very good in English. I also don't teach my children Filipino history. I don't see what's the point. The Filipinos haven't made many contributions in terms of the world. Take inventions, for instance. Filipinos are just noncreative." But most others did not teach their children Tagalog because they did not want to retard their children's academic progress. The following comment by an accountant is typical:

I did not want my children to be confused growing up with two languages. I wanted them to do well in school. I also didn't want them to speak Filipino at school because they might be mistaken for somebody who is an immigrant. And besides, where they grew up, it's an area where there's no Filipino neighbor. All of our neighbors speak English and all of their friends speak English. (Author's interview)

The low level of language maintenance among Filipino professionals is attributable partly to their economic status. For example, in a study of Hispanic ethnicity, Nelson and Tienda found "lower levels of Spanish retention among the more successful members of the community." [60] However, given the historical colonial relationship between the Philippines and the United States, Filipino linguistic assimilation is also a product of the pervasive Americanization of Filipino culture. An important legacy of this cultural colonialism is the institutionalization of English as the lingua franca. Because English is the medium of instruction in secondary and higher education in the Philippines, most Filipino immigrants speak a fair amount of English. According to the 1980 census, over 91 percent of post-1970 Filipino immigrants reported that they speak English well or very well.[61] Describing his ease with English, an editor of a community newspaper said, "I was so English-oriented that when I came to America, I was in a world that I knew all along." Because it is "natural" for them to speak English, most Filipinos feel no need to converse with their children in the Filipino language. As an accountant explained, "We don't teach the children Tagalog because we're comfortable in English also. English comes out almost automatically when we speak to them. Even the grandparents speak English."

When asked what is "Filipino" about their household, most immigrants interviewed mentioned food and family closeness. Food and family often converge at get-togethers with nearby relatives and periodic reunions with family members in other parts of the United States as well as in the Philippines. Although few Filipinos desire to retire in the Philippines, most have maintained ties with family and friends in the home country through occasional visits, telephone calls, remittances, and humanitarian contributions. In so doing, they have assumed the role of transmigrants, generating and sustaining multistranded relations that link the Philippines and the United States.[62] On the other hand, because second-generation Filipinos are not as able as their parents to draw on the knowledge of an alternative way of life or on the social ties back "home," their identities are shaped largely by the dialogue of racial domination in the United States. It is important to note that, while the family get-togethers and the trips to the Philippines allow second-generation Filipinos to experience ethnic Filipino culture, they perceive these events to be intermittent, brief, and disconnected from most of the other areas of their lives. As a result, the ethnicity of second-generation Filipinos remains largely symbolic—one that "does not need a practiced culture, even if the symbols are borrowed from it."[63]

Narratives of Conformity

Of the life stories I collected in San Diego County, in almost all cases, second-generation Filipinos contended that their ethnicity has changed in both its importance and in its content over time. Before college, most Filipino Americans saw themselves as "an average American teenager" and wanted to "assimilate, to be like the other Anglos." To these Filipinos, "assimilate" means to speak only English, to date and associate primarily with white people, and to slight the Filipino culture. As a thirty-year-old high school counselor explained:

> When I was in high school, I did a lot of things that were al-
> most anti-Filipino. I didn't hang around Filipinos. I didn't join
> Filipino organizations. I just wasn't very proud to be Filipino.
> I hung around mostly Anglos. I did a lot of Anglo things, like
> surfing, skiing, and I listened to not real Filipino-type music.
> (Author's interview)

The three storytellers in this paper trace their limited knowl-edge of Filipino culture to the lack of active cultural socializa-tion—the deliberate teaching of the language, traditions, and history of the Philippines—in the home. With some bitterness, Armando tells of the cultural void in his family:

> Not much was going on in my home. Nothing. It wasn't
> made explicit that Filipino culture is something that we
> should retain, that we should hold on to, as something that's
> valuable. There wasn't that sense that we should keep the
> language. So you don't really get taught you know. And I
> found that to be a real common experience among Filipinos
> my age. Our parents don't realize that we don't know any-
> thing about the old country: who was the first president,
> when was Independence Day, who was José Rizal.[64] Some-
> times I feel a bitter envy toward other Asian groups because
> there's a sense of culture there that I am not sure is empha-
> sized for Filipinos.

Armando attributes the lack of cultural socialization in his and other Filipino families to the influence of U.S. colonial rule on his parents' generation:

> They were raised in an environment that valued American and Western things. The Philippines has a political system, a government system based on the United States, a religion which is western; it has a language which is a hodgepodge that is heavily influenced by Western languages, and an educational system run by Americans. I've talked to a lot of Filipinos who know more about the American Civil War, about George Washington and Abraham Lincoln than they do about their own history. I've got aunts and uncles who were raised on John Wayne, Gary Cooper, and Clark Gable. Those were the heroes. So if you have that mind-set, it makes the American culture, the American perspective more important than the Filipino.

For Elaine and Ruby, the lack of cultural transmission in their homes stems from their parents' desire—for themselves and for their children—to succeed in mainstream society. According to Elaine, "I guess my parents faced a lot of discrimination when they first came here. So they felt that our culture would hold us back and that it wasn't something to be proud of. They felt that we needed to melt with everybody else, and everybody else was white." In Ruby's case, active cultural socialization seldom occurred because of her parents' busy work schedules. To pay for their suburban home and their children's private school tuition, Ruby's parents took on second jobs at a nearby coliseum selling beer and nachos to game attendees.

This is not to say that cultural socialization did not take place in these families. As discussed above, interviews only identify the "ethnic" characteristics that the respondents are aware of and may miss some traits they are unaware of or do not perceive to be ethnic. Because family cultures—manifested in subtle interpersonal styles, child rearing patterns, and mind-sets—are difficult to quantify and often difficult for the respondents to articulate, they may not "show up" in the respondents' answers. On the other hand, it is important to note that, whatever the actual content of their family cultures, all three storytellers stressed that the pressures of the larger society had the strongest influence on their ethnic identification. This attitude probably had to do with that stage of their life—the adolescent years—in which peer pressure rather than family culture was of paramount importance. For example, Armando attributed the decreasing significance of his Filipino ethnicity during his adolescent years to his largely white environment: "I think you learn very early on that being different doesn't contribute to acceptance, it just doesn't. So part of surviving is learning not to accentuate differences. Given that most of my environment was such that being Filipino wasn't salient, it just faded out in the background." Similarly, when asked if her family celebrated Filipino holidays, Ruby replied, "I am afraid not. We don't celebrate these holidays because growing up in . . ., whitewashed suburbia, we just couldn't." However, this does not mean that their world is devoid of Filipino culture. As indicated above, through family get-togethers, visits to the Filipino markets, and trips to the Philippines, the second generation does experience Filipino culture via food, cultural artifacts, family celebrations, and overheard conversations in Tagalog. However, from their perspective, these "ethnic" experiences are periodic and thus have little or no relevance to their daily life. As Armando explained:

> Being Filipino was an event; it was going to a party on the weekend with my parents and eating Filipino food; that's when I was Filipino. It was periodic and external. It wasn't internalized to the point where I could bring that with me across situations. When I was in high school, we only associated with Filipinos, mostly my parents' friends, two, three, or maybe four times a year. The rest of the year, it didn't come into play.

Although these personal narratives document on the individual level an acceptance of the given rules of U.S. society, they are important because they are part of a dialogue of domination.[65] They reveal that Filipinos, both in the United States and in the Philippines, live within and in tension with a racist system that defines white middle-class culture as the norm.[66] This system of domination coerces and entices Filipinos to "become simply a mimicry of the white American."[67] But this is not a unilinear process. For these three Filipino Americans, repeated encounters with the inequalities of a race-based social world at first puzzled and wounded them but led them ultimately to reconsider their relationship to and understanding of their assigned place in U.S. society.

Narratives of Ethnic Change

In a study of ethnicity among white people in the United States, Richard Alba concludes that for white ethnic groups, all in all, ethnic prejudice and discrimination "does not seem potent enough to do much for ethnic identities on a mass scale."[68] But this is not the case for people of color, since "a European-non-European distinction remains a central division in [U.S.] society."[69] This division—as manifested in institutional discrimination and personal prejudice—shapes not only the life outcomes but also the eventual identities of immigrants of color and their descendants.

In their narratives, Armando, Elaine, and Ruby detail the social costs of being Filipinos in the United States. Besides witnessing the economic discrimination faced by their immigrant parents, all three were teased and harassed by others for their perceived racial differences. Growing up in largely white neighborhoods, Armando was ostracized because of his racial difference:

> There was a theme in the early part of my life of people asking me questions that I couldn't quite fully answer like, "Where did you come from? I've never heard of that place." "Are you Mexican? Are you Black? Are you Chinese?" "Why do your parents speak funny?" And when I talk about it even now I get angry because, as a child, I was forced very early on to justify who I was.

Similarly, Elaine recalled being rejected by her boyfriend's parents in high school:

> I was dating this white guy in high school. His parents basically forced him to stop going out with me because I wasn't white. They didn't even know I was Filipino. They thought I was Chinese. It broke my heart. I was pissed. You know, you hear it happening to other people and you say, "Oh, I am so sorry," but when it's you, you feel like, "Goddamn it! I am really mad!" Because of that incident, I was insecure for a long time. Any white guy that was interested in me, I was like, "No, I don't want to go through that again."

Whereas Armando and Elaine experienced prejudice in largely white settings, Ruby was "the butt end of a lot of tricks and jokes" at her predominantly African American elementary school in West Oakland: "I remember being teased because I didn't look the same, ya know, being accused of being Chinese and not knowing how to talk. I still remember a lot of the pain."

Adding to the indignity of these epithets, is, of course, the fact that these names are inaccurate. In all three cases, the offenders did not refer to Armando, Elaine, or Ruby as Filipino, but rather as black, Mexican, or Chinese. While these mistakes may reflect genuine ignorance, they also are symptomatic of a society that is racialized and yet indifferent to and ignorant of the racial differences and hybridization of its peoples.[70] Ruby told of her confusion growing up in a society that ignores her ethnic background:

> In elementary school, we had to make a mask for our face and the plate was white and we only had black and white crayons to work with. I didn't know what to do. All I knew was that I wasn't black and I wasn't white. And the same thing happened when I was applying for citizenship, I was seven years old at the time. I remember this vividly because I can feel my parents' chill when I asked them, "Mom and Dad, are we Negro?" because I knew we weren't white, I knew we weren't other, so that makes us Negro. I didn't know what Negro was. I didn't. I could feel all the heads turn and my parents getting nervous. I could feel it but I couldn't understand it.

Although these childhood incidents are not catalytic, they are nevertheless key events in the ethnic experiences of these Filipino Americans, a background against which they interpret subsequent incidents and reevaluate their assigned place in U.S. society.[71]

It was not until the beginning of young adulthood that these Filipino Americans sought a return to their ethnicity—a process sparked largely by their increasing racial awareness. For Ruby, the process of ethnic awareness began in her senior year in high school when an academic counselor discouraged her from applying to the University of California. An active and above-average student, Ruby was baffled by the counselor's advice. "I remember coming home crying. My self-confidence was really low." When Ruby asked her friends about their experiences with the same counselor, she discovered that while her white friends received ample information on colleges and scholarships, her Asian friends were advised against applying to prestigious universities, even though the latter had higher grades. "It started clicking in my head. They are picking us out just because we are not white. This was the first time that I ever started getting any sense of awareness or consciousness that I am different." But Ruby did not accept the counselor's prognosis of her future. Instead, she sought out other counselors, attended college open houses, and poured over the myriad entrance requirements. Ruby recalled her joy when she found out that she had been accepted to the University of California. "I remember screaming and dancing in the street when I got the acceptance letter in the mail and I felt so good when I came up to that same counselor and said, 'Look, I am going to do well.' And that's exactly what I did."

Ruby's growing sense of racial and ethnic consciousness crystallized during her college years. She considers her involvement with the Student Affirmative Action/Economic Opportunity Program (SAA/EOP) and the Filipino American Club as catalytic. The SAA/EOP sensitized her to issues of student retention and multiculturalism and forged her identity as a student of color. "I was out there in the front line, you know, helping students of color pass classes and talk out their problems." And through the Filipino American Club, Ruby found "a cultural niche" where she "hooked up" with Filipino friends, learned about Filipino history, and performed in the Filipino dance troupe.

Institutional support also was critical in Armando's development. Because he grew up in predominantly white neighborhoods, college was the first place he was exposed to other Asian Americans. "I've never been among that many Asians before, a lot of Vietnamese, Chinese, and Koreans. That was strange in a very good sense." He recalled that college

> was one of the first places where, not just myself as a Filipino but a lot of other students, we were given permission to associate with other Asian students. There were actual clubs for us. There was even an Asian Awareness Week, you know, and Asian American classes. I think for me one of the more liberating things that I did in my development was when I took a class called Asian American Psychology.

Elaine's ethnicity became salient when she involved herself in student politics in college, fighting for the retention and recruitment of students and faculty of color. She attributes this activism to her relationship with her two roommates (a Latina and an African American) and to the general racially conscious atmosphere of her college campus:

> When I first went to college, I think I really was an assimilationist. But living with my roommates who were very active, I felt I had to get involved. One of my roommates, she was African American, I learned a lot from her about the Civil Rights movement and about racial discrimination. I think African Americans are made more painfully aware of their race than Asian Americans are. And we also had a lot of really bad race problems on campus at that time. The students of color wanted more professors of color, more women and gay and lesbian professors. So, it started causing all these problems. People started throwing food in the cafeteria and writing racist things on the walls such as, "I could have gotten this one scholarship but I wasn't black."

Thus, the ethnic consciousness of these Filipino Americans crystallized when they made the transition from living at home with their parents to being independent. This pattern is not unique to Filipino Americans. Census and survey data on later generation white ethnic groups in the 1970s and 1980s have yielded a similar finding—that the beginning of young adulthood is a time of ethnic flux.[72] This period is critical because it marks, for many people, their first exposure to and contact with people from different ethnic groups. In a study of white ethnic groups, Waters contends that it is through meeting people different from oneself—in terms of approaches of life, values, food, and personality—that one's own ethnicity becomes clearer.[73] The above narratives suggest a more complex explanation of ethnic differences, in particular the recognition that these differences lead to differential treatment. In other words, their process of ethnic awareness is intimately linked to their awareness of racial domination. Thus, the ethnic aspect of identity formation "must be understood in relation to the societal production of enduring categorical distinctions and not simply in terms of individuals adopting and 'shedding' particular manifestations of those categorical identities."[74]

This recognition of racism provides a frame of reference not only for understanding contemporary incidents, but also for reinterpreting childhood episodes. Noting that the experience of racism is cumulative, Armando revealed "My personal understanding of things in the present has allowed me to give names and labels to my experiences in the past. Before, I could only describe it as a 'weird experience.' I didn't understand why they didn't understand, why they didn't like me, why they kept calling me Jap or Gook when I am a Filipino." Echoing this sentiment, Elaine related, "When I was growing up, some of the kids used to snub me. At the time, I thought there was something wrong with me, you know, that it was because I wasn't fun to be with. But now, I realize that it was because I wasn't white."

Also, what is striking in these narratives is the critical role that supportive institutions—ethnic clubs, ethnic studies programs, affirmative action services—play in the process of ethnic identification. These institutions are important because they provide a setting for students of color to establish social ties and to discuss their common problems and experiences; in so doing, they have an opportunity to develop a racial/ethnic consciousness out of their shared history of discrimination.[75] As they come together to coordinate, plan, and participate in the activities of these organizations, they become involved in a cohesive interpersonal network. More important, these institutions are not only avenues for the caretaking of unique, static identities, but also sites for the unfolding of multiple, expanded identities, as Filipino Americans come to identify their own situation with the collective needs and interests of diverse groups. However, it is important to point out that while these institutions help young Filipinos to develop a positive sense of self in a racially conscious, hierarchical environment, they also promote certain models of the United States—including ethnic pluralism, nationalism, and racial identity of people of color—that do not challenge structural oppression in the United States and in the world.

Narratives of Ethnic Construction

Both the assimilationist and pluralist perspectives focus on the quantitative transformations of ethnic consciousness—that is, the degrees to which individuals or communities assimilate into American life or retain their community of origin ties. This conceptualization of identity—as bipolar and linear—overlooks the emergence of distinct new cultures that are qualitatively different from those of the immigrant homelands as well as from traditional American identities.[76] Settling for neither nativism nor assimilation, these Filipino Americans, in their narratives, describe the ongoing construction of ethnic identity as a process of selecting, rejecting, and redefining both "ethnic" and mainstream notions of being Filipino American.

For Elaine and Ruby, the making of Filipino American culture necessitates the rewriting of cultural traditions that, at times, are patriarchal and restrictive. An outspoken young woman, Elaine deviates from her family's notion of a traditional daughter:

> I am very outspoken and it is not something that is approved of by most Filipinos. My grandfather tells me that I am too "Americanized." I wonder what he means by that. Does he mean that I talk back to my parents too much or that I go out too much? I feel he equates being Americanized with being independent. My sister and I do a lot of things on our own. We make decisions for ourselves. I think my grandfather is really surprised by that.

Similarly, Ruby described her struggle to reconcile family expectations with individual ambition. "In graduate school, I was getting a lot of pressure from my parents to get married and have children. And I am like, 'Wait a minute. Is this what I really want?' I had a hard time identifying with my parents' demands for me as their eldest daughter." It was through her involvement with Asian American Women's Support Group that Ruby eventually learned "that it's okay to stand up to Mom and Dad and that it doesn't mean that I love them any less or that I am any less Filipino."

Also, to assert a Filipino American identity is to insist that the process of incorporation is multidimensional, and that one needs not choose between being "Filipino" and being "American." When asked about his ethnicity, Armando was adamant that "I am not Filipino and I am not American. I am both." Describing herself as "hybrid," Ruby related,

> Up through high school, I was mostly all-American white. And then in college, I started to identify with the ethnic self. It was

not until graduate school that I learned, yes, it's okay to have a little bit of both. It was then that I started resolving between my Filipino and my white selves.

Elaine gave an example of how she reconciled her "Filipino" and her "American" worlds:

> I am American because of my independence; I don't buy into the traditional Filipino way of not questioning authority. But I am also Filipino in the sense that I do recognize those positions of authority and I will not cross those boundaries. The elders, people in my family that are older than I am, I give them respect.

These narratives, then, suggest that the ongoing construction of Filipino American identity requires the breaking with not only restrictive cultural traditions but also practices of cultural domination—practices that deny the existence of a distinct Filipino American culture that is neither an extension of the "original" culture nor facsimile of mainstream "American" culture.

In their narratives, Armando, Ruby, and Elaine stress that the making of their Filipino American ethnicity involves not only cultural inheritance but also active cultural construction. Having grown up largely without assigned roles or groups that anchor ethnicity, their ethnicity becomes "something that they have to study in order to acquire 'knowledge about' it and in order to 'appreciate' it."[77] As Armando explained,

> Not being readily connected to a Filipino community, learning through books, learning through discussion, that's probably the most structured way that I can educate myself about the Filipino culture and history. This knowledge gives me a factual understanding of what it means to be a Filipino, and right now maybe that's as good as I can get at this point in my life.

For these second-generation Filipinos, ethnicity has come to approximate an "object of cognitive orientation,"[78] something that does not require a commitment to a culture that must be practiced daily. This is not to say that their ethnicity lacks meaning or that it will necessarily disappear in the near future. Cognizant of the intermittent aspects of their ethnic identity, these Filipino Americans struggle to give it substance, to move it beyond the level of symbolic ethnicity. According to Armando:

There was a time when I used to say that "I am a Filipino because I eat lumpia and pancit." It was very much at that level. There was nothing underneath, no substance. But now, I want to dig a little bit deeper. Food is important , but so is language, history, literature, and all that. Part of the history that you need to know is the history of the Philippines and the history of Filipinos in America. I think those are two different things but very related. So what are the differences? How are they important to me? How have they been affecting me? How do I trace myself through these different periods? These are questions that I am trying to answer. I believe that until you are willing to explore all these questions, you might be trivializing what it means to be a Filipino American.

Another way to combat the trivialization of ethnicity is to give it a political content. According to Elaine, "For me, being Filipino American means fighting racism and discrimination, hate crimes, anti-Asianism, and all that. It does not mean attending cultural events like the beauty pageants. You have to be politically involved." Along the same line, Ruby was adamant that

Filipinos ought to be more organized and more issue-oriented. I don't want to discount the Filipino charismatic groups or the Filipino beauty pageants committees but I would much rather see them coming together to address their social and political needs. I can feel it happening in my own generation—people in their twenties and thirties, college-educated—they are aware and are coming forth.

In sum, the immigrant and the second generation may differ among themselves not only in *degree* but also in the *nature* of their identification with ethnicity.[79] For the immigrant generation, ethnicity is deeply subjective, concrete, and cultural, born out of "common life experiences that generate similar habitual dispositions";[80] for the second generation, it is largely cognitive, intermittent, and political, forged out of their confrontation with and struggle against the dominant culture.

Another important aspect of being Filipino American is the desire to transmit to the next generation the Filipino American culture.[81] Because their own ethnicity does not include a practiced culture, these Filipino Americans have to construct for their

41

children the meaning of what it means to be Filipino. Although uncertain as to what they themselves can teach, all three want to make sure their children know more than they did about Filipino culture. As Armando stated,

> I don't know exactly in terms of the content of what I'll teach my children. But I want them to know a hell of a lot more than I did. I want them to know the language, the history. I'd like Filipino to be more than just an experience that they have at dinner. I'd like them to feel more connected with their relatives back in the Philippines, which I never got the chance to do.

Similarly, Elaine related,

> I can honestly say that when I get older and have children, I am not going to be able to cook the Filipino food or speak the language. But I hope my children can learn about Filipino culture through stories. Both my grandfathers and my uncle are very good storytellers, so they can pass along the family history and the Filipino history. I also hope that I will have enough money so that I can travel to the Philippines with my children.

These narratives suggest that for third-generation Filipinos, the cultural manifestation of their ethnicity, like those of their parents, will be largely intermittent and symbolic—though consciously maintained. One should also note that the transmission of culture is not only unidirectional—a passing of ethnic traits from parents to children—but is also multidirectional, an intergenerational transfer of inherited as well as invented cultural practices. For example, Elaine reported that her interest in and involvement with Filipino culture and history have "ethnicized" her family:

> I think my whole family considers ourselves Filipino American now. I feel good about that because ever since I went off to college, I would come home talking about all these racial issues going on at campus; now the whole family is into this Filipino American awareness. My parents have always been very aware of their ethnicity but they never talked to us about it when we were little. And now, they do.

Finally, these Filipino Americans emphasize the multiplicity and situationality of their ethnic identity, suggesting that cultural difference is always simultaneously bound up with color, gender, economics, and other distinctions.[82] In the following excerpt, Elaine affirmed that her identity is never purely and exclusively ethnic:

> When white women say stuff like, "it's race versus gender; you have to decide what you're fighting for," I feel like saying, "Excuse me! You can separate that because you're white. I wear who I am and my color defines me." And I will never trade that in. I will never say that I am a woman first and a Filipino second. It just doesn't work; I will be selling myself short. Fighting against racism, and sexism, and classism, and homophobia are all tied together and I don't know how anyone can ever separate those things.

When asked to list their closest friends, all three named individuals from a wide array of backgrounds. Armando's social network provides an example:

> My circle of friends includes like-minded individuals from various races—Latinos, African Americans, whites, and some Asian Americans—and so a lot of my identity has been shaped not strictly along racial lines but across more social political binding and bonding. So a lot of what I am doing now is to work to integrate and stretch each one of these different identities.

These interracial relationships are noteworthy because, contrary to assimilationist prediction,[83] they do not appear to dissolve, but, instead strengthen ethnicity. As Armando related, "Now I have a group of people who, despite the fact that they are not Filipino, encourage me to find out as much about my own ethnicity as I can. We all encourage each other to find out more about our own respective group." These narratives indicate that the construction of ethnic identity is a migratory process, taking place not only within but also between cultural sites.[84]

In particular, as stated earlier, the ethnicity of second-generation Filipinos is intimately linked to their racial awareness. Mindful that outsiders generally lump all Asians together, these Filipino Americans herald their common fate to build political unity with other Asian Americans. Ruby explained the importance of organizing as Asian Americans. "I really do see myself as part of the Asian American group. I think it is important that we identify as such because unless we have some umbrella group to call ourselves, we'll have no means to build a united front and to be politically effective." Although the Asian American identity is foremost, it is not solely political. In the following excerpt, Elaine described the affinity that she shares with other Asian American women:

> I think a lot of my Asian American female friends, we have a lot to relate to in terms of like family upbringing. It's kind of interesting, you know, we all had the same dating background when we were in high school. I found that a lot of the Asian American friends of mine, we don't date like white girls date. We don't sleep around like white girls do. Everyone is really mellow at dating because our parents were constraining and restrictive. Also, almost all of my Asian friends come from two-parent families, their parents are still married, and they are all professionals. And so, yeah. Those are the commonalities that we share. The most important commonality is, of course, that we are all becoming aware politically.

Studies on the racial and ethnic identity of recent black immigrants to the United States have found that they often adopt an ethnic identity based on their country of origin to distinguish themselves from racial categorization—or, more specifically, from the racial stigma of being categorized as African American, a group branded with low status by U.S. society.[85] Prior to the 1960s, Asian immigrants in the United States similarly practiced ethnic disidentification, the act of distancing oneself from other groups so as not to be mistaken for a member and suffer any negative consequences.[86] However, given the pervasiveness of pan-Asian lumping, these attempts at disidentification generally failed, thus clearing the way for the eventual emergence of pan-Asian consciousness. By the late 1960s, pan-Asianism was possible partly because of the large number of native-born, U.S.-educated political actors in the Asian American community. Since then, pan-Asianism has continued to be most salient among U.S.-born, college-educated, and politically oriented Asians.[87] The Asian American example suggests that the relationship between ethnicity and race among more recently arrived black populations will depend largely on the pervasiveness of racial lumping and on the political and racial consciousness of the second and later generations.

Conclusion

In this chapter, I examined the construction of identities among the children of highly trained professional immigrants from the Philippines. As a people of color, these second-generation Filipinos have to confront simultaneously the political pressure to assimilate and the racism that signals to them that they will never be accepted. On the other hand, as children of middle-class, acculturated parents, they have grown up largely without the presence of strong ethnic networks that reinforce their culture of origin. Thus, like later generation members of white ethnic groups, their ethnic behavior is largely symbolic and intermittent, though consciously maintained. Yet, because Filipinos are dark skinned, their ethnic/racial role is ascriptive rather than voluntary and thus their ethnicity is often politicized; it is something more than a leisure-time activity. Because of their class background, racial status, and ethnic origin, most of these Filipinos *simultaneously* conform to the forces of acculturation and assimilation, resist the dominant ideologies about their place in U.S. society, and construct a Filipino American culture that is neither an extension of the "original" culture nor a facsimile of mainstream "American" culture. As such, their experience provides an interesting case study of the intersection of race, ethnicity, and class in contemporary U.S. society.

The assimilationist school predicts that with each succeeding generation, American ethnic groups will move up the economic ladder, acculturate further, and become progressively more similar to the "majority culture." In contrast, the pluralist position posits that assimilation is *not* inevitable, noting that many immigrants and their descendants have remained as distinct national communities. While predicting opposite outcomes, both models are unilinear in that they do not allow for ethnic flux over the life course and intergenerationally: the "straight-line" assimilation model overlooks the dynamics of resistance of people of color; the pluralist model downplays the evidence of cultural Americanization—particularly among middle-class members of ethnic groups and among those from former U.S. colonies or territories. More important, because both models ignore the issue of race and thus deny the historically specific experiences of people of color, they are inadequate to address the experiences of Filipino Americans. Through the prism of the life stories presented in this paper, we can see that ethnic identification is, in fact, a more dynamic and complex social phenomenon than has been predicted by either the assimilationist or pluralist model. These narratives point to a reconstructed model of ethnic and racial identities—one that underscores multiple, simultaneous identities rather than a country divided into mutually exclusive but equivalent groups as proposed by the pluralist model.

The point of these stories and my analysis of them is not to determine the extent to which these Filipino Americans have retained their "original" culture or adopted the "American" culture. To do so would be to accept the essentialist position that identity is bipolar—that is, one gravitates toward either the pole of nativism or the pole of assimilation. Rather, my interest is in the strategies these Filipino Americans have used to construct distinct new cultures and subcultures and to rework dominant ideologies about their place in U.S. society. Stressing flux rather than continuity and multilinearity rather than unilinearity, these narratives show that ethnic identity can change in both its importance and its content over the life course and intergenerationally. They also show that the making of a Filipino American culture and identity is not done in isolation, but in dialogue with and in opposition to the racist ideologies and practices within the United States.

Each of the stories in this chapter reveals ways in which Filipino American identity has been and continues to be shaped by a colonial history and white-dominated culture. It is through recognizing how profoundly race has affected their lives that Filipino Americans forge their ethnic identity—one that challenges stereotypes, undermines practices of cultural domination, and involves inherited as well as invented cultural practices. It is in this sense that the ethnic experiences of Filipino Americans resemble those of communities of color and diverge from those of European ethnic groups. In the late twentieth century, when immigrant and ethnic communities are no longer discrete and impenetrable, and when the "minorities" rapidly become the new majority, the recognition of intergroup linkages is crucial for the development of alliances not only within but across groups.

In talking about their multiple identities in terms of race and gender, as well as ethnicity, second-generation Filipinos challenge a U.S. model of multiculturalism that divides the populace into discrete, tightly bound groups, and they resist the subordinate status the U.S. system ascribes to Filipinos and Asian Americans. At the same time, it is important to stress that to accept multiple identities as part of a U.S. racial group (e.g., Asian) or as a "racialized" U.S. ethnic group (e.g., Filipino American) is *not* to challenge the economic forces that structure power and inequality in the United States, including the category of "race" that capitalist economic structures tend to use.[88] In other words, to accept the label "Asian," to struggle to win recognition for the contributions of Filipinos to "American" culture, or to move against gender domination is *still* to accept the domination of the system of global capitalism—one that has structured the historical oppression of the Filipinos both in the Philippines and in the United States. The ethnic/racial experiences of second-generation Filipinos remind us that people of color, as actors in conditions not of their own choosing, both resist and accept the structures of class and racial domination in this country and in the world.

Notes

1. John Liu, Paul Ong, and Carolyn Rosenstein, "Dual Chain Migration: Post-1965 Filipino Immigration to the United States," *International Migration Review*, 25 (1991): 487–513.

2. David M. Reimers, *Still the Golden Door: The Third World Comes to America* (New York: Columbia University Press, 1985), 100–102.

3. Ronald Takaki, *Strangers from a Different Shore: A History of Asian Americans* (Boston: Little, Brown, 1989), 432; Alejandro Portes and Ruben G. Rumbaut, *Immigrant America: A Portrait* (Berkeley: University of California Press, 1990), 20.

4. Alvar W. Carlson, "The Settling of Recent Filipino Immigrants in Midwestern Metropolitan Areas," *Crossroads*, 1 (1983): 13–19.

5. E. San Juan Jr., "Mapping the Boundaries: The Filipino Writer in the U.S.A.," *The Journal of Ethnic Studies*, 19 (1991): 117–31.

6. William J. Pomeroy, "The Philippines: A Case History of Neo-classicism," in *Remaking Asia: Essays on the American Uses of Power*, ed. Mark Dreden (New York: Pantheon, 1974), 192.

7. This is the title of a 1983 book on Filipino American history authored by Fred Cordova, a Filipino American public historian.

8. See Elena Yu, "Filipino Migration and Community Organizations in the U.S.," *California Sociologist*, 3 (1980): 76.

9. San Juan, "Mapping the Boundaries," 120.

10. Cordova, *Filipinos: Forgotten Asian Americans*.

11. Amado Cabezas, Larry H. Shinagawa, and Gary Kawaguchi, "New Inquiries into the Socioeconomic Status of Filipino Americans in California," *Amerasia*, 13 (1986–87): 1.

12. Oscar Penaranda, Syquia Serafin, and Sam Tagatac, "An Introduction to Filipino American Literature," in *Aiiieeeee! An Anthology of Asian American Writers*, ed. Frank Chin, Jeffrey Paul Chan, Lawson Fusao Inada, and Shawn Hsu Wong (Washington, D.C.: Howard University Press, 1974), 49.

13. Oscar V. Campomanes, "The Institutional Invisibility of American Imperialism, the Philippines, and Filipino Americans." Paper presented at the 1993 Annual Meeting of the Association of Asian Studies, Los Angeles, Calif., 1993.

14. Cecil V. Cruz, "Relocating Myths: An Analysis of Two Filipino Transmigrants," (Unpublished paper, University of California, San Diego).

15. Renato Rosaldo, "Ideology, Place, and People without Culture," *Cultural Anthropology*, 3 (1988): 78.

16. Roberto V. Vallangca, *Pinoy: The First Wave* (San Francisco: Strawberry Press, 1977); Edwin B. Almirol, "Filipino Voluntary Associations: Balancing Social Pressures and Ethnic Images," *Ethnic Groups*, 2 (1978): 65–92; Yu, "Filipino Migration and Community Organizations in the U.S.," 76–102.

17. Jonathan Y. Okamura, "Beyond Adaptationism: Immigrant Filipino Ethnicity in Hawaii," *Social Process in Hawaii*, 33 (1991): 56–72; Amefil Agbayani, "Community Impacts of Migration: Recent Ilokano Migration to Hawaii," *Social Process in Hawaii*, 33 (1991): 73–90; Virgie Chattergy and Belen C. Ongteco, "Educational Needs of Filipino Immigrant Students," *Social Process in Hawaii*, 33 (1991): 142–52.

18. Susumu Awanohara, "Filipino Americans: High Growth, Low Profile," *Far Eastern Economic Review*, 7 (1991): 39–40.

19. Gans, "Second-Generation Decline," 175.

20. Chan, *Asian Americans: An Interpretive History*.

21. W. Lloyd Warner and Leo Srole, *The Social Systems of American Ethnic Groups* (New Haven, Conn.: Yale University Press, 1945), 245; Robert E. Park, *Race and Culture* (Glencoe, Ill.: Free Press, 1950).

22. Michael Omi and Howard Winant, *Racial Formation in the United States* (New York: Routledge and Kegan Paul, 1986).

23. Andrew Greeley, "The Ethnic Miracle," *Public Interest*, 45 (1976): 20–36.

24. Stanley Lieberson and Mary C. Waters, *From Many Strands: Ethnic and Racial Groups in Contemporary America* (New York: Russell Sage, 1988).

25. Lieberson and Waters, *From Many Strands*, 248.

26. Andrew Greeley, *Why Can't They Be More Like Us? America's White Ethnic Groups* (New York: Dutton, 1971); Michael Novak, *The Rise of the Unmeltable Ethnics: Politics and Culture in the Seventies* (New York: Macmillan, 1973).

27. E. San Juan Jr., *Racial Formations/Critical Transformations: Articulations of Power in Ethnic and Racial Studies in the United States* (Atlantic Highlands, N.J.: Humanities Press, 1992).

28. John H. Stanfield II, "Epistemological Considerations," in *Race and Ethnicity in Research Methods*, ed. John H. Stanfield II and Rutledge M. Dennis (Newbury Park, Calif.: Sage, 1993), 29.

29. Brackett Williams, "A Class Act: Anthropology and the Race to Nation Across Ethnic Terrain," *Annual Review of Anthropology* 18 (1989): 401–44.

30. Lisa Lowe, "Heterogeneity, Hybridity, Multiplicity: Marking Asian American Differences," *Diaspora* (Spring 1991): 30.

31. See Takaki, *Strangers from a Different Shore*, 474–84.

32. Sharon Lee, "Asian Immigration and American Race-Relations: From Exclusion to Acceptance?" *Ethnic and Racial Studies*, 12 (1989): 368–90.

33. Robert W. Gardner, Bryant Robey, and Peter Smith, "Asian Americans: Growth, Change, and Diversity," *Population Bulletin*, 40 (Indianapolis: Indiana University Press, 1985).

34. Charles Hirschman and Morrison Wong, "Trends in Socioeconomic Achievement among Immigrants and Native-Born Asian Americans," *Ethnic Groups*, 3 (1981): 495–513; Morrison G. Wong, "The Cost of Being Chinese, Japanese, and Filipino in the United States, 1960, 1970, 1976," *Pacific Sociological Review*, 25 (1982): 59–78.

35. Stanley Lieberson, "Unhyphenated Whites in the United States," *Ethnic and Racial Studies*, (1985): 159–80.

36. Lee, "Asian Immigration and American Race-Relations," 368.

37. Peter Rose, "Asian Americans: from Pariahs to Paragons," in *Clamor at the Gates: The New American Immigration,* ed. Nathan Glazer (San Francisco: IGS, 1985).

38. Espiritu, *Asian American Panethnicity*.

39. Nina Glick-Schiller, Linda Basch, and Cristina Szanton Blanc, "Transnationalism: A New Analytic Framework for Understanding Migration," *Annals of the New York Academy of Sciences*, 645 (1992): 14.

40. Micaela di Leonardo, *The Varieties of Ethnic Experience: Kinship, Class, and Gender among California Italian Americans* (Ithaca: Cornell University Press, 1984).

41. Steven Steinberg, *The Ethnic Myth: Race, Ethnicity, and Class in America* (New York: Atheneum, 1988), 261.

42. Waters, *Ethnic Options*, 5.

43. Herbert J. Gans, "Symbolic Ethnicity: The Future of Ethnic Groups and Cultures in America," *Ethnic and Racial Studies*, 2 (1979): 1–20.

44. Waters, *Ethnic Options*, 5.

45. Lieberson and Waters, *From Many Strands*, 253.

46. Personal Narratives Group, "Truths," in *Interpreting Women's Lives*, ed. Personal Narratives Group (Bloomington: Indiana University Press, 1989), 261.

47. Greeley, *Ethnicity in the United States*, 32.

48. Waters, *Ethnic Options*, 94.

49. di Leonardo, *The Varieties of Ethnic Experience*, 1984.

50. Waters, *Ethnic Options*, 94.

51. Vladimir Nahirny and Joshua Fishman, "American Immigrant Groups: Ethnic Identification and the Problems of Generations," *American Sociological Review*, 13 (1965): 323.

52. The empirical work reported here is based on a preliminary analysis of forty in-depth interviews. This is part of a larger study in progress that compares the ethnic experiences of Filipino Americans of different classes, generations, and genders.

53. For a discussion of the difference between a narrator's own plot and the expected story, see Faye Ginsburg, "Dissonance and Harmony: The Symbolic Function of Abortion in Activists' Life Stories," in *Interpreting Women's Lives: Feminist Theory and Personal Narratives*, ed. Personal Narratives Group (Bloomington: Indiana University Press, 1989), 64–66.

54. John Liu and Lucie Cheng, "Pacific Rim Development and the Duality of Post-1965 Asian Immigration to the United States," in *The New Asian Immigration in Los Angeles and Global Restructuring*, ed. Paul Ong, Edna Bonacich, and Lucie Cheng (Philadelphia: Temple University Press, 1994).

55. Paul Ong and Tania Azores, "The Migration and Incorporation of Filipino Nurses," in *The New Asian Immigration in Los Angeles and Global Restructuring*, ed. Paul Ong, Edna Bonacich, and Lucie Cheng (Philadelphia: Temple University Press, 1994).

56. To protect the privacy of these individuals, their names have been changed in this chapter.

57. Takaki, *Strangers from a Different Shore*, 43–46.

58. Ong and Azores, "The Migration and Incorporation of Filipino Nurses," 189.

59. In San Diego County, retired Navy men are the most active members of the ethnic organizations. This is partly so because at this stage in their life cycle, these men no longer have to adhere to a rigid work schedule or tend to the demands of young children.

60. Candace Nelson and Marta Tienda, "The Structuring of Hispanic Ethnicity: Historical and Contemporary Perspectives," *Ethnic and Racial Studies*, 8 (1985): 68.

61. Portes and Rumbaut, *Immigrant America: A Portrait*, 199.

62. Glick-Schiller, Basch, and Szanton Blanc, "Transnationalism: A New Analytic Framework," 3–4.

63. Gans, "Symbolic Ethnicity," 12.

64. José Rizal is the most honored patriot and martyr of the Philippines. Shot by a firing squad in 1896, Rizal has become a symbol of justice, courage, and wisdom to the Filipino people.

65. Personal Narratives Group, "Origins," in *Interpreting Womens' Lives*, ed. Personal Narratives Group (Bloomington: Indiana University Press, 1989), 8.

66. David Mura, "Strangers in the Village," in *The Graywolf Annual Five: Multi-Cultural Literacy*, ed. Rick Simonson and Scott Walker (St. Paul, Minn.: Graywolf Press, 1988), 137.

67. San Juan, "Mapping the Boundaries," 123.

68. Richard Alba, *Ethnic Identity: The Transformation of White America* (New Haven: Yale University Press, 1990), 163.

69. Lieberson and Waters, *From Many Strands*, 248.

70. Lowe, "Heterogeneity, Hybridity, Multiplicity."

71. See Philomena Essed, *Understanding Everyday Racism* (Newbury, Calif.: Sage, 1991).

72. Waters, *Ethnic Options*, 44.

73. Waters, *Ethnic Options*, 45.

74. Williams, "A Class Act," 428.

75. Espiritu, *Asian American Panethnicity*, 35–38.

76. Glenn Omatsu, "Asian Pacific Americans: in 'Motion' and 'Transition,'" *Amerasia Journal*, 18 (1992): 84.

77. Nahirny and Fishman, "American Immigrant Groups," 323.

78. Nahirny and Fishman, "American Immigrant Groups," 323.

79. Nahirny and Fishman, "American Immigrant Groups," 312.

80. Carter G. Bentley, "Ethnicity and Practice," *Comparative Studies in Society and History*, 29 (1988): 32–33.

81. It is important to note the life cycle aspect of ethnic identifications. In my interviews, I found that second-generation Filipinos were most reflective about their ethnicity when they discussed marriage and raising families. Many respondents stated that they returned to their Filipino "roots" out of a desire to transmit the Filipino "culture" to their children.

82. Lowe, "Heterogeneity, Hybridity, Multiplicity," 38.

83. Gordon, *Assimilation in American Life*; Alba, *Ethnic Identity*.

84. Lowe, "Heterogeneity, Hybridity, Multiplicity," 39.

85. Virginia R. Dominguez, "From Neighbor to Stranger: The Dilemma of Caribbean Peoples in the United States," in *Occasional Papers*, no. 5, by Antilles Research Program (New Haven: Yale University Press, 1975); Nancy Foner, "The Jamaicans: Race and Ethnicity among Migrants in New York City," in *New Immigrants in New York*, ed. Nancy Foner (New York: Columbia University Press, 1987), 131–58; Glick-Schiller and Fouron, "'Everywhere We Go We are in Danger'," 329–47.

86. David Hayano, "Ethnic Identification and Disidentification: Japanese-American Views of Chinese Americans," *Ethnic Groups*, 3 (1981): 157–71; Roger Daniels, *Asian America: Chinese and Japanese in the United States Since 1850* (Seattle: University of Washington Press, 1988), 113.

87. Espiritu, *Asian American Panethnicity*.

88. Perry Anderson, "The Origins of the Present Crisis," *New Left Review*, 23 (1964): 26–35; Glick-Schiller and Fouron, 1990, 342.

FORMATION OF ETHNIC IDENTITY AMONG SECOND-GENERATION VIETNAMESE AMERICANS

Hung Cam Thai

The new "second-generation Americans," a term technically referring to the children of contemporary immigrants, has just recently been given attention by immigration scholars. Only a few studies have looked at the subjective experiences of children of these immigrants, particularly with regard to identity issues and how the youth negotiate between "new" and "old" worlds. The future demographics of the United States will include a large percentage of children of immigrants. Among Asian American children, for example, it is estimated that over 90 percent live in a household with at least one immigrant parent. In fact, in some states such as California and Texas, children of immigrants will soon outnumber whites.[1]

This chapter examines the ways Vietnamese Americans form ethnic identity through a cultural ideology. Given the need for a wider focus on the subjective experiences of children of contemporary immigrants, this chapter attempts to join existing discussions by exploring how second-generation Vietnamese American college students and young working adults portray and interpret their experiences of growing up as children of immigrants, and for some, as immigrants themselves. Drawing on eighteen open-ended interviews, my data indicate that young adult second-generation Vietnamese Americans experienced the classic *marginal man* situation in their childhood and adolescent years, but in early adulthood, they began to shift in their cultural self-perceptions. Initially conceptualized by Park and later formalized by Stonequist, the marginal man situation is one in which "the individual who, through migration, education, marriage, or some other influence, leaves one social group or culture making a satisfactory adjustment to another finds himself on the margin of each but a member of neither."[2]

Research on contemporary immigrants has generally been structural in nature, ignoring cultural ideology and devoting more consideration to such dimensions as the labor market and educational attainment. Until recently, immigration scholars have focused on adult immigrants and the ways they cope with social and economic changes. Much of this research is organized around the straight line assimilation model, a theoretical perspective that assumes immigrants eventually abandon their ethnic culture and enter into the host society as a way of ensuring upward mobility and economic security.[3] My informants began to challenge traditional patterns of immigrant assimilation when they entered college and the workforce. Instead of continually identifying themselves with the host culture, they began to form a strong ethnic identity.

By now, many scholars have observed that the resurgence of ethnicity in the United States and around the world has challenged the assimilation model. For instance, scholars who examine the lives of children of immigrants have begun to explore how "new" ethnic minorities resist hegemonic notions of assimilation, often creating new identities and images of themselves. In my exploration, I seek to understand ways in which second-generation Vietnamese Americans experience bipolar marginality—the sense of being on the margins of two cultures—and how as young adults, they utilize cultural ideologies to help them construct, create, and recreate ethnic identity. This study adds their voices to the discussion of the new second generation, putting a new dimension to research on contemporary immigrants for at least two reasons. First, it offers a glimpse of how contemporary children of immigrants perceive their ethnic identification via relationships with family and friends and via the larger society. Second, the Vietnamese, either as refugees or as members of family reunification programs, are a unique set of immigrants because of the nature of their departures from their old world. Strictly speaking, many were not voluntary migrants and this provides an interesting angle into questions of their ethnic identification.

The Ideology of Collectivism

The Vietnamese are contemporary immigrants to the United States since few actually arrived before 1965. Since then, Vietnam has been one of the top countries to send immigrants, along with Mexico, the Philippines, China/Taiwan, and South Korea.[4] Unlike other contemporary immigrants, the Vietnamese were mostly forced out of their homeland because of political turmoil, and the majority of Vietnamese immigrants arrived in the United States after South Vietnam lost the war to the North in the mid-1970s. As a result, regardless of their economic standing prior to migration, most experienced some level of poverty and were forced to depend on government assistance upon arrival in the United States.[5] Vietnamese immigrants in the United States and elsewhere can be categorized into six different waves. The first exodus of Vietnamese immigrants who arrived as political refugees began shortly after April 30, 1975, after the South had lost the war in Vietnam.[6] The second wave, which included mostly ethnic Chinese, left in 1978 and 1979; the third wave included those who escaped by boat or overland between 1978 and 1982. The fourth and fifth waves occurred between 1983 and 1989 and after 1989 respectively; most members of these waves were asylum seekers and those who sought resettlement from refugee camps in countries such as Thailand and the Philippines. Currently, those arriving in the United States come from refugee camps abroad or as participants in family reunification programs.[7]

Different waves of Vietnamese immigrants are closely associated with social class and the urban/rural background. In general, the earlier waves came from more affluent, urban backgrounds. Since 1975, a short period of time relative to the broader picture of U.S. immigration history, over 1.2 million Vietnamese have made the United States their new homeland.[8] Of this total, over 56 percent live in California and Texas, two states in which children of immigrants will soon outnumber whites.[9] Because the Vietnamese arrived in such a large number in a relatively short period of time, their visibility in the dominant culture and their reactions to adaptations have been extensively researched by social scientists and the popular media.

Few, however, have focused on the second generation's subjective experiences as children of immigrants, as immigrants themselves, and as minorities.

Researchers have often separated the children of Vietnamese immigrants into various generations. Among the foreign born, for example, three groups are categorized by age on arrival: the "second generation," those arriving before their fifth birthdays; the 1.5 generation, those who arrived between the ages of five and twelve; and the "first generation," those arriving in adolescence.[10] For the purpose of this study, second-generation Vietnamese Americans are classified as those who were either born in the United States or those who came here before they reached the age of twelve.[11]

Vietnamese immigrants have drawn extensively on the Chinese Confucian ideology of family collectivism. The process of migration creates much uncertainty about life in their new world, with respect to both social and economic resources. In this transitional period, Vietnamese immigrants often merge resources from different relatives to support each other, including members of the extended kin group. For the Vietnamese, the ideology of family collectivism is also practiced in the realm of friendship and, as such, friends are often spoken of as family.[12]

The collectivist ideology around family carries with it several definitions. Traditional Confucian notions of collectivity place a great emphasis on hierarchical relations in terms of both age and gender. Children and younger siblings are expected to pay great respect to their elders and older siblings and women to show deference to their husbands, older brothers, parents, and parents-in-law. Despite new and often altered patterns of hierarchical relations in the family as indicated by the younger generation's desire for autonomy and adults' lack of parental control—an empirical statement that has not been widely supported by the literature—[13]this study indicates that young adult second-generation Vietnamese Americans continue to maintain a strong sense of family obligation and patchworking, especially when they reflect on childhood migration experiences and young adulthood.

For instance, adult children of Vietnamese immigrants often criticize their American peers' plans for filial care of elderly parents. In a study of adult children of Vietnamese and Korean immigrants, Karen Pyke found that many plan to help their parents financially prior to their elderly years by living with them once they get old, with the fifties commonly regarded as old. Those who wanted to maintain autonomy reported that they would live near their parents as neighbors to help in their care during their elderly years.[14] Because few Vietnamese arrived in the United States before 1965, the second generation's experience with biculturalism is a relatively new phenomenon and it is no surprise that experiences of new and old worlds with no frame of reference from earlier generations of Vietnamese immigrants often put them in situations of negotiating with their identities. I have found that the meanings and significance of family life and friendship patterns drawn from a collectivist ideology allow them to cast their own identity against and next to the dominant culture.

Ethnicity and the Social Construction Perspective

The principal theoretical perspective that guides this study is the social construction of ethnicity that conceptualizes ethnicity as a fluid, situational, volitional, and dynamic phenomenon. Through social interactions, individuals are able to define and express their identity as "ethnic actors."[15]

Two of the basic building blocks of ethnicity are identity and culture.[16] In everyday social arenas, we use culture to give meanings to our identity and we use identity to construct affiliations and boundaries with other individuals and groups. The complex interplay of identity and culture is a salient feature of the experiences of ethnicity for immigrants, especially when their marginality is highlighted by the host society. For example, in a discussion of Korean and Chinese Americans' reflections on intermarriage, Nazli Kibria observes that second-generation Asian Americans often experience a sense of "not belonging."[17] Growing up as children of immigrants, for Kibria's informants the problem of "not fitting in" was often easily recollected and acted as constant reminders of their identity as ethnic individuals. Unlike the experiences of second-generation European Americans, such as Italian Americans who eagerly invoke honorific experiences of growing up "American,"[18] Asian Americans more often than not identify themselves as being different and not fitting in with their peers, especially whites.

Thus, to a large extent, second-generation Asian Americans are in the position of the marginal man while growing up, an experience similar to those of first-generation immigrants when they are "pulled in the direction of the mainstream culture but drawn back by cultures of their own."[19] The experiences of second-generation Asian Americans are often centered around the "immigrant story," a discourse that effectively positions them as both outsiders and insiders.[20] Experiences of marginality help them understand the different layers of their identity. As young adults, reflections on these experiences allow them to see how, as children of immigrants, they were ethnic and at the same time they were on pathways into being Americans. In many ways, these reflections help them process cultural ideologies and practices that are central to their ethnic self, which later help to produce a heightened sense of ethnic continuity.

In discussing ethnicity, it is useful to look at culture and how it helps to manufacture meanings of ethnicity. When individuals engage in constructing culture, they are also in the process of building ethnic boundaries that will determine who they are and what they are. For example, Pyke argues that in their young adulthood, children of immigrants identify "differences" between themselves and their American peers by defining their beliefs in maintaining certain cultural ideologies and practices.[21] She found that as children, Vietnamese and Korean second generations fantasized about having "American" parents; but, as young adults, they switched to an Asian ethnic framework when asked about their future plans for filial care.

In my exploration of the lives of children of Vietnamese immigrants, I found the metaphor of the shopping cart to be useful in understanding how culture operates as a vehicle to shape ethnic identity:

We can think of ethnic boundary construction as determining the shape of the shopping cart (size, number of wheels, composition, etc.); ethnic culture, then, is composed of the things we put into the cart—art, music, dress, religion, norms, beliefs, symbols, myths, customs. It is important that we discard the notion that culture is simply a historical legacy; culture is not a shopping cart that comes to us already loaded with a set of historical goods. Rather, we construct culture by picking and choosing items from the shelves of the *past and the present*.[22] (emphasis added)

Norms and beliefs are mechanisms of culture that help to create our sense of ethnic identity. As we engage in relationships with those who are both close and distant to us, we might alter, negotiate, or revise our identity, including the categories of our ethnicity. I like to suggest that for second-generation Americans, intimate relationships with family and friends act as important arenas for merging both past and present experiences and ideologies, the "old" and "new" worlds. In this chapter, I illustrate how constructions of ethnic identity are processes that are interwoven in experiences of culture and identity for the new second generation, particularly Vietnamese Americans. By looking at the ways they describe their experiences of marginality as both children of immigrants and young adults, we can see how relationships with friends and family help shape processes of ethnic identity formation. In this process, we also see how they draw on and utilize cultural ideologies to help them construct and maintain boundaries from the larger society.

Methods

The analyses presented here are drawn from eighteen open-ended interviews with young adult second-generation Vietnamese Americans in the San Francisco Bay area, which is the area of the second highest concentration of Vietnamese in the United States.[23] The study was limited to young adults between the ages of eighteen and twenty-seven with an average age of twenty-two. Eight were undergraduate students (although two were part-timers), two were professional/graduate students, seven were in the workforce, and one was an unemployed recent college graduate. There was an equal number of men and women. None of the informants was married nor had children. Three were born in the United States, while the rest immigrated prior to the age of twelve with the average age of arrival being five-and-a-half-years-old. Informants were located through three organizations, a student club at two universities and a volunteer association. I created a sample for my study based on principles of theoretical sampling, a strategy in which the sociologist "may begin the research with a partial framework of local concepts, designating a few principal or gross features of the structure and processes in the situations that he [or she] will study."[24]

I wanted to get a wide variety of waves of immigration, college majors, and age. I also wanted to get a balance of females and males and those in the workforce. In general, the wide variety of year of arrival in the United States also reflects a range of social class, with those arriving earlier coming from urban, more affluent backgrounds. Although they come from homes that varied in economic standing, the sample consisted of college students or graduates—those headed toward middle- and upper-middle-class occupations. As such, we would expect the second generation in this sample to be more acculturated than individuals in the larger immigrant population. Interviews were conducted between August 1997 and May 1998 and were done in English, although most shifted to Vietnamese (often slang terms) to express or clarify certain points to me since I am fluent in the language. The interviews took the form of a life history lasting one to four hours and were mostly unstructured. I asked questions about friendship and family life in the various spheres of their lives including experiences during childhood, adolescence, and college, and at work. I conducted second interviews with eleven of the eighteen informants to get further clarifications on important issues. These latter interviews usually lasted less than one hour and most were about thirty minutes long. With their informed consent, I taped all the first interviews and later transcribed them. Most of the second interviews, except for two, were recorded only as field notes.

I read and analyzed the interviews using the strategy of the "constant comparative method of analyses," a strategy of data analysis that calls for continually "making comparisons" and "asking questions."[25] I coded the interviews with phenomena labeled and sorted into emerging themes, which were then compared to each other for generalizability. I noted categories that were exceptions, but relevant to the study, such as differences in gender. In general, as I was conducting the interviews, I probed into the possible significance of age, class, wave of immigration, and (in one case) sexual orientation, especially where I felt these factors might play a role in experiences. However, the coding of data revealed only subtle differences, and these dimensions became peripheral to my analysis of ethnic identity.

Marginality and the Formation of Ethnic Identity

My findings show that, during the childhood and adolescent periods ranging from elementary to high school, my informants experienced a heightened sense of marginalization, often having conflicting images of who they were and feeling a sense of "not belonging" to either their "old" or "new" social worlds. As children and adolescents, pressured by both outsiders and insiders to acculturate as fast and as much as possible, they attempted to blend into the dominant culture in various ways through their dress, language, and consumer patterns. In their accounts, they remembered often feeling uncomfortable, especially at "acting white," during these episodes. At the same time, they were often reminded by individuals of their own ethnicity to remain loyal to traditional cultural ideologies and practices. Many recalled being reprimanded by older relatives for being *my qua* (too Americanized), especially during adolescence when peer pressures were particularly strong.

However, when adulthood approached, my informants began to reassemble and reevaluate their own feelings about ethnicity and, at times, even nationality.[26] As they navigated through new institutional experiences such as college and work, they formed a new sense of ethnic identity. Thus, the sense of being on the margins of two cultures ended when they began to recreate their identity in early adulthood, a crucial stage resulting in a cognitive decision to selectively choose to maintain certain traditional cultural ideologies. In their everyday life, my informants have challenged U.S. mainstream cultural beliefs of individualism and in their relationships with family and friends specifically, they subscribe to a collectivist ideology. I argue that when they subscribe to a collectivist ideology in the various spheres of their lives, a formation of ethnic identity takes place.

Being the Marginal Man

Most of my informants described their childhood and adolescent years as a time often characterized by ambiguity about who
they were culturally. They spoke of "public spaces" such as
schools as areas where they were pressured into being an "American kid" and homes where parents and relatives insisted that
they should not "lose" their culture. Especially where older and
traditional relatives lived in the same household,[27] constant encouragement, and often even reprimands, were given to remind
them not to be *my qua*. Mong-Cam,[28] a twenty-two-year-old
teacher who came to the United States when she was five, described a representative experience of growing up. Like most respondents, she gave an account of how at times the marginal man
situation created tension in family life. In Mong-Cam's case, identity and marginality were also flavored with gender issues:

> I think throughout my life, thinking back now, I've always bat-
> tled with the two sides of me. Always at home, I was the Viet-
> namese daughter and sister; at school I was supposed to be like
> everyone else: I'm a student, I'm supposed to be independent
> and think for myself. But, when I'm at home, you are expected
> to act within the tradition, right. I always had problems when
> these two values conflicted. And for a while, my father and I
> didn't get along because of that, especially when my father let
> my brother do something and not me.

In general, the women I interviewed did not recall a stronger
sense of marginality, compared to the men, arising from gender hierarchy in their households. A few explained that during childhood, their parents restricted them from doing certain things, such
as walking alone late at night; at the same time, they noted these
practices were just as likely if they were Americans. For some of
the women informants like Mong-Cam, the double ambivalence
about who they were culturally often resulted from the expectations of Vietnamese parents to be traditional and the respondent's
own initial desire to acquire American values of independence and
self-sufficiency. Some explained that during childhood, particularly the teenage years, the expectations of parents and their own
personal desires became the core of intergenerational conflicts.
Hue, a twenty-two-year-old education senior who came to the
United States when she was six, gave the following account:

When I was in high school, my father was afraid that I would have a boyfriend, because in Vietnam, girls don't date, they're only "given off" to their husbands' families. I guess when my American friends started dating at the beginning of high school, I wanted a boyfriend, too. I wanted to do my own things, sort of being independent from my parents, like my American friends.

For one of my informants, sexuality was central to his identity, an identity marked by uncertainty and often depression. Loi, a twenty-year-old gay male who immigrated when he was six, spoke of how difficult it was for him to initially acknowledge his sexuality to his friends and to himself. He emphasized that the process was even more complex when he realized he had to explain it to his Vietnamese family:

It's funny, but most Asian people I know consider that being gay is an American thing, a white thing. Asian people, especially Vietnamese, don't talk about gay issues because for some reason they believe that only American people can be gays. When I was growing up and when I realized I was gay, I would never dare tell anyone in my family about my feelings and my frustrations. My mom always wanted me to have American friends when I was younger, but she always told me to not be too "Americanized"; so when I was growing up, to me, being gay was being too Americanized!

Both U.S. and foreign-born informants recalled often contradictory patterns of encouragement from their parents; for the foreign born, these contradictions were especially apparent during the early years of settlement. On the one hand, they were encouraged to make American friends in order to learn the language and culture rapidly;[29] but on the other, making too many American friends meant that they were trying to lose their *nguon* (roots). Minh, a twenty-three-year-old computer sales agent who came here in 1975 right after the war, says that these double insistences often left him unsure of what his parents wanted him to be and as a result produced identity conflicts:

In middle school, I saw myself as the all-American kid when I was out in the neighborhood playing football and chasing people with our bicycles and doing your typical suburban American things. And my parents at first wanted me and my brothers to hang out with the white kids a lot. When we were beginning to use English in the house more than Vietnamese, both of my parents, especially my mom, became scared and set aside special hours for us to learn Vietnamese. They also took us to these Vietnamese cultural centers almost every weekend at one point so that we could meet other Vietnamese kids and do Vietnamese things. So then I had weekend Vietnamese friends and weekday American friends.

Some informants asserted that marginality led to undesirable impressions of both cultures. They spoke of being different or "unequal" to American and Vietnamese peers. Oanh, a twenty-two-year-old U.S.-born law student, interpreted the constraints of her bicultural experiences:

There were times when I just wanted to say I didn't belong to both and others where I wanted to see myself as equal to everyone (in both cultures). [What do you mean by equal?] The kids I hung out with at school were white, but I didn't have many of the things they had because my parents didn't know about it. You know, like the nice trendy clothes and everything. At home, when I met other Vietnamese kids who were FOBs [Fresh Off the Boat] I felt like I was such a foreigner to them. I mean, you know, I didn't know how to behave like they did to the adults and the way I spoke was different. I hated feeling different.

Acting and Being White

The second-generation Vietnamese Americans I interviewed spoke of trying to "act" or "be" white during the early stages of their lives in the United States. Embedded in their everyday life as children of immigrants was a belief that being "American" was equivalent to being white. As one of my informants, Nam, a twenty-four-year-old graduate psychology student, exclaimed, "I mean, all the prom kings and queens year after year were white. All the leaders in the school were white and so you knew that if you act or behave like one of them, you, too, could be those things or at least be one of their friends!"[30] Trung, a twenty-seven-year-old human resource manager, who came here at age eight, explained, before he moved to California to work, how he saw himself as a white person. He noted later in the interview how working in California has made him much more "culturally aware" of his Vietnamese identity:[31]

> Before coming out here to work, I didn't have any Vietnamese friends, although at home my mom made sure I didn't lose the language. Most of the friends I had in high school and college were white and so I always saw myself as one of them. Although I don't think I was like a token minority to those friends, not really, there were times when I clearly made a big effort to be white, you know, with my posture, the ways I talked, the clothes I wore and things like that. [What did being white mean to you?] I don't know, American I guess. I mean all the cool guys, the jocks, were white at my school, they were tall and they wore nice clothes . . . they were Americans.

Similarly, Huong, a twenty-five-year-old sales clerk who immigrated here at the age of three, explained how she saw herself as being white even though there were quite a large number of Asian students at her high school:

> All the Asian girls in high school thought it was so cool to have a white boyfriend. It was so retarded of me, but I thought I was one of the white girls. I tried dying my hair blonde once and I put on makeup to look like one of them! (laughs) There was a period I would say that I felt very white and I guess at the time it was cool, because I got to be friends with the white kids and I did have a white boyfriend.

For some, the "acting and being white" stage lead to temporary negative images of the self and of Vietnamese culture.[32] Loi explained how he didn't like himself and, consequently, felt alone in high school because he constantly compared himself to his white peers:

> Before coming to college I was very afraid of people and I felt alone because I didn't have friends. [Why?] I really disliked myself, because I disliked my culture. I disliked my parents, I disliked all the things that happened to me, all the Vietnamese things. Now I see it in terms of me basically comparing myself, the distorted self-image I got because I compared myself to a white person, a white standard. And I wanted to be white. That's why when I first came out as being gay, the only people I was attracted to were white men and I thought that Asians

and Vietnamese were not attractive. But, that's why right now I'm so keen into the race issue—so keen on the Vietnamese identity, because I have realized that that was the crux of my problem and not just mine, but a lot of other (Vietnamese and Asian) people.

For my informants, the acting and being white phenomenon was a temporary period in their lives lasting from a few years after migration, usually once they were acclimated in elementary school, until they entered college or the workforce. Young adulthood provided new social arenas in which to understand and, perhaps, transform themselves. In these new social arenas, most of my informants underwent a typical process that Loi called "deprogramming the self."

Search for Ethnic Identity in Young Adulthood

Deprogramming the Self

All of my respondents described the entrance into college and to a lesser degree for some, the workforce, as periods of identity change, periods that were highly marked by critical observations of the ways their American peers subscribed to and practiced mainstream U.S. cultural values of individualism. In many ways, the college campus was seen and understood as a site of ethnic recovery, and for some, ethnic discovery. The processes of "deprogramming the self" and assessing mainstream cultural practices with their own cultural lens were largely interactional. In other words, while they gradually ceased from acting and being white, they began to draw upon traditional cultural ideologies to help them see differences and, more often than not, preferences for Vietnamese over American values. Loi explained this process for himself since entering college:

> Basically, I have been deprogramming myself for over two years now. Actually this self-deprogramming thing is not a very uncommon thing. So I got involved with the Vietnamese students at school [college] because I just wanted to be with Vietnamese people. I had a theory—that if I was exposed enough and if I saw enough faces, just as when I learned the piano or when I picked up classical music, because I was ex-

posed I realized its subtlety and I realize the beauty and the differences in it.

Similarly, Hue gave the following account:

Near the end of high school, I began to see Vietnamese culture as cool. [How so?] I mean I liked it more than me trying to be American. When I started making really good friends . . . now that I look back, I had chosen to make good friends with the Vietnamese girls. [Why?] The ways we did things were different than the Americans [white]. [How so?] I mean, when we went out to eat, we didn't have to split the bills; someone just paid. Gosh, I think splitting things in half is so white! (laughs) I used to do that and I hated it and I'm trying to get away from that. When I began college, living in the dorm and stuff, I liked the ways Vietnamese folks do things, especially when it comes to helping your friends.

Why was college a physical and social space for deprogramming the self? The second-generation Vietnamese Americans I interviewed maintained that college provided coursework where they could talk openly about issues of race and ethnicity; they noted that courses in such departments as Asian American Studies and Ethnic Studies were crucial in helping them see who they were relative to the larger dominant society. College life presented possibilities for participation in issues such as politics and economic mobilization for Vietnamese minority communities. However, the most important and most often cited reason for deprogramming of the self and constructing a new identity were the formations of new friendships with other Vietnamese individuals; most informed me that they had chosen to participate in their college ethnic clubs to meet other Vietnamese people and many spoke of not "being conscious" of trying to act and be white until college. As Mong-Cam recalled:

I mean I grew up thinking that I'll somehow be white one day! I think I was conscious of this since, probably since college, and since I've taken Asian American courses and ethnic studies courses. Before that I mean, you know this is a phenomenon where a lot of people go through where you know where you're conscious of the fact that you're different and that you are who you are except there's no name for it.

Another informant, Theo, a twenty-three-year-old recent physics college graduate who emigrated from Vietnam when he was seven, affirmed his identity in the following statement:

> Yeah, I had that white phase. I even picked a white name [Andy] for people to call me in high school, because I thought Americans [whites] would see me as someone like them. When I came here [college], I got rid of Andy, because I wanted people to see me as a Vietnamese person. Man, it was like coming out of the closet, like once being a closeted gay person or something.

Articulating Ethnic Identity through a Collectivist Ideology

Boundaries and Construction of Ethnic Identity

It is well known that the notion of boundaries is often used to study ethnic groups who undergo differentiation and identity formations. Individuals and groups create boundaries as a way of differentiating themselves from the larger society and as a way of affirming their ethnic identity. Ethnic boundaries are situational and changeable, resulting from external and internal sources; that is, how we see ourselves relative to the larger society and how the larger society positions us are both important factors in the shaping of ethnic identity. Through reviewing past and present relationships, my informants consistently assembled new ways of seeing themselves, resulting in new identity formations. After the elementary and adolescent school years of being the "marginal man" in which they bargain with meanings of biculturalism—who they were relative to whom—introduction into college and the workforce became important social territories for viewing mainstream U.S. culture in relation to their own.

When reviewing their current and past friendships, for instance, most of my informants pointed out that as they got older, they acquired and kept more Vietnamese friends than they used to and they perceived that it was not due to rejections by non-Vietnamese individuals. A few also stated that they gradually drifted away from their previous friendships with non-Vietnamese individuals, especially white Americans, and many maintain intimate friendships almost exclusively with other Vietnamese individuals. They attributed this transition, forming and maintaining strong friendships with other Vietnamese, to different cultural ideologies about the rules and practices of friendship, which became more salient once they emerged into their young adulthood. Likewise, as adults, all of my informants provided divergent and often negative feelings about the ways their non-Vietnamese peers approached family life. Most explained that during childhood, these feelings were often not troubling because they were taught to glorify all American values in the process of being "Americanized."

While most informants described their friends and family as people to whom they could turn for emotional support, they also saw friends and family in utilitarian interpersonal relationships embodied in a collectivist ideology. It was clear and unequivocal that friends and families are individuals they could turn to and depend on for practical assistance, including financial support; in turn, they said they were readily available for their friends and families. Most informants explained that they were frequently disturbed and appalled by the economic boundaries their American peers practiced with friends and family, such as the calculation and division of financial expenses during their leisure moments.[33] My inquiry shows that for these second-generation Vietnamese Americans, the contrast between a collectivist familial ideology and an "American" identity led them to reassert a Vietnamese ethnic identity.

The Family over the Individual

Most of my informants emphasized that their family, especially their parents, was the most crucial influence to the development of their self-identity. What they wanted to be, what they might become, and how they relate to people in interpersonal relationships were all directly affected by the connection they had to their family. Most also made clear that the central reason why they had high aspirations for a college education was because of their parents. Individual goals were also important, but they were of secondary significance; family, especially parents, determined such things as what they would study and where they would go to school. In fact, those who were in graduate or professional schools asserted that if it weren't for their parents' desire, they probably would not have gone on to pursue an advanced degree. It was not uncommon for informants to say that they had future plans to live with or near their parents so that they could support them. For instance, those who had already begun working said they regularly sent money home to their parents and younger siblings who were attending college. Viewed in these ways, relationships with family are in part utilitarian among second-generation Vietnamese Americans. When they compared themselves to their "American" counterparts, those who they claim practice a culture of individualism and egalitarianism, my informants emphasized that a collectivist ideology helps them recapture a sense of ethnic identity. Manh, a twenty-four-year-old chemistry technician who immigrated here by himself at age seven and later sponsored his parents and younger sister to the United States, gave the following account:

> My little sister is a freshman in college now in the South and I know she's working hard in school and doesn't have a lot of money. I send her money each month and I tell her, "here's this and this amount of money, go and have some fun." My parents can't help us out because they don't make a lot of money. [Do you help your parents?] Yeah. [How so?] I mean they live with me so I pay for everything, the rent, food. They help me out when they can but I want them to enjoy. They are getting old, you know.

One might conjure up images of immigrant families who only pool resources in times of economic insecurity, as a reciprocal "moral economy," but this is not necessarily true as suggested by the descriptions of my informants. For example, Bach-Lan, a twenty-year-old engineering sophomore who was born in the United States, said all four of her college-educated older siblings understood that if anyone needed money to buy a bigger house or invest in a business, the capital was readily available within the family. Likewise, she said she often received monetary gifts from siblings for leisure activities:

> When I went to Europe last summer, I could have lived off $800, but when I told my older sister how much I had, she was shocked (laughs). [Why?] She didn't think I would have enough money to spend. A week later, I received a check from

all four of my brothers and sisters for the trip . . . this is one of the cool reasons to be the youngest in a Vietnamese family. (laughs)

My informants consistently spoke about family life as generated, as well as regulated, by the meanings of collectivism. In these accounts, they saw these meanings as ethnically defining. That is to say, most viewed obligation, nonegalitarianism, and pooling resources to the family unit as deriving from Vietnamese culture, and sharply contrasted with American values. Lien, a twenty-three-year-old senior education major who immigrated here at the age of three, explained how all her family members live together to support her polio-ridden brother:

I have five siblings including me. My older brother, he has polio. He's like thirty-five or thirty-six, around there. All of my siblings live together to help him out, especially after my mom died. Two of them are married and so there are a lot of people in the house, but it's fun . . . It's sad how the Americans leave their handicapped family living by themselves. I mean the other day I saw a sign at school of someone looking for an attendant because he was quadriplegic. I mean, where is his family?!

Similarly, when Le-Thuy, a twenty-four-year-old sales clerk who immigrated here at age six, told me she considered herself more imbued with Vietnamese ideologies than American ones, she gave the following explanation:

I like to *oi nha voi ong ngoai* (stay home with maternal grandfather) because he's eighty-nine years old and he needs someone to play with him. [Why do you think this is more Vietnamese than American culturally?] I don't think American people stay home with their grandparents. They usually put them in the old people's home anyways. None of my American friends live with their grandparents. I mean I don't see anything wrong with that, but I wouldn't do it [putting grandparents in nursing homes]. I know Vietnamese people wouldn't do it.

Friends as Family

When I asked my informants about their friendship patterns, the overall picture that emerged was that friends are treated "just like family." Friendships, like relations with family, are permeated by a sense of obligation to share resources. When I asked my informants in what ways were they close to their best friends, most gave answers such as "they will help me when I need it" or "I can depend on them." Sharing feelings and common interests were important, although secondary to material help and support.

In fact, when I inquired about intimacy in friendship, such as what kinds of things they talk about and what emotions they share with their friends, most of my informants were uncertain about what I meant. Some were surprised that I asked such questions. Many saw their friends as people with whom they share similar activities, but "true" or "best" friends were people who shared material support with each other, including money and who provided for each other in noncalculating terms. Mong-Cam, who said she didn't have Vietnamese friends until entering college, described how her new Vietnamese friends take care of each other, creating a sense of "familization" through friendships and, at times, there might be conflicts where non-Vietnamese friends were part of the picture:

> They (Vietnamese friends) truly do it because that's who they are and that's how they were raised . . . to take care of one another. They'd cook for me, they'd clean. The guys and girls. The only way I can view it is that it was communal. Nothing's like "this is mine, this is yours." The weird thing with this American friend of mine . . . when she and two of my other Vietnamese friends were living together, we shared all the food, there was no question about it and cleaning up, we shared all of those deals; right now there's some problems. The first thing the American friend said was that "I'm not gonna share food." I had asked her and she said, "I want to keep it separate because I like to eat different things." And I was like, "All right." I don't like counting everything—just being more free with things. I don't like people who count everything, who make you aware that "Oh, you owe me this, you owe me that."

Like their convictions about the rules and practices in family life, the ideology of collectivism in the realm of friendship was also regarded as a culturally bound affair. This was reflected in Le-Thuy's account:

Once I needed to pay my insurance, but I was short fifty bucks, a Vietnamese friend gave it to me. She offered me a hundred bucks so that I would have an extra fifty bucks in my account in addition to paying for the insurance. I told her I didn't need it. Vietnamese when you *muon tien* (borrow money), they don't ask for it right away. Most of the times, they don't even ask for it. *My* (Americans), they want it right away. That's why it's so *co* (difficult) to borrow from them. If you borrow from them, even if it's only two dollars, they will ask for it. That's why I get very *ngay* (uncomfortable) with sharing with American friends.

Constructing and Maintaining Boundaries

The cultural ideology of collectivism acts as a tool for the second-generation Vietnamese Americans I interviewed to see differences between them and their American peers. In recognizing these differences, I suggest boundaries are often put into place and are interwoven into the formation of ethnic identity. Most of my informants explained that at some point in their lives, particularly once they reached college and into adulthood, they began critically to look at "American" lives with their own cultural lens. While growing up as children of immigrants, they contended, they saw American ideals as glorifying and appealing, but the pathways into adulthood with new ways of viewing family life, friendship, and intimate relationships presented divergent feelings. These feelings often resulted in the construction and maintenance of boundaries. Lam, an American born twenty-three-year-old computer programmer, discussed how he began to view American individuals as distant, cold, and often removed from intimate ties with family and friends:

I think as we get older, we look at friends differently . . . I think we expect more out of people. American people are very *lan va mac cam tinh* (cold and lack feelings). [How so?] I don't know, I feel very *ngay* (uncomfortable) about asking *My* (Americans) for something, I always feel like I have to pay them back. You know, I can ask my Vietnamese friends for anything and I know I will get it. If they can't get it for me, they will ask other people. That's what *ban* (friends) are for, they *hie sinh* (sacrifice) for each other. That's why I prefer Vietnamese friends.

Lien explained how she began to label herself as being a Vietnamese, and not Vietnamese American:

Just the other day, I was talking to some of my [Vietnamese] girlfriends and we were arguing about politics in the United States. And, I ended up saying that I thought of myself as a Vietnamese and not Vietnamese American. And I was surprised that they all were thinking about the same things. I mean I just don't term myself Vietnamese American. I don't like that term. I am Vietnamese. Vietnamese to me is like believing in your culture. I hate it when Americans try to teach immigrants they should call themselves Americans. [Why?] I mean they shouldn't lose their *nguon* (roots). [When did you begin labeling yourself as Vietnamese?] When I got to college and I started to getting really close with Vietnamese people. It's hard to explain, but you know, just the way we do things. [Such as?] Like when we go out to eat, everyone would fight over to see who would pay for each other, but with Americans, we have to fight over how to divide the tab equally. That's being Vietnamese to me.

Similarly, Ngu, a twenty-year-old chemistry major who came here at the age of eight, explained how a difference in the ideology of family obligation created boundaries between her and an American friend:

There was this girl (American) I knew in high school who had so many problems at home. We were becoming good friends and I remembered when her mom was abused by her father, the first thing she thought about was leaving home for college. I told her not to, I thought that was so selfish! [Why?] If that was me, you know like, I would try to get a job and stay home and get my mom the hell out of there. I mean if that's how she treated her own mom, what is a friend to her then? That's so a white thing to do, to want and just leave your family as soon as you turn eighteen. I hate that. We stopped hanging out with each other because she didn't like the advice I gave her. That's fine with me. I guess I'm just too Vietnamese for her.

About one fourth of my informants have recently been back to Vietnam and they claimed the trip "back home" made their critical observations of American ideologies in family life and friendships more pronounced. Some even noted how families and friends in Vietnam appeared to be more intimate than their own. Oanh exclaimed, "They help each other with everything over there! It's just amazing what friends do for each other. It's not uncommon to see children of friends living with your family." A few of my informants actually spoke of going back to Vietnam to live once diplomatic ties are solidly developed with the United States. As Manh said, "I went back there, and when I came back to the United States, I was so homesick; I missed the warmth of the people, especially the friends and family who were willing to help each other, no matter how rich or poor they were. That is one thing that most Americans don't do. They sometimes help, but only when someone is suffering."

This process of constructing and maintaining ethnic boundaries is inextricably linked to Vietnamese Americans' understandings of family life and friendship. Beneath these meanings and feelings were the intense belief in and practice of the collectivist family ideology. As young adults, these boundaries may be set as continuous symbols of ethnic identity for second-generation Vietnamese Americans—what they believe in and what they practice in social relationships determine who they are. If these ethnic boundaries are indeed dynamic and changeable, then we might argue that the lives of these Vietnamese Americans are characterized by certain conditions that are affected by a particular time and place and more specifically, those conditions that are built around the new second-generation experience.

Conclusion

By tracing second-generation Vietnamese American descriptions of growing up as children of immigrants and their experiences as young adults, my findings suggest that the experiences of ethnicity involve the fluid and complex interplay of culture and identity. Working under the social constructionist perspective on ethnicity, I argue that the experiences of ethnicity for the children of Vietnamese immigrants are shaped largely by rules and practices in past and present relationships, which they pick from their cultural shopping cart. These experiences are situated under a specific context. For second-generation Vietnamese Americans, this context may be understood as a stage in the life cycle, a stage characterized by constant sifting and assembling of new identities and identities that have been put into place.

Growing up as children of immigrants, the second-generation Vietnamese Americans I interviewed described their childhood as often infused with ambiguity, uncertainty, and tension about who they were. Given the opportunities and constraints presented to them from both their old and new worlds, they experienced the classic marginal man situation in which constant negotiations of identity took place. Under these conditions, they equated "American-ness" with "whiteness." As children and adolescents, like other "racialized" minority groups, they tried to "be" American by acting and being white in order to fit in with peer groups. Once they progressed into their adulthood, they undertook a process of "deprogramming the self" as they challenged notions of American-ness.

As young adulthood introduced new possibilities for friendship patterns and as they began to reevaluate meanings they assigned to family life, the collectivist familial ideology became a crucial mechanism for ethnic identification. This reevaluation was particularly active during the college years, a time when many second-generation Vietnamese adults first leave their family. In short, friendship and family life turned into social arenas where a collectivist ideology acts as an articulator of ethnic identity. My findings show that ethnic identity formation may contribute to reducing internalization of negative self-images during young adulthood relative to childhood experiences of marginality. But it is important to recognize that in these processes, boundaries with a pejorative emphasis are often put into place.

While I only paint a picture of how second-generation Vietnamese Americans use cultural ideology to form and recapture ethnic identity and to position themselves next to members of the host society, it might be argued that ethnogenesis, or "collective identity shift," occurs for the children of Vietnamese immigrants in this process. Kibria shows that ethnogenesis among second-generation Korean and Chinese Americans takes place through their reflections on intermarriage. She found that most Korean and Chinese second generations wanted to preserve "ethnic purity," even when they used an Asian American identity.[34] With similar insights, using friendships and family life as the center of analysis, I found that for second-generation Vietnamese Americans, relationships act as powerful devices for maintaining ethnic values as indicated by the boundaries they construct.

Drawing on these eighteen interviews, this study interprets and illustrates how second-generation Vietnamese Americans draw upon the ideology of collectivism in their family life and friendships, especially during their young adulthood, to turn more exclusively to their "original" ethnicity. I argue that ethnic identity gets assembled and produced, where it otherwise might not for children of immigrants under an "assimilation track" into adulthood. If they were to apply hegemonic values such as individualism, egalitarianism, and self-sufficiency that are embedded in everyday life in the United States, they believe loss of ethnic identity will inevitably be the result.

As many have pointed out, research on immigrants in much of the past century has focused on the experiences of Europeans.[35] Much of this research applies the straight line assimilation model, which holds that immigrants move on a continuum of change—contact, competition, conflict, accommodation, and assimilation—where they eventually lose their ethnic identity and locate themselves in mainstream U.S. culture once acculturation and assimilation have been achieved. In addition, most of this research maintains that change is often necessary for successful upward mobility. Rejecting this approach, a lively discussion of the lives of contemporary immigrants and their children who are mostly immigrants of color proposes that ethnic continuity can help contribute to mobilizing rather than inhibiting the successful pathways into U.S. society.

One of the clearest examples of how ethnic continuity helps to mobilize rather than inhibit minority groups is when children of Vietnamese immigrants challenge hegemonic American values of individualism, egalitarianism, and self-sufficiency to show that they intend to provide care for family members and friends who are in need. Given the diminishing care from the state and other public spheres in the past decade, care that comes from the family and the private sphere is increasingly important.[36] For immigrants, ethnic continuity may help facilitate and balance the necessary forms of care in private life.

The data presented here are preliminary, given the small and distinct nature of this sample—the interview participants live in

California in a highly populated Vietnamese and Asian metro area. Clearly, given the ways Vietnamese Americans have settled in the United States since the mid-1970s, the next step in this research should be to examine second-generation Vietnamese Americans from different geographical areas. California is not a typical U.S. state, and it is well known that social and political activism from the Asian American community originated here in the 1960s and has since remained alive.[37] Part of this activism has led to a resurgence of ethnic identity and the maintenance of boundaries.

The social forces built around the new second-generation experience, especially for Asian Americans, provide a myriad of complex questions about immigrant lives. For example, how will second-generation Vietnamese Americans choose where they live, in terms of neighborhoods and cities, given their social experiences as children of immigrants? Whom will second-generation Vietnamese Americans' children (the third generation) interact with in schools and neighborhoods? By looking at the subjective experiences of a specific group of the new second generation, we see how trajectories into young adulthood can often result in rigid constructions of boundaries, which seemingly and possibly cannot be removed. The ways identity and culture grow in relationships with second-generation Vietnamese Americans rely heavily on the influence of institutions such as schools, neighborhoods, and the workforce in the host society. Thus, a proper and useful analysis of immigrant lives should explore the dynamics of relationships within these terrains to see how negotiations with, and often challenges to, mainstream cultural values take place. It is necessary, as many have done, to go beyond the assimilation model in order to explore both processes of ethnic identification and ethnic boundary constructions. To do otherwise would simply ignore or minimize the experiences of members of the new second generation.

Notes

Many thanks to Arlene Kaplan Daniels, Jerome Karabel, Hien Le, and Pyong Gap Min for comments on earlier drafts; to Allison Pugh for suggestions; to Ajay Deshmukh, Sergey Ioffe, Chris King, Tram Le-

Nguyen, Anil Reddy, Aman Sappal, Sheila Swaroop, and Alice Wong for discussions; and to Barrie Thorne for numerous discussions, comments, and guidance.

1. Contemporary immigrants are those individuals who arrived in the United States after the Immigration Act of 1965. Since then, most immigrants have come from Asia or the Americas. See Min Zhou, "Growing Up American: The Challenge Confronting Immigrant Children and Children of Immigrants," *Annual Review of Sociology*, 23 (1997): 63–95. For a brief discussion of the Immigration Act of 1965, see Alejandro Portes and Ruben G. Rumbaut, *Immigrant America: A Portrait*, 2d edition (Berkeley: University of California Press, 1996), 8–15. For recent studies focusing on children of contemporary immigrants, see Ruben Rumbaut, "The Crucible Within: Ethnic Identity, Self-Esteem, and Segmented Assimilation among Children of Immigrants." *International Migration Review* 28 (1994): 748–94. Min Zhou and Carl L. Bankston III, "Social Capital and the Adaptation of the Second Generation: The Case of Vietnamese Youth in New Orleans," *International Migration Review*, 28 (1994): 795–820; Kibria, "The Construction of 'Asian American'," *Ethnic and Racial Studies* 20 (1999): 523–44. Portes and Rumbaut, *Immigrant America: A Portrait*, 2d edition; Zhou, "Growing Up American." Although there are distinctions, depending on the interpretation, the terms "second generation" and "children of immigrants" will be used interchangeably in this paper for ease of presentation. And, for an in-depth discussion of the "coming white minority" in California, see Dale Maharidge, *The Coming White Minority: California Eruptions and America's Future* (New York: New York Times Books, 1996).

2. Robert E. Park and Ernest W. Burgess, *Introduction to the Science of Society*, 2nd ed. (Chicago: University of Chicago Press, 1924), 161–64, 280–87; and Everett Stonequist, *Marginal Man* (New York: Scribner's, 1961).

3. Informed by classical theory of urbanism, the assimilation model began with the Chicago School sociologist Robert E. Park. For a critique of the assimilation model and the limits of using structural analyses to discuss immigrants' lives, see Nagel, "Constructing Ethnicity," 152–76; Jean Bacon, *Life Line: Community, Family, and Assimilation Among Asian Indian Immigrants* (New York: Oxford Press, 1996); Karen Pyke, "'The Normal American Family' as an Interpretive Structure of Family Life among Children of Korean and Vietnamese Immigrants." Paper presented at the annual meeting of the American Sociological Association, San Francisco, 1998; Kibria, "The Construction of 'Asian American'"; and Zhou, "Growing Up American."

4. Zhou, "Growing Up American," 63.

5. Darrel Montero, *Vietnamese Americans: Patterns of Resettlement and Socioeconomic Adaptation in the United States* (Boulder, Colo.: Westview, 1979).

6. Between April and December 1975, the United States admitted 130,400 Southeast Asian refugees, 125,000 of whom were Vietnamese. Annual arrivals of Southeast Asian refugees have increased exponentially: 20,4000 in 1978, 80,700 in 1979, and 166,700 in 1980. Refugees quickly earned "legal" status as immigrants, but tensions had arisen from the public and refugees themselves about resettlement programs, including unorganized mass resettlement. For a discussion of refugee law and policies on the Vietnamese American community, see Bill Hing, *Making and Remaking Asian America through Immigration Policy*, chapter 4, 121–38.

7. Prior to 1965, there were about 18,000 Vietnamese in the United States, mainly as university students or as war brides to U.S. servicemen. See James Freeman, *Changing Identities: Vietnamese Americans 1975-1995* (Boston: Allyn and Bacon, 1995), 30.

8. This number may exclude over 200,000 persons from Vietnam who identified themselves as Chinese for the U.S. census. See Nazli Kibria, *Family Tightrope: The Changing Lives of Vietnamese Americans* (Princeton, N.J.: Princeton University Press, 1993), chapter 1, 3–23.

9. See Maharidge, *The Coming White Minority*.

10. Rubén Rumbaut, "The Agony of the Migration and Adaptation of Indochinese Refugee Adults and Children" in *Refugee Children: Theory, Research, and Services*, ed. Frederick Ahearn Jr. and Jean Athey (Baltimore: Johns Hopkins University Press, 1991).

11. Researchers have used this age bracket to classify second-generation children of immigrants. See Zhou and Bankston III, "Social Capital and the Adaptation of the Second Generation"; Zhou, "Growing Up American"; Leif Jensen and Yoshimi Chitose, "Today's Second Generation: Evidence from the 1990 U.S. Census," *International Migration Review*, 28 (1994): 714–35; Maria Patricia Fernandez-Kelly and Richard Schauffler, "Divided Fates: Immigrant Children in a Restructured U.S. Economy," *International Migration Review*, 28 (1994): 662–89; and Kibria, "The Construction of 'Asian American.'"

12. Hien Duc Do, "The New Outsiders: The Vietnamese Refugee Generation in Higher Education" (Ph.D. dissertation, University of California at Santa Barbara, 1995).

13. For further discussion of the apparent "generation" gap among Vietnamese children and their parents, see Kibria, *Family Tightrope*, chapter 6, 144–66; and Pyke, "'The Normal American Family' as an Interpretive Structure of Family Life among Children of Korean and Vietnamese Immigrants."

14. Pyke, "'The Normal American Family' as an Interpretive Structure of Family Life among Children of Korean and Vietnamese Immigrants."

15. Lyman and Douglas, "Ethnicity: Strategies of Collective and Individual Impression Management," 344–65.

16. Nagel, "Constructing Ethnicity," 152–53.

17. Kibria, "The Construction of 'Asian American,'" 535.

18. See, for example, Gans, "Symbolic Ethnicity," 1–20; and Richard Alba, *Italian Americans: Into the Twilight of Ethnicity* (Englewood Cliffs, N.J.: Prentice-Hall, 1985).

19. Zhou and Bankston, "Social Capital and the Adaptation of the Second Generation," 822.

20. Bacon, *LifeLine*; Kibria, "The Construction of 'Asian American.'"

21. For example, one of Pyke's informants explained, "With the *American* culture, it's . . . not much frowned upon to put your parents in a [nursing] home when they grow old. In *our* culture, it is a definite no-no." ("'The Normal American Family' as an Interpretive Structure of Family Life among Children of Korean and Vietnamese Immigrants," 22).

22. Nagel, "Constructing Ethnicity," 162.

23. The site of this study—the San Francisco Bay area—has the second highest concentration of Vietnamese in the United States. In addition, over 46 percent of all Vietnamese in the United States reside in California, according to the 1990 census. See Freeman, *Changing Identities: Vietnamese Americans*, 11.

24. Barney Glaser and Anselm Strauss, *The Discovery of Grounded Theory: Strategies for Qualitative Research* (Chicago: Aldine, 1967), 45.

25. Glaser and Strauss, 1967, 101; and Anselm Strauss and Juliet Corbin, *Basics of Qualitative Research: Grounded Theory Procedures and Techniques* (Newbury Park, Calif.: Sage, 1990).

26. Although this topic is not a focus of this paper, some informants referred to citizenship and nationality as salient issues for them in their identity formation. Many pointed to globalization and transnational relations with extended kin as opportunities to see themselves as "truly" Vietnamese rather than Americans or Vietnamese Americans.

27. One third of my informants reported that an extended relative, usually a grandparent, lived in the same household with them while they were growing up.

28. All names have been changed in order to protect the anonymity of informants.

29. Among recent immigrant Vietnamese parents, as Fernandez-Kelley and Schaulffler (1994) discovered, encouraging their children to make American friends was a way to quickly learn the language and culture of their new country. My informants explained that this was true in the early years of settlement for them, but tensions often resulted if they acculturated too quickly.

30. Scholars studying minority students in schools have discussed the ways minority students face the "burden of acting white" in order to succeed. See Signithia Fordham and John U. Ogbu, "Black Students' School Success: Coping with the Burden of Acting White," *The Urban Review*, 18 (1986): 176–206; Donna Y. Ford, John L. Harris, Karen S. Webb, and Deneese L. Jones, "Rejection or Confirmation of Racial Identity: A Dilemma for High-Achieving Blacks?" *Journal of Educational Thought*, 28 (1994): 7–33. Although Fordham, Ogbu, and Ford focus on African American students, they point out that other minority groups, including immigrants, are also faced with similar problems. Ogbu and Matutue-Bianchi also explain how Mexican American students see themselves and their peer groups as doing the "Anglo thing" and those who resist say these "linear acculturation" mechanisms are detrimental to the integrity of their cultures and identity. See Ogbu and Matute-Bianchi, "Understanding Sociocultural Factors in Education: Knowledge, Identity, and Adjustment," in *Beyond Language: Sociocultural Factors in Schooling, Language, and Minority Students* (Los Angeles: California State Department of Education, 1986), 71–143.

31. Although sixteen of the eighteen individuals I interviewed experienced secondary migration in the United States, only three said they were raised in neighborhoods and went to elementary and secondary schools where the majority consisted of whites. Secondary migration refers to the process in which the Vietnamese moved from one state to another (the latter having more Vietnamese people) after being settled in arbitrary parts of the United States in the mid-1970s and throughout the 1980s.

32. In a thoughtful collection of essays written by Asian American professionals, editors Pyong Gap Min and Rose Kim found that despite their strong ethnic identity, some second-generation Asian American adults felt more comfortable making friends with and dating whites, rather than coethnics or other Asians. See Min and Rose, *Struggle for Ethnic Identity: Narratives by Asian American Professionals* (Walnut Creek, Calif.: AltaMira Press, 1999). While these children of immigrants were also likely to have experienced the acting white phenomenon, they did not feel that it was inhibiting to their ethnic identity formation. Two of the writers who identified strongly with their ethnicity ended up marrying white Americans. Min and Rose suggest that neither of these Asian Americans, who were Japanese and Bangladeshi, "were forced to relinquish their Asian and ethnic cultures as a precondition for marrying white partners. They married white men who accepted their Asian and ethnic backgrounds. This indicates that in contemporary America, intermarriage and multiculturalism go together" (p.112). Although I am not arguing here that adult children of Vietnamese immigrants are

unable or unwilling to have a strong ethnic identity while at the same time developing friendships and intimate ties with white Americans, I point out the "acting and being white" phenomenon, especially during childhood, did lead them to view "American-ness" as a monolithic cultural category—that of "whiteness." The crucial point is that as young adults, these reflections are evidence of a "bicultural dilemma" during childhood and adolescence. For second-generation Vietnamese Americans, cultural ideology and practices during young adulthood *within* the realm of family life and friendship act as powerful articulators of ethnic identity.

33. Unlike friendships in most Western cultures, where expressions of emotions and feelings are arguably the most important components of the intimacy in friendship patterns, friendships for my informants are very much utilitarian in nature in addition to the sharing of emotions and feelings. For a discussion of how friends in Western culture practice economic and social boundaries, see Lillian Rubin, *Just Friends: The Role of Friendship in Our Lives* (New York: Harper & Row, 1985).

34. Kibria, "The Construction of 'Asian American.'"

35. For example, see Kibria, *Family Tightrope*; Kibria, "The Construction of 'Asian American;'" Zhou and Bankston III, "Social Capital and the Adaptation of the Second Generation"; Zhou, "Growing Up American"; and Pyke, "'The Normal American Family' as an Interpretive Structure of Family Life among Children of Korean and Vietnamese Immigrants."

36. For a thoughtful discussion of the decline of "public" or state care and the need for public and private care, see Arlie Hochschild, "The Culture of Care: Traditional, Postmodern, Cold-Modern, and Warm-Modern Ideals of Care," *Social Politics* (1995): 331–46.

37. For a discussion of Asian American activism in California, see William Wei, *The Asian American Movement* (Philadephia: Temple University Press, 1993).

CHAPTER THREE

DISCIPLINING DESIRE IN MAKING THE HOME: ENGENDERING ETHNICITY IN INDIAN IMMIGRANT FAMILIES

Sharmila Rudrappa

What could be closer than my own body, my body image? Yet what could be more permeable to the currents of the world, the rough waves of ideology? Gender, the social construction of sexuality, flows as an intrinsic portion of this current. I see myself, to some extent, as I am seen, as bodily being. Struggling against the way I am seen, I remake myself, rework images that encode the symbolic valences of self. I might whisper this or shout it out aloud, but the truth comes to me through the sensorium of a gendered body.[1]

In the documentary film *The Color of Fear*, a group of men of varied racial backgrounds gets together to discuss what "whiteness" in twentieth-century United States means. Among them is a white man who just does not understand the privileges white skin bestows on him. In frustration and anger, one of the black participants screams at him, "Get ethnic, and you will understand." In this chapter I provide a partial explanation of what it means to "get ethnic." Ethnicity—in this case among Indian Americans—is not a pregiven entity but is, instead, actively recreated within an American context. Indians, like myself, arrive from India with no conception of ourselves in racial terms; instead, our caste/class is crucial. Religion matters. Gender and region of origin within India are significant to the ways in which we conceive of our self. Upon arrival in the United States we postcolonial immigrants suddenly become racialized. We have to rethink ourselves in different ways than we did in the past to negotiate the racial hierarchies that structure American society. From being persons with no tangible race—for we do not think of ourselves in racial terms in India—we become people of color in this society.

Indian immigrants see the world outside, the public sphere, as an alienating space where, as nonwhites, they have to conform to a white standard. They are not able to set the public normative context in this new country to which they have arrived, but instead are expected to follow existing racial norms. On the other hand, the home or the private sphere is perceived as a free space, autonomous from outside influences. The public sphere, where whiteness is the norm, can be kept away from the privacy of the home. In the home nonwhite immigrants have the power to be what *they want* to be and become "ethnic" once again.

In the home they draw selectively on their notions of an authentic culture that ostensibly exists in India to build repertoires of racial practices here in the United States that mark them as authentically ethnic. Central to this discourse on ethnicity are notions of "Indian womanhood" and sexuality, leading to the curtailment of women's sexual autonomy for the stability of the good, immigrant family. Hence, sexuality is imbricated in Indian Americans' attempts to get ethnic, with uneven repercussions on men and women.

In conclusion, I argue that Indian immigrants' orientation to the past—through disciplining women's sexuality and building the normative immigrant home—has repercussions for the way Indians project their identity to the American public world. They argue that their "good" families give their children solid foundations to become good American citizens. Therefore, though Indian immigrants would like to see the home and the outside world as two distinct spheres, we see that the private world of the Indian home and the public world of American citizenry are not really that disparate, but instead they mutually reconstitute each other.

Agency within Existing Racial Structures

American society is a racialized society. Any cursory glance at popular culture, everyday interactions on streets, the actions of state institutions, immigration laws, the layout of urban landscapes, and so on will indicate the racialization of the American polity. Indians arrive in the United States, which is already structured by race. Race here exists as rules and resources that "make it possible for discernibly similar social practices to exist across varying spans of time and space and which lend them 'systemic' form."[2] These social rules give meaning to human actions within specific contexts, and sanction modes of social conduct, thereby laying out procedures for social action. Actors are not self-consciously aware that their everyday lives are structured by rules, but instead, they have a tacit understanding of these rules. Actors have a practical consciousness—that implicit knowing of "rules and tactics whereby daily social life is constituted and re-constituted across space and time"[3]—and they use this practical knowledge "in the production of day-to-day social encounters."[4] People rationalize their acts based on their practical conscious-ness and live their everyday lives accordingly. This practical consciousness can be an overlapping set of ideas that constitute the group, such as the ways to conduct oneself in public, the ways children are raised, notions of masculinity/femininity, and the like. Or, this practical consciousness can be a set of beliefs some social groups have regarding another group, which guides the way they conduct themselves toward the other.[5]

Though Indian immigrants have a fair inkling about race in America through mass media, they are unprepared for the ways in which race rhetoric permeates everyday living here in the United States. They also cannot conceive of the ways in which their self itself will be changed. In moving from a national space where one is the norm to a location where one is not, immigra-tion involves a radical rupture in the way immigrants think of themselves. Taken-for-granted cultural ideals, ways of raising children, interacting with others, the use of public space, bodily conduct, and, fundamentally, conceptions of the self (i.e., who they are at the very core) are disrupted. In order to understand how they fit into the imagined American community, immi-grants begin to reconceptualize themselves. Upon arrival here Indian immigrants are characterized racially. Most Indian immi-grants, because of phenotypic characteristics, certainly cannot pass as white and become "average" Americans as perhaps Ger-man or Irish immigrants are able to do.

What Ruth Chung, a Korean American, says of her early days in the United States holds true for many Indian immigrants:

It didn't take long before I became painfully conscious of being different. I quickly experienced the consequences of being a

minority in America. One day in second grade, I looked wist-
fully at the blond hair of a classmate who was sitting in front
of me, wondering, "Why couldn't I have been born in America
to white parents?" "Why couldn't I have blond hair and blue
eyes like her, and a 'normal' sounding name like Smith?" Instead, I was subject to a litany of well intended but humiliating
questions such as "Where are you from?" "How come your
eyes look different?" "What do you eat at home?"[6]

Like Ruth Chung, Indian immigrants are more or less incorporated into the American polity as people of color. But what
does it mean for this minority that never conceived of itself in
terms of race to begin reconceptualizing itself as having a race?
Within this nation organized along color lines what race are
they? Who are they really? And based on their conceptions of
their self, how do they exercise their agency in attempting to fit
into this new world that they will eventually claim as their own?

Building primarily on George Herbert Mead, Emirbayer and
Mische define agency as "the temporally constructed engagement by actors of different structural environments . . . which
through the interplay of habit, imagination, and judgment, both
reproduces and transforms those structures in interactive response to the problems posed by historical situations."[7] According to them, agency can be understood as having three broad
components based on its different orientations: *iteration, projec-
tivity*, and *practical evaluation*. Iteration is the capacity of persons
to actively select and incorporate patterns of thought and social
practices from the past, to give stability to their present situation
so that they may cope with the temporal/spatial transitions of
perhaps migration and immigration. The iteration of past social
practices gives persons a sense of continuity in self-identity and
fosters a sense of belonging to a larger community. The projec-
tive element of agency refers to the imaginations of persons. Received traditions of thought and social practices from the past
are recast in relation to the persons' hopes and desires for the future. The past is reconfigured to organize the future. Practical
evaluation is the ability of people to make judgments among the
various possible trajectories of action in response to present social situations. Received traditions and schema of thought from
the past are selectively utilized in building sets of social practices
for the present. Hence, agency centrally involves the selective re-

casting of the past in order to make sense of the future so that social actors may proceed with everyday living. Meena Alexander, whom I quote at the beginning, speaks of remaking her self:

> I see myself, to some extent, as I am seen, as bodily being. Struggling against the way I am seen, I remake myself, rework images that encode the symbolic valencies of self. I might whisper this or shout it out aloud, but the truth comes to me through the sensorium of a gendered body.[8]

Though she is cast in particular race/gender categories based on how she looks, she recasts herself in ways she wants to be perceived. Likewise, Indian immigrants may be labeled as non-white, minor partners in the American nation, but they resist the categories in which they are placed and "rework images that encode the symbolic valences of self." Their racialized bodies may be viewed suspiciously in a nation that is becoming increasingly anti-immigrant in its public sentiments, but Indian immigrants recast themselves as good immigrants who contribute to the American polity.

However, at this point, one should stop and ask—from where does the imagination arise by which Indian immigrants recast themselves? How is this imagination mobilized to rework identities in a racialized world? What are the repercussions of reworking ethnic identities for Indian immigrant women?

The Public and Private Practices of Race

Sayantini DasGupta, a second-generation Indian American, tells us of her childhood in a midwestern suburb. She says:

> I grew to recognize the corrosive effects of being Indian on the weekends and American during the school week, the cultural juggling act that each second generation Indian American must learn to perform. . . . The effect was exacerbated for Indian American young women, who felt the pressure of a white beauty standard at school, and the pressure of being a dutiful, very "Indian" daughter at home. It depresses me still to remember how many of my lighter-skinned Indian sisters tried to pass themselves off as Italian or Greek during school, while dancing in *bharata natyam* recitals and going to *pujas* on the weekends.[9]

Three points emerge here. First, DasGupta's narrative reveals that white racial practices are not unique to white people alone. Instead, they form a part of nonwhite immigrants' repertoire of everyday practices as they attempt to become American. The broad range of academic work spanning various fields from critical legal theory to literature, called "whiteness" studies, examines the social construction of race with a central focus on how race structures white people's lives. The existence of large, disadvantaged African American communities, under apartheid conditions for much of U.S. history, has shaped white people's racial ideologies, identities, and subsequent political struggles. Studies on whiteness discuss how white people's various social practices construct the white race.[10] While this scholarship on whiteness has been an absolutely crucial contribution to our understanding of race, it primarily examines the cultural practices of people currently classified as "white" and then proceeds to examine how these groups practice race.[11] However, we see that nonwhite immigrants, too, grapple with notions of whiteness as they attempt to become part of the American public.

Second, DasGupta's words show that racial practices are not uniform in all spaces. On the weekends, in the private sphere of the home, she says her Indian "sisters" performed *bharat natyam* recitals and went to *pujas*, all ostensibly Indian practices. On the other hand, during the week in the public sphere of the school the Indian American girls felt the pressures of a white norm, performed whiteness. The workplace and the home—corresponding to the public and the private—remain clearly separated in most societies. Such a dichotomy is far more pronounced for immigrants. With an increasing backlash against immigration in American politics, the average Indian in the United States strives hard to reproduce herself/himself in the public sphere as a model minority. The workplace, the school, the playground are examples of public spaces where immigrants need to prove their ability to fit into a "white" world. On the other hand, in the private sphere of the home the immigrant individual attempts to cultivate his/her Indian-ness self-consciously.

Within the racial hierarchies that exist in the United States we are categorized and our bodies are invested with racialized meanings. We often resist such categorization, attempt to self-define and empower ourselves as "Indian," and try to articulate a singular Indian American community identity. Contrarily, even as we want to emphasize our particularities, we attempt to become part of the larger imagined national American community. We perform whiteness in public and become Indian in the private sphere. DasGupta's account exemplifies how nonwhite South Asian immigrants like me try to make a sense of place in the racial economy of this nation to which we have arrived. We strive to show, in the public sphere, how well we conform to a society structured by whiteness. On the other hand, the private sphere of the home is an autonomous space where we can be our ethnic selves once again. We immigrants resist the negative connotations ascribed to the categories in which we are placed and draw our inspiration to "rework images that encode the symbolic valencies of self"[12] from the home, the source of our ethnic identities.

The third point I draw from DasGupta's essay is that "whiteness" and "Indian-ness" are not a priori categories, but instead are actively created through various practices taken to signify white or Indian. Many autobiographical essays, novels, and so on, such as DasGupta's essay, written by the Indian diaspora, speak about conforming to whiteness in public. Yet, few speak of what they mean by "whiteness." How does one perform "whiteness"? Is it simply by calling ourselves "Greek" or "Italian"? Or is there a set of practices that go along with it? "Indian-ness" remains marked and categorized, and the practices of "Indian-ness" are easy to name—*pujas* and *Bharat Natyam* on weekends. Yet, what practices constitute "whiteness"?[13] While the question of "whiteness" is an interesting question to pursue, it is in the former, the private practices of race that I am interested (i.e., Indian Americans "becoming Indian" in the private sphere).

In his essay titled "Is the Ethnic 'Authentic' in the Diaspora?" Radhakrishnan speaks to second-generation Indian Americans and comes to realize that Indian Americans seem to lead a double life in the United States.[14] He writes:

> During the last few years, I have talked and listened to a number of young, gifted Indian children of the diaspora who, like my son, are born here and are thus "natural" American citizens. I was startled when they told me that they had grown up

with a strong sense of being exclusively Indian, and the reason was that they had experienced little during their growing years that held out the promise of first-class American citizenship. Most of them felt that they could not escape being marked as different by virtue of their skin color, their family background, and other ethnic and unassimilated traits. Many of them recited the reality of a double-life, *the ethnic private life and the "American" public life,* with very little mediation between the two.[15]

Radhakrishnan does not question American public life but turns his critical gaze onto the ethnic private life and explains that ethnicity is not a given thing but is, instead, renegotiated constantly. The Indian diaspora constantly ascribes to "authentic" Indian practices within the home but Radhakrishnan casts a dubious eye on any claims of "authentic Indian-ness." Instead, he questions this whole notion of authenticity and asks—"who and by what authority is checking our credentials [as Indians]? Is 'authenticity' a home we build for ourselves or a ghetto we inhabit to satisfy the dominant world?"[16]

The private space/home is one of the most crucial anchors for the nonwhite immigrant family as we negotiate our ways through a sea of American "whiteness." Indian immigrants perceive the home as a utopia, an autonomous space outside the influences of a competitive, uncertain, and potentially alienating world where they are marginal to a public discourse that takes the white society as the norm. The home remains a safe haven to which the immigrant retires from public scrutiny. This private sphere is seen as a separate social universe, unsullied by the happenings of the public world. In the privacy of their homes Indian Americans are able to practice their religion, speak their language, cook their Indian foods, and, crucially, reproduce their families in what is considered to be the "Indian" way. The Indian family becomes a repository of cultural values, exemplar family ideals, and, I subsequently argue, idealized heterosexuality in opposition to "American values" existing outside the home.

Much of the earlier academic writings on race and family have focused on how racial stratification affects structures of families. Jacqueline Jones's *Labor Of Love, Labor of Sorrow: Black Women, Work, and the Family from Slavery to the Present* (1985),

Nakano Glenn's *Issei, Nesei, War Bride* (1986), a study of Japanese American families, and Zavella's *Women's Work and Chicano Families* (1987) are all examples of such work. In my work I reverse the question. I do not disagree that racial stratification affects family structures. However, I think our conceptions of family and "authentically" ethnic familial practices also affect our understandings of race/ethnicity as we strive to belong to the imagined American community. Who we think we are at our very core, in other words our essence, is based on who we are at home. As immigrants in a "white" country, and in an unfamiliar cultural context, we acutely feel the need for free spaces such as the home and family where we think we can become Indian once again. Homes provide an anchoring for minority identities and are crucial sites from which immigrants "begin to describe, defend or justify themselves and their acts."[17]

The Past is in the Present: Agency in Expressing Ethnicity

And how shall I speak for myself without memory—my memory and the memories of my people, however dispersed, however distanced?[18]

Is the dichotomy between a hostile and alienating public world and sacrosanct private home a new cultural configuration among Indian immigrants here in the United States? No, not necessarily. Writing about Indian independence struggles at the turn of the century, Partha Chatterjee describes how Indian nationalism, led by a nascent bourgeoisie, divided the social world into material and spiritual domains. "The material is the domain of the 'outside,' of the economy and of statecraft, of science and technology," in which the West was superior. The West was to be carefully studied if the Indian bourgeoisie was to succeed in the public domain. On the other hand, the spiritual was "an 'inner' domain bearing the 'essential' marks of cultural identity."[19] The colonial state had no power in this inner domain, and it was here that the national bourgeoisie launched what Chatterjee considers its most creative and powerful project. The home, the family, and the Indian woman—elements of the private sphere—were crucial sites on which an Indian national culture was constructed. The nationalist period saw the rise of a new patriarchy where the woman was supposed to be educated and modern, but had to have all the bearings of a traditional Indian woman that set her apart from the so-called evils of Western norms. Chatterjee writes:

> The world is the external, the domain of the material; the home represents one's inner spiritual self, one's true identity. The world is the treacherous terrain of the pursuit of material interests. . . . It is also typically the domain of the male. The home in its essence must remain unaffected by the profane activities of the material world—and woman its representation.[20]

Hence, the ideologies of gendered public and private spheres, and the centrality of home and "woman" to notions of Indian culture, are not exclusive to immigrants here in the United States but also exist in India, the sending country. Indian immigrants draw on individual and collective memories of the past to condition their actions in the present. The past's "presence is exhibited in memory, and in the historical apparatus that extends memory."[21] The past continues into the present, conditioning how we perceive both the present and future, and directs our cultural practices in the living present. Indian immigrants recall and selectively mobilize past cultural schemas they were familiar with in India. These cultural schemas can be bodily actions and cognitive patterns, or they can consist of "mental categories, embodied practices, and social organization."[22] Through reiteration the past "becomes a stabilizing influence that shapes the flow of effort and allows us to sustain identities, meanings, and interactions over time."[23] Therefore, Indians here in the United States are able to continue thinking of themselves as Indians because of the ways in which they understand their personal and collective histories, giving them a sense of a shared past, and a shared identity.

However, these cultural schemas are not simply transplanted from India, but instead are refashioned within the specificities of life here in the United States. Indian Americans focus on directing their future possibilities in responding to the challenges of a racialized American society. They direct inherited schemas of cultural practices and habitual ways of doing things *selectively* to help them get incorporated into larger racial structures. Given the uncertainties of social life, Indian immigrants are "capable of distancing themselves . . . from schemas, habits, and traditions that constrain social identities and institutions. This capacity . . . enables them to reconstruct and innovate upon those traditions in accordance with evolving desires and purposes."[24]

Indian immigrants dig into their memories of what constitutes home and recast their "authentic" cultural scripts to make new homes in this nation to which they have arrived. The concept of home itself takes on new meanings that they never thought of before. Home can refer to just the nuclear and extended family, or the suburban home. The private sphere can mean the four walls that guard the powerful secrets of a normative, nuclear family. Or home can also mean the neighborhoods in which they shop, buying spices, saris, and gold jewelry. Home is sometimes the South Asian business district on Devon Avenue in Chicago, where immigrants purchase the necessary accouterments that make them Indian. Or home can mean even the entire nation of India itself.

Vivek Bald, a young second-generation biracial man, tells us that India to him signified a space where his inner, spiritual self could reside. He often told himself that by returning to the homeland of his mother, he would become "whole" once again. The United States, on the other hand, remained an alienating space that was corrupt and decadent. Bald says:

> I had planned to go back to India where most of my mother's family lived. Yes, I was born in the United States, but I did not want to consider myself American. In my mind, America stood for violence, arrogance, hypocrisy, and greed. So ignoring my birth here, my whole childhood here, and a much-loved side of my own family that was from California, Australia, and before that Scotland, I chose India as my "place of origin." I imagined India as America's polar opposite. I saw it as the place of my true roots, my true politics, my true home. So all I had to do was "go back" and everything would be all right.[25]

We see that the notion of home itself is not an a priori concept for Indian immigrants, but instead is actively reinterpreted. Home can either mean the house in which the family resides, or it can mean the entire subcontinent of India as Bald theorizes.

Whatever home is taken to mean, migration causes radical ruptures in immigrants' conceptions of who they are and what their ethnic practices are. Radhakrishnan says of immigration—"the very organicity of the family and the community, displaced by travel and relocation must be renegotiated and redefined." As immigrants, "the issue then is not just 'being Indian' in some natural and self-evident way, . . . but 'cultivating Indian-ness' self-consciously."[26] Hence, homes and origins are actively reinvented, building on what are perceived to be the markers of an authentic identity.

While ethnic homes are no doubt central nodes for expressing race/ethnicity, we must also recognize that they are built on networks of power and domination that allow certain kinds of activities, but foreclose other liberties among members within the ethnic group. For the ethnic family to endure immigrants have to produce the normative texts on which homes are produced. These normative texts are disciplinary heterosexualities according to which both men and women are expected to conform. To build the immigrant home, disciplinary measures are imposed to a far greater degree on women's sexuality than men's. I specify normative *het-ero*sexuality because it is not just queerness that is subject to censure. A heterosexually active woman, for example, is also subject to the strictures of the family. She is subtly, but more often not so subtly, coerced into complying with familial discipline regarding her sexual activities, and also, the race/ethnic background of her sexual partners. Normative sexuality forms the very grid lines on which immigrant homes are mapped and immigrant families reproduced. Yet, even as the family is based on normative sexuality, it is also the site in which such normativity is reproduced. The Indian immigrant family and normative sexuality are mutually constitutive. The home becomes a site for disciplining sexuality, and in turn, the immigrant home so essential for expressing ethnicity, is based on disciplinary sexuality. Normative sexuality then is central to making race a social reality for nonwhite immigrants.

Disciplining Women's Sexuality

Anthias and Yuval-Davis say that women's sexuality is central to ethnic/national processes.[27] Firstly, women are biological reproducers of members of ethnic collectivities since they give birth to children, who are future members of an ethnic group. In addition, women are seen as the bearers of culture for the ethnic group. Women are the "main socialisers of small children, but in the case of ethnic minorities . . . they may be required to transmit the rich heritage of ethnic symbols and ways of life to other members of the ethnic group, especially the young."[28] Hence, women's everyday conduct, their associations with people within and outside the group, types of associations, and so on are all scrutinized to greater degrees than are men's associations. In addition, Anthias and Yuval-Davis point out that women are not just passive receivers of these traditions, but instead, many women are willing participants in the ideological reproduction of their ethnic collectivity.

Speaking of Indian immigrants, Bhattacharjee says that the site for Indian tradition and culture here in the United States is the home. The home is "a place to reaffirm one's Indian-ness and the Indian woman is expected to be responsible for maintaining this Indian home in diaspora by remaining true to her Indian womanhood."[29] To make the ideal Indian home, girls are taught to be good mothers and wives, which often translates into self-sacrifice and accommodating everyone's needs in the family. DasGupta and Das Dasgupta comment that in the cultural schooling of Indian American youth there is careful preservation of gender roles. The chastity and purity of "daughters is much prized, evidenced by unequal parental restrictions."[30] Monisha Das Gupta writes that the second-generation women she interviewed for her research were expected to be more careful of their conduct in social interactions than were men. The women were carefully monitored by their parents into adulthood until their marriages. For example, they had to put up with strictly imposed curfews where they returned home much earlier than their male siblings. Or in more extreme cases, women might not be allowed to leave the parental home in pursuit of an education. Says one young woman she interviewed: "I was never allowed to go away from home to study. But my brother has got away with a lot. Right now he is away at college. He worked night shifts and returned at three in the morning. Or he goes out at ten at night, saying he would be back in half-an-hour but he stays out until twelve. That does not create a problem."[31]

The immigrant Indian family becomes a repository of cultural values, exemplar family ideals, and idealized heterosexuality in opposition to "American" values existing outside the home. Monisha Das Gupta writes that Indian parents feel the need to protect their families, especially their daughters from the American world lying outside their chaste Indian home. Dating among young teenagers is a major concern for Indian American parents who view it as a uniquely American practice. The disciplining of teenage daughters' sexuality is a major source of contention in families. An interviewee to Das Gupta says, "From an early age I understood that dating, smoking, drinking, staying out late were simply not done."[32] Dating is explicitly forbidden by parents, because women's reputations and marriageability within the community depend on their perceived chastity.

Many Indian American girls are sent back to India to the extended family in an effort to regain familial control of their sexuality. Growing up in India is seen as the best prescription for getting control over a young woman's sexuality. In addition, parents negotiating matrimonial alliances for their sons prefer young brides from India, because these women are more "authentically" Indian, and their sexuality ostensibly more disciplined within families. India, in contrast to America, is recast as a nation where women's sexuality is disciplined and hence, a space where families thrive.

Daughters from an early age bear the weight of the family's and community's honor. Maira says that women are believed to be the repositories of the immigrant family's *izzat*, or reputation, and immigrant parents maintain more conservative standards for their daughters than their sons.[33] Gibson observes of Punjabi Sikh immigrants in California:

> Punjabis worry in particular about their daughters' reputations. "All our respect is in their hands," the parents told us. A girl's indiscretions could jeopardize marriage arrangements not only for herself but for her siblings as well. A family's good name is of paramount importance in arranging a marriage, and parents expressed a heavy responsibility to keep their daughters', and thus, family's, name untarnished.[34]

In addition to raising the specter of premarital sex, dating also creates anxiety among first-generation Indians regarding the possibilities for interracial marriage and the reproduction of biracial offspring who are not "wholly" Indian. Says Monisha Das Gupta—"The issue stirred up the parents' worst apprehensions about exogamy and assimilation."[35]

Writing as a Korean American woman, Chung says that when she was dating a white man, her father threatened to disown her. This threat meant not only separation from her immediate family, but also from Korean culture. Moreover, she knew that even without this ultimatum, she would invariably drift from Korean culture if she married a non-Korean.[36] What Ruth Chung says also holds true for many Indian American women who date non-Indian men; they often self-discipline themselves so that they may feel part of a larger community. An immigrant woman's immediate family and ethnic community are meaning-giving contexts. Family and community give her a sense of grounding and structure her ethnic self. The familial location actualizes her ethnicity, and she may find it hard to go against familial/communal gendered norms set for her.

In addition, Indian American women self-discipline themselves because they do not want to bring dishonor to their parents in the eyes of the larger community. If they exercise sexual choices independent of their immediate family's wants, their parents, especially their mothers, are blamed for their "bad" upbringing and could be ostracized by the larger Indian American community. As primary caregivers, mothers in the immigrant family are responsible for raising their children, especially their daughters, in traditional ways. Rayaprol shows in her research that immigrant women are responsible for "memory work," giving concrete shape to Indian ethnicity. Women are responsible for cultured activities such as performing *pujas*, cooking ethnic foods, and wearing ethnic clothes.

The women Rayaprol studied, however, were not forced into these roles, but instead participated in gendered roles willingly. Her research participants derived meaning from the various rituals of ethnicity and felt a sense of empowerment by raising their children here in the United States in ways they deemed proper.[37] The sense of accomplishment that women feel in raising their children to be "truly Indian" in the face of an overwhelming American world outside can be considerable, for against all odds they have been successful Indian mothers in the eyes of the larger diasporic Indian community as well as the extended family back home in India. The onus of raising children, especially daughters in sexually disciplined ways, falls more on mothers than on fathers. Successful motherhood often translates to maternal disciplining of daughters' sexuality, and "thus it is the mothers who most often come into conflict with second generation young women regarding sexuality."[38]

Speaking of immigrant women in general, Espin explains how immigrant women negotiate questions of ethnic identity and sexual identity. Decisions regarding sexuality taken independent of the family are associated with "becoming Americanized." Espin points out that immigrant women have to deal with both the racial oppressions from outside the racial/ethnic community, as well as the pressures from having to conform to tradition within the community.[39] She writes that "Young women's independent sexual choices, made without family approval, [are] labeled as 'Americanization' and [are] considered synonymous with unprincipled immoral behavior."[40] The home then, which is presumed to be a utopian space and which allows an immigrant to be his or her ethnic *ur* self, is a gendered space that is far more limiting for Indian American women. Retiring from a public white gaze, she returns home to all the sexual/gendered disciplinary norms imposed on her in the name of a reimagined Indian culture.

Private Disciplines Public Successes: Becoming an Ethnic American

So far I have discussed how the home becomes a central space for expressing ethnicity. At this point, one must stop and ask— Are the public and private worlds so completely separate as immigrants believe them to be? Or instead, are the two worlds connected, wherein private familial disciplines are perceived to make a successful American? We see that Indian immigrants, at one level, voice that their homes are separate from the public world outside. Yet, at another level, especially within a context of anti-immigrant backlash, they posit their sexually disciplined, ethnic families as the fundamental reason for their development into successful American citizens. The Indian American family, precisely because of its isolation from the American world, is idealized as a virtuous space from which good American citizens arise.

If we cast even a cursory glance at the traditional academic literature on assimilation of immigrants, we will notice that the underlying concern is with how the ethnic home either impedes or aids Americanization. Americanization of new immigrants—speaking English; the adoption of American customs of sanitation, hygiene, and time management; cooking "nonsmelly" foods; modification of child rearing practices—was seen as a prerequisite for their socioeconomic mobility in this nation. Immigrant women especially were perceived as the main hindrance to immigrant families' assimilation and subsequent social/economic mobility. A small group of middle-class Americans,[41] mainly women social workers, sought to change immigrant families to bring progress to the tenements. These social workers intervened into the private sphere, focusing their reformatory efforts on immigrant women. They had "firm scientific ideas about proper infant care, family life, parent-child relationships, diet, and hygiene."[42] They sought to change the fundamental patterns of the everyday lives of the new immigrants, with the hope that by becoming American culturally, they could progress economically and achieve social mobility.

The perception right up to the 1960s was that customs, cultural practices, and traditions—things immigrants practiced in their homes—were "backward" and impeded immigrants' assimilation into the United States. Milton Gordon was among the first to question this linear progression of assimilation. He claimed that cultural assimilation (i.e., Anglo conformity) did not necessarily lead to civic assimilation or acceptance into mainstream social institutions.[43] By the mid-1960s and 1970s, the concept of assimilation had fallen into disrepute because of its strong ethnocentric tendencies.[44] In the 1980s, however, the term reared its head once again in academic and popular parlance. This time the concept was not deployed ideologically, but instead "assimilation" was used to describe the processes by which post-1965 immigrants grappled with arriving into the United States and got incorporated into the American civic body. Focusing especially on second-generation nonwhite immigrants, the prevailing academic perspective was the exact opposite of the turn of the

century nationalist discourse that prescribed wholesale acculturation. The 1980s perspective cast a skeptical eye and posited that
indiscriminate cultural assimilation was perhaps not the best
possible means for social mobility in the United States. Recent
studies on the post-1965 second generation showed that assimilation into some aspects of American culture was detrimental to
their academic achievement. Instead, retention of ethnic characteristics and ethnic networks could facilitate school performance
and social mobility.

Among these studies was Margaret Gibson's *Accommodation
Without Assimilation* (1989) focusing on Punjabi immigrants,
originally from northwestern India, who had settled in northern
California. Gibson posits a *selective* assimilation model to describe a situation where second-generation immigrants judi-
ciously adopted only positive American values and were therefore successful. She explains that these second-generation
Punjabi immigrants achieved academic success in spite of viru-
lent racism directed against them because they retained their
parents' cultural values but also took on desirable American
traits. Parents urged their children to abide by school rules, develop strong English language skills, and learn other useful
skills. On the other hand, the parents also pressured their children against too much contact with white peers because they
could become too Americanized and leave home at eighteen,
and begin dating, dancing, and making decisions for their lives
without parental consent. The Punjabi second-generation youth
were seen to selectively acculturate, picking up certain American
values, but also retaining strong ethnic identities, which led to
their success in school performance here in the United States.[45]

Theories on assimilation have come full circle. Retention of
ethnic cultures and ethnic networks, instead of hindering the
economic outcomes of immigrants as perceived at the turn of the
century, is now seen as potentially facilitating the economic mobility of new post-1965 immigrants.[46] The immigrant home as
the primary site of ethnic culture and the immigrant woman as
the progenitor of this culture were previously seen as the main
impediments to American acculturation and social mobility. Today, instead, we see a reversal. The immigrant home—that ven-
erated site of ethnic culture—is now understood to be the main
reason for immigrant success.[47] Private familial practices in im-

migrant homes, such as the ones described by Gibson, are seen to bolster public social/economic successes.

Indian immigrants understand their homes to be completely beyond the influences of the outside world. In their sanctified homes, standing in self-imposed isolation from the negative influences of the outside world, they believe that they can raise their children to follow Indian values such as respecting elders, abiding by parental rules, not dating, and working hard. These ostensibly Indian values lead to Indian immigrants becoming public successes as adults. The family is perceived as the node on which the Indian American community's "model minority" status rests. Indian American family structures, idealized as strong and moral, are perceived to be the building blocks of economic and social success of Indian Americans in the public sphere. Indian Americans perceive themselves to be "good" immigrants who have good work ethics and by extension become good Americans, precisely because of the values inculcated in the private sphere of the family. Hence, ethnic values are actually seen to make them successful Americans.

Indian immigrants simply do not blend into a racialized, American world, but instead they actively exercise agency in a mediating fashion, working the cultural practices they carry from their sending county within the American cultural context. They do not transform the racial context of this nation, but they are active agents in resisting the ways in which they are negatively categorized. They arrive into an American world that expresses strong anti-immigrant sentiment. A common refrain in mass media, school boards, environmental agencies such as Sierra Club, welfare agencies, hospitals, and other such public spaces is that the new, nonwhite immigrants are unassimilable. They do not learn English. They have different cultural values. They are a threat to traditional American institutions. Immigrants are blamed for the overall decline in American standards of living.[48] In such a context, Indian immigrants vigorously exert themselves back into the American public sphere as minorities, but as *good* minorities who will contribute to the American nation.

Take the example of an article titled "Indian-Americans are industrious, resourceful, and prudent" in the news magazine *India Worldwide* (January 31, 1995). The author, Sandhu, points out that as the U.S. economy worsens, immigrant minorities are subject to racism. He questions why immigrants are blamed for America's economic ills, especially when this nation also receives immigrants such as Indians who are

> hard-working, industrious and resourceful. They produce wealth, live prudently save and plough their wealth in productive enterprises, qualities that are the hallmark of success in all spheres of business and industrial undertaking. To cap it all they are law-abiding and peaceful citizens and abhor violence. They will be the last to look to social services and welfare to provide them with sustenance, as such dependence is considered a disgrace and stigma, however legal such dependence may be.[49]

Indian immigrants perceive their families as the main reason for their success here in the United States. Hence, even as they posit the privacy of the home as an insular, utopic site untouched by the happenings of the world outside, the home and the family birth them as good public citizens. They believe they have moral families that inculcate virtuous values, and therefore they are able to merge into the American public world as exemplary individuals. As an example, let me reproduce a news article published in the March 10, 1997, issue of the *Indian Express*, forwarded to me over e-mail by an Indian American friend. The subject line of the e-mail read "NEAT NEWS!! DISTRIBUTE," and the article title proclaimed "Indian brilliance dazzles Americans."

> Continuing their dazzling good form that has electrified and bemused the American academic world, two Indian students in the United States rank among the top four Westinghouse science talent prize winners this year. The superb Indian performance follows up last year's remarkable feat when three Indians ranked among the top ten, leading many educationists to question and study *the proclivity of Indian families and systems to foster academic brilliance.* . . . . [W]hat has baffled and impressed American educationists is the frequency and ease with which Indian students figure in this list, completely out of proportion with their numerical strength. The Indian population in the US is only about a million with less than half-a-million students and certainly less than 100,000 school going kids. Yet they fig-

ure prominently in any sphere of academic excellence from spelling bee contests to chess tournaments. . . . Many attribute it to *family values and high ideals inculcated in Indian homes.*

Though viewed as polar opposites, Indian immigrants posit a causal relationship between the home and the world. Their frequent understanding is that, precisely because of their private disciplines, especially strictures on women's sexuality, they are able to succeed in the world outside, thus making for a successful model minority community.

Conclusion

Indian Americans feel they have to conform to white norms in the public sphere. Such racial conformity feels alien to their ethnic being. Hence, they retire to the privacy of their homes, away from a racially disciplining gaze of an American public. In the privacy of their homes they can resist the disciplinary norms of American race rhetoric and become Indian once again. The production of home as the ethnic node, however, is based on normative heterosexuality, imposing strict regulations on men and women. The precepts regarding women's sexuality are far more severe than they are for men. Yet, even as the home—so central to expressing ethnicity—is seen as separate and unsullied by the world outside, immigrant success in the public world is attributed precisely to the home. It is the home, with all its disciplined sexuality, that is posited as the chief reason for immigrant successes. On the one hand, the immigrant sees the home as separate, but at another level, the home is the fundamental node on which immigrant success rests.

As immigrants Indian Americans refuse to be subordinated by the categories into which they are placed. They balk at assimilation into a public "whiteness," where they are incorporated as minor partners. In a white world they can never set the context, but only toe the line. The home, on the other hand, is the site of Indian immigrants' resistance—it is that space that allows them to become their *ur* self. At home they can become Indian. They therefore strive hard to reproduce their families, their sites of resistance to "whiteness." Yet, in the reproduction of "Indian-ness" in families they are still conscious of our locations here in the United States, and the ways in which they interpret their racial practices ultimately have the unintended consequences of bolstering the existing structures of race in the United States. They do not challenge or try to intervene in any manner in the racial debates that rage through the nation, but instead retreat to the privacy of their homes, in a quiet manifestation of everyday resistance. The unintended consequence of such resistance is that it leads to fortifying racial hierarchies in the United States, rather than destabilizing them.

Speaking of African diasporic filmmakers in the Americas, Stuart Hall says:

> It is because this "new World" is constituted for us [immigrants] as place, a narrative of displacement, that it gives rise so profoundly to a certain imaginary plenitude, recreating the endless desire to return to "lost origins," to be one again with the mother, to go back to the beginning. . . . And yet, this "return to the beginning" is like the Imaginary in Lacan—it can neither be fulfilled nor requited, and hence is the beginning of the symbolic . . . the infinitely renewable source of desire, memory, myth, search, discovery—in short, the reservoir of our cinematic narratives.[50]

Likewise, the Indian diaspora in the United States is endlessly creative in narrating its origins so as to make sense of the here and now. But there can be no return to what we have left behind, for we as individuals as well as India itself have moved on. In the sending country, India, we do not find the Indian cultural norms that first-generation immigrants practice here in the United States. First-generation immigrants tend to freeze "Indian-ness" to what existed when they were children in India, but that nation has moved on from those times. In an appropriately titled book, *Imaginary Homelands*, Salman Rushdie cautions us immigrants from looking back to the sending country to constantly reimagine ourselves. He says:

> It may be that writers in my position, exiles or emigrates or expatriates, are haunted by some sense of loss, some urge to reclaim, to look back, even at the risk of being mutated into pillars of salt. But if we do look back, we must do so in the

knowledge—which gives rise to profound uncertainties—that our physical alienation from India almost inevitably means that we will not be capable of reclaiming precisely the thing that was lost; that we will, in short, create fictions, not actual cities or villages, but invisible ones, imaginary ones, Indias of the mind.[51]

While the imagination of the immigrant in the New World can no doubt be endlessly creative as Hall indicates, I have shown that it can also be immensely conservative especially in the politics of holding onto an *ur*-identity, to which immigrant women are expected to conform. Indian immigrants cannot presume that their ethnic practices stand in stark resistance to the normative pressures of whiteness outside the home. Instead, the repertoire of racial practices they perform actually bolsters their public performances. Moreover, these racial practices are inherently gendered, imposing greater sexual strictures against women than men. In resisting the mainstreaming pressures of "whiteness" outside the home, they reproduce gender ideologies with all the dictates of differential disciplining of men and women's sexuality.

Getting ethnic, then, is not a way out for destabilizing the structures of power that shape them. Indeed, in remaking their ethnic selves—"reworking the images that encode the symbolic valencies of self"[52]—they draw on memories that further discipline them in ways they do not expect. Fanon's words, written in the mid-1960s when newly independent nations were forging new national identities, still hold a warning to immigrants such as Indians in the United States. Fanon cautions:

We must not . . . be content with delving into the past of a people in order to find coherent elements that will counteract colonialism's attempts to falsify and harm. A national culture is not a folklore, nor an abstract populism that believes it can discover a people's true nature. A national culture is the whole body of efforts made by a people in the sphere of thought to describe, justify and praise the action through which that people has created itself and keeps itself in existence.[53]

Instead of freezing culture into normative practices and rituals, Indian immigrants need to understand that culture is an ever-changing entity. Indian culture is a whole body of historic/present efforts made by Indians both here and there, involving a plethora of subaltern movements, feminist ideals, anticaste agitations, and antiracist struggles that influence the philosophies of our everyday lives, thus helping create us, and keeping us in existence. As immigrants, we need to truly engage with the politics of the home and of the world, and grapple with issues that happen every day, instead of retreating to notions of a glorious cultural past that somehow makes us good Indians, and therefore, good Americans. Reflective judgment on who we are ethnically and where we racially fit into an American world as persons of color—getting ethnic, in other words—is not simply a matter of aesthetics and the application of authentic cultural practices. Instead, getting ethnic represents some of our most political mental abilities.[54]

Notes

1. Meena Alexander, *The Shock of Arrival: Reflections on the Postcolonial Experience* (Boston: South End, 1996), 155.i.
2. Anthony Giddens, *The Constitution of Society* (Berkeley: University of California Press, 1984), 16–18. Giddens points out that these rules are subject to contestations.
3. Giddens, *The Constitution of Society*, 90.
4. Giddens, *The Constitution of Society*, 21.
5. Patricia Williams, *The Alchemy of Race and Rights: Diary of a Law Professor* (Cambridge: Harvard University Press, 1991).
6. Ruth Chung, "Reflections on a Korean American Journey," in *Struggle for Ethnic Identity: Narratives by Asian American Professionals*, ed. Pyong Gap Min and Rose Kim (Walnut Creek, Calif.: AltaMira, 1999), 60.
7. Mustafa Emirbayer and Ann Mische, "What Is Agency?" *American Journal of Sociology*, 103 (1998): 962–1023.
8. Alexander, *The Shock of Arrival*, 155.
9. Sayantini DasGupta, "Thoughts from a Feminist ABCD," *India Currents*, 6 (1993): 26.
10. See David Roediger, *The Wages of Whiteness* (London: Verso, 1991); Frankenberg, *White Women, Race Matters*; Theodore Allen, *The Invention of the White Race* (New York: New York University Press, 1994); Noel Ignatiev, *How The Irish Became White* (New York: Routledge, 1995).

11. For detailed discussions on racial practices see, Haney Lopez, *White by Law: The Legal Construction of Race* (New York: New York University Press, 1996); Frankenberg, 1993.

12. Alexander, *The Shock of Arrival*, 155.

13. For an interesting discussion on this issue of not marking whiteness, see Williams, 1991, 88–89.

14. R. Radhakrishnan, "Is the Ethnic 'Authentic' in the Diaspora?" in *The State of Asian America: Activism and Resistance in the 1990s*, ed. Karin Aguilar-San Juan (Boston, Mass.: South End, 1994).

15. Radhakrishnan, "Is the Ethnic 'Authentic' in the Diaspora?", 223. My emphasis.

16. Radhakrishnan, "Is the Ethnic 'Authentic' in the Diaspora?", 229.

17. Winona Giles, "Remembering The Portuguese Household in Toronto: Culture, Contradictions, and Resistance," *Women's Studies International Forum*, 20 (1997): 387–96.

18. Alexander, *The Shock of Arrival*, 156.

19. Partha Chatterjee, *The Nation and its Fragments*. (Princeton, N.J: Princeton University Press, 1993), 6.

20. Chatterjee, *The Nation and its Fragments*, 263.

21. George Mead, *The Philosophy of the Present* (1932), 17. Quoted in Emirbayer and Mische, "What Is Agency?", 975.

22. Emirbayer and Mische, "What Is Agency?", 975.

23. Emirbayer and Mische, "What Is Agency?", 975.

24. Emirbayer and Mische point out that social actors *are* able to hypothesize their experiences and reconfigure received schema "by generating alternative possible responses to the problematic situations they confront in their lives" ("What Is Agency?", 984).

25. Vivek Bald, "Taxi Meters and Plexiglass Partitions" in *Contours of the Heart: South Asians Map North America*, ed. Sunaina Maira and Rajini Srikanth (New York: Asian American Writers' Workshop, 1996), 66–73.

26. Radhakrishnan, "Is the Ethnic 'Authentic' in the Diaspora?", 223–24.

27. Floya Anthias and Nira Yuval-Davis, eds., *Woman-Nation-State* (New York: St. Martin's Press, 1989), 7.

28. Anthias and Yuval-Davis, *Woman-Nation-State*, 9.

29. Annanya Bhattacharjee, "The Habit of Ex-Nomination: Nation, Women, and the Indian Immigrants Bourgeoisie," *Public Culture*, 5 (1992): 19–44.

30. Shamita Das Dasgupta and Sayantini DasGupta, "Astride the Lion's Back: Gender Relations in the Asian Indian Community," in *Contours of the Heart: South Asians Map North America*, ed. Sunaina Maira and Rajini Srikanth (New York: Asian American Writer's Workshop, 1996).

31. Monisha Das Gupta, "What Is Indian About You? A Gendered Transnational Approach to Ethnicity," *Gender and Society*, 11 (1995): 572–96.

32. Das Gupta, "What Is Indian About You?", 584.

33. Sunaina Maira, "Chaste Identities, Ethnic Yearnings: Second Generation Indian Americans in New York," (Ph.D. thesis, Graduate School of Education, Harvard University, 1998).

34. Gibson, *Accommodation Without Assimilation*, 120.

35. Gibson, *Accommodation Without Assimilation*, 586.

36. Chung, "Reflections on a Korean American Journey," 63.

37. Aparna Rayaprol, *Negotiating Identities: Women in the Indian Diaspora* (New Delhi, India: Oxford University Press, 1997).

38. Sayantini DasGupta and Shamita Das Dasgupta, "Sex, Lies, and Women's Lives: An Intergenerational Dialogue," in *A Patchwork Shawl: Chronicles of South Asian Women in America*, ed. Shamita Das Dasgupta (New York: Routledge, 1998), 113.

39. Oliva M. Espin, "'Race,' Racism, and Sexuality in the Life Narratives of Immigrant Women," *Feminism and Psychology*, 5 (1995): 223–38.

40. DasGupta and Das Dasgupta, "Sex, Lies, and Women's Lives."

41. Elizabeth Ewen, *Immigrant Women in the Land of Dollars: Life and Culture on the Lower East Side, 1890–1925* (New York: Monthly Review Press, 1985).

42. Ewen, *Immigrant Women in the Land of Dollars*, 85.

43. Gordon, *Assimilation in American Life*.

44. See Nathan Glazer, "Is Assimilation Dead?" *Annals of the American Political and Social Sciences*, 530 (1993): 122–36; Richard Alba and Victor Nee, "Rethinking Assimilation Theory for a New Era of Immigration," *International Migration Review*, 31 (1997): 826–72.

45. Gibson, *Accommodation Without Assimilation*.

46. Alejandro Portes and Robert Bach, *Latin Journey: Cuban and Mexican Immigrants in the United States* (Berkeley: University of California Press, 1985); Kenneth Wilson and W. Allen Martin, "Ethnic Enclaves: A Comparison of the Cuban and Black Economies in Miami," *American Journal of Sociology*, 88 (1982): 135–60.

47. Pyong Gap Min, "A Comparison of Post-1965 and Turn-of-the-Century Immigrants in Intergenerational Mobility and Cultural Transmission," *Journal of American Ethnic History*, 18 (1999): 65–94; Portes and Zhou, "The New Second Generation," 74–97; Min Zhou, "Segmented Assimilation: Issues, Controversies, and Recent Research on the New Second Generation," *International Migration Review*, 31 (1997): 975–1008.

48. Rita Simon, "Old Minorities, New Immigrants: Aspirations, Hopes, and Fears," *The Annals of The American Political and Social Science*, 530 (1993): 61–73.

49. G. S. Sandhu, "Indian-Americans are Industrious, Resourceful, and Prudent," *India Worldwide* (Jan. 31, 1995), 1.

50. Stuart Hall, "Cultural Identity and Cinematic Representation," in *Black British Cultural Studies: A Reader*, ed. Houston Baker Jr., Manthia Diawara, and Ruth Lindeborg (Chicago: University of Chicago Press, 1996), 221.

51. Salman Rushdie, *Imaginary Homelands* (London: Penguin, 1991), 10.

52. Alexander, *The Shock of Arrival*, 156.

53. Fanon, quoted in Hall, "Cultural Identity and Cinematic Representation," 221.

54. Emirbayer and Mische ("What Is Agency?", 996) quote Hannah Arendt: "reflective judgment is not limited to aesthetics but represents 'the most political of man's mental abilities.'"

CHAPTER FOUR

ETHNIC ATTACHMENT AMONG SECOND-GENERATION KOREAN AMERICANS

Pyong Gap Min and Joann Hong

The massive immigration of people from Third World countries to the United States since the late 1960s has contributed to revival of research on immigrants and their children. In the 1970s and the early 1980s, research focused exclusively on first-generation immigrants' adjustments, especially their economic adjustments. But social scientists began research on the children of post-1965 immigrants, or the so-called new second generation, in the late 1980s, often using high school students as a database. As a result, as documented in the introductory chapter, a number of articles and several books that shed light on the new second generation have been available as of 2000.

As emphasized in the introductory and other substantive chapters of this book, ethnographic research is more helpful than survey research in understanding the dynamic, changing, and multiple characteristics of ethnic identity among second-generation Asian Americans. Yet, survey research is necessary to examine overall trends in different aspects of their ethnic attachment, such as their fluency and frequency of using mother tongue, preference for coethnic members as dating partners, and choice of primary ethnic identity among second-generation Asian Americans. More important, survey research is useful in determining the relationships between their background characteristics and the levels of their ethnic attachment.

Major survey data on the new second generation were collected in Miami and San Diego using high school children.[1] The two data sets include information about retention of mother tongue and choice of ethnic identity. Yet data were largely based on the children of Latino, Caribbean, and Filipino immigrants and Indochinese refugees heavily concentrated in the two cities.

There is no major survey study that has focused on the children of other major Asian immigrant groups, namely Chinese, Korean, and Indian, who represent a higher class background than Indochinese refugees.[2] This chapter bridges the gap in information about second-generation Asian Americans' ethnic attachment by using survey data. It examines ethnic attachment among second-generation Korean adolescents based on results of a survey conducted in the New York area.

Ethnic attachment indicates the degree to which members of an ethnic or immigrant group are integrated into the ethnic community culturally, socially, and psychologically. This article has two interrelated objectives with regards to second-generation Koreans' ethnic attachment. First, it describes the levels of second-generation Korean adolescents' cultural, social, and psychological dimensions of ethnic attachment. Second, this article examines, using t-test analyses, the major factors that are highly correlated with two of the three dimensions of ethnic attachment: use of the Korean language and Korean friendship. Respondents' sex, country of birth, age, place of residence, frequency of attending a Korean church, and coresidence with a grandparent will be considered as major factors that are highly correlated with these two dimensions of their ethnic attachment.

Data Sources

A questionnaire was administered to Korean junior and senior high school students in the New York area in 1989 and 1996. "Convenient sampling" characterized the sampling technique used because Korean adolescents were located for administration of the questionnaire by the convenience of those who collected the data. In the majority of the cases, the questionnaire was administered to small groups in public high schools with a large number of Korean students, Korean churches, and other organizations. In other cases, the questionnaire was administered to Korean American adolescents individually by a number of volunteers who knew those students. To mix Korean enclaves with those in suburban areas, the respondents were located not only in Queens but also in other New York City boroughs, Long Island, and the New Jersey area. The respondents may have been a little biased in that most of them were located in settings where they had more interactions with coethnics than Korean American adolescents in general.

In all, 485 respondents completed the questionnaire; 134 respondents were born in the United States, 340 were born in Korea, and the remaining eleven were born in a third country. In this study, second-generation Korean adolescents were defined as those Korean-born children who came to the United States at the age of five or before as well as those who were born in the United States or a third country.[3] Ninety-two of those 340 Korean-born respondents immigrated to this country at the age of five or before. Thus, 237 respondents who met the definition of the second generation were selected for data analysis. Many of these second-generation Korean respondents failed to respond to one or more of the items included in the questionnaire. Therefore, the number of cases for most variables involved in data analysis was less than 237.

The survey was conducted to collect general information about Korean American adolescents. The questionnaire included forty-nine items, which were related to Korean children's relationships with their parents, teachers, and peers; their extracurricular activities; future educational plans; and demographic and family backgrounds, as well as those dimensions of their ethnic attachment. *ethnic attachment*
It included several items that measure the respondents' fluency and frequency of using English and Korean. Language is the most salient aspect of ethnic subculture.[4] Thus, the responses to the items measuring the respondents' fluency and frequency of using the Korean language were used as indicators of their cultural ethnic attachment. The questionnaire also included an item asking about the ethnic composition of the respondents' three best same-sex friends, another item about the ethnic composition of their dating partners, and a third item about feeling more comfortable making Korean friends than non-Korean friends. The responses to these three items were used to measure the respondents' social ethnic attachment. Finally, one item asked the respondents to report their primary ethnic identity by choosing one of the following categories: Korean, Korean American, Asian American, American, and others. If a respondent identifies himself or herself as "Korean," he or she can be considered to have strong psychological ethnic attachment. If he or

she chooses the "American" category, he or she should be considered to have almost no psychological attachment. We expect most second-generation Korean students to identify themselves as "Korean American."

The questionnaire was not created particularly to measure Korean American adolescents' ethnic attachment. Thus, the measurement of the three major components (cultural, social, and psychological) of the dependent variable (ethnic attachment) is not as accurate as we wanted it to be. Yet the responses to these items are likely to provide useful information about second-generation Korean adolescents' ethnic attachment in a large Korean community not available in other sources.

Levels of Ethnic Attachment

Table 4.1 provides data on second-generation Korean adolescents' fluency in English and Korean based on their self-evaluations. The majority of the respondents evaluated themselves to be fluent in all three components of the English language. The data indicate that a language barrier may be a problem for Korean immigrant students, but that at least second-generation Korean students do not have difficulty at all with the English language. In their survey study of language patterns of second-generation Latino and Caribbean black children in Miami, Portes and Schauffler found that 73 percent of respondents reported that they were able to speak, read, and write English very well.[5] A much larger proportion of the Korean respondents, nearly 90 percent, reported that they were proficient in English.

Table 4.1. Respondents' Self Report of the Degree of Their Fluency in English and Korean (percent)

| | English | | | Korean | | |
	Speaking	Reading	Writing	Speaking	Reading	Writing
Fluent	91.1	89.5	86.9	9.4	1.7	1.3
Good	7.6	8.0	9.3	28.9	23.8	11.9
Fair	0.8	1.7	3.0	39.6	39.6	41.7
Poor	0.4	0.4	0.4	26.4	26.4	33.2
Not at all	0.0	0.4	0.4	8.5	8.5	11.9
Total	99.9	100.1	100.0	101.0	101.0	100.0
	(N=237)	(N=237)	(N=237)	(N=235)	(N=235)	(N=235)

The right-hand panel of table 4.1 shows the degree of the respondents' fluency in the Korean language. Overall, the majority of the respondents rated their Korean speaking as good or fair, and lower proportions of the respondents, but still the majority, rated their Korean reading and writing skills to be good or fair. A very small proportion of the respondents chose either of the extreme categories (fluent or not at all). This suggests that most second-generation Korean adolescents have learned the Korean language at some level, but that few of them have achieved a high level of proficiency. Korean American adolescents need to speak Korean to communicate with their parents because almost all Korean immigrants speak it at home.[6] Korean American children also seem to have advantages over other Asian American children for learning their mother tongue because Koreans have only one language. While Indian, Filipino, and even Chinese communities with multiple languages use English for their ethnic media, major Korean communities have several Korean language dailies and several TV and radio stations.

In addition, Korean American children have advantages for learning their parental language because most of them have the convenience of participating in the Korean language program offered by a Korean church. More than 75 percent of Korean immigrant families regularly participate in Korean Christian churches, and most Korean churches have established a Korean language program.[7] Ninety-five percent of the respondents listed Catholicism or a Protestant denomination as their religion and all attended a Korean congregation. In order to give their children Korean language and other Korean cultural education, Korean immigrants with one or more school-attending children tend to attend a Korean immigrant church in higher proportion than other Korean immigrants.

Table 4.2 shows respondents' frequency of using the Korean language versus English with their parents at home and their Korean friends outside of school. The predominant majority of the respondents use English more often than Korean or use the two languages equally when they communicate with their parents, with a small proportion using the Korean language more often. Considering that most Korean parents cannot speak English very well,[8] we can imagine that Korean

Table 4.2. Respondents' Frequency of Speaking Korean with Their Parents and Korean Friends (percent)

	With Parents	With Korean Friends
English always	6.1	36.4
English most of the time or more often	28.9	48.3
English and Korean half-and-half	42.5	13.6
Korean most of the time or more often	15.4	1.3
Korean always	7.0	0.4
Total	101.0	100.0
	(N=228)	(N=236)

American children's proclivity to use English for communication with their parents causes serious problems. Often Korean parents speak to their second-generation children in Korean, while their children respond in English. Approximately eighty-five of the respondents reported that they used English always or more often to communicate with their Korean friends even outside of school.[9] This finding reflects the preference of second-generation Korean adolescents to use English as the everyday language.

Table 4.3 shows the ethnic compositions of the respondents' three best friends and dating partner, which reflect their social ethnic attachment. The majority of the respondents reported that a Korean was their best friend. The proportion of those who chose a Korean as their second best or third best friend was close to the majority. Although 107 re-

Table 4.3. Racial Composition of Respondents' Three Best Friends and Dating Partners (percent)

Ethnic Category	Best Friend	Second Best Friend	Third Best Friend	Dating Partner
Korean	57.0	48.0	47.5	56.9
Chinese	10.5	10.2	9.4	8.6
Other Asian	4.6	5.8	4.0	3.4
White	22.3	30.2	35.9	31.0
Latino	2.2	4.0	2.2	0.0
Black	0.9	1.8	0.9	0.0
Total	100.0	100.0	100.0	99.9
	(N=229)	(N=225)	(N=223)	(N=59)

spondents (47 percent of them responded to the item) reported that they had ever dated an opposite sex partner, only 59 responded to the question about the ethnic category of their dating partner. Again, the majority of them reported that a Korean was their partner. As reflected by their use of language, second-generation Korean adolescents have achieved a high level of cultural assimilation. However, they show preference for Koreans as close friends and dating partners. Thus, the distinction between cultural and social assimilation is very useful to understanding second-generation Korean adolescents' adjustment patterns.

Second-generation Korean adolescents prefer whites next to Koreans for close social relations. About one-third of the respondents had a white person as their best, second best, third best friend, or dating partner. Second-generation Korean students accept whites as close friends far better than Korean immigrant students do. A little more than 10 percent of Korean immigrant student respondents included in the same survey indicated a white person as their best, second best, third best friend, or dating partner. The close friendships that second-generation Korean adolescents maintain with white students suggest the possibility for a high level of intermarriage between the Korean and white populations in the future. In fact, 1990 census data show that U.S.-born Koreans have the highest rate of intermarriage (72 percent) among all Asian ethnic groups and that the vast majority of them marry white partners.[10]

Data in table 4.3 also reveal that many second-generation Korean adolescents maintain close friendships with Chinese students. Because of cultural and physical similarities, Korean, Chinese, and Japanese Americans accept one another very well through a close friendship and intermarriage.[11] Several public schools in New York City have many Chinese and Korean students. Thus, Korean students in many high schools in New York City have the opportunity to make friends with Chinese students. As demonstrated in many other chapters of this book, second-generation Asian Americans develop stronger ethnic and pan-Asian racial identities as they enter college. As the respondents advance to college, they are likely to maintain closer relations with Chinese American friends, away from white American friends. It is a well-known fact that Korean

Table 4.4. Respondents' Choice of Ethnic Identity Categories (percent)

Korean	21.3
Korean American	72.2
Asian American	3.0
American	3.5
Total	100.0
	(N=230)

immigrants do not maintain close relations with blacks and Latinos.[12] Our data show that even second-generation Korean children rarely interact with members of these minority groups either.

Table 4.4 shows the respondents' choices of ethnic identity labels. As expected, the vast majority (72 percent) chose the "Korean American" label. A significant proportion (21 percent) selected the national origin label, "Korean." There is a significant difference between second-generation and immigrant Korean adolescents in their ethnic identity. For the immigrant sample, 73 percent chose the national origin label and only 26 percent chose the "Korean American" label. However, even second-generation Korean adolescents hold a strong Korean identity as more than 90 percent of the respondents considered themselves "Korean" or "Korean American."

Studies of ethnic identity using other second-generation samples show that much larger proportions of the respondents thought of themselves as "American" and that smaller proportions used the national origin label. For example, an analysis of two major survey data collected in San Diego and Miami reveals that about 20 percent of U.S.-born—mostly Latino and Caribbean—high school respondents identified themselves as "American."[13] Second-generation Korean adolescents seem to maintain a strong Korean ethnic identity mainly because of the cultural and historical homogeneity of the Korean group characterized by one language and no subcultural differences.[14] The group homogeneity has negative effects on the adjustments of Korean immigrants by isolating them from the mainstream society and other minority groups. But it has positive effects on the adjustments of second-generation Korean Americans by helping them maintain a strong ethnic identity and solidarity without losing interactions with other groups.

Correlates of Ethnic Attachment

Using frequency tables, we have thus far examined the levels of second-generation Korean adolescents' cultural, social, and psychological ethnic attachment. In this section, we examine major factors that are highly correlated with two of the three dimensions of their ethnic attachment—use of the Korean language and Korean friendship—using t-test analysis. A value between 1 and 5 was given to each of their five categories in the ascending order for the three items measuring the respondents' proficiency in the Korean language and the two items measuring their frequency of using it. The five items were combined to create an index indicating use of the Korean language. The responses to the three items indicating the ethnic categories of the respondents' three best friends and to an additional item asking about their opinions of feeling more comfortable with making Korean friends were combined to create a scale of Korean friendship. A value of 2 was given to a Korean friend and 0 to a non-Korean friend for each of the first three items. Also, a value between 1 and 5 was given to each of the five categories of responses to the question about whether they feel more comfortable with making Korean friends than non-Korean friends. Table 4.5 shows results of t-test analyses to determine the statistical significance of the differentials between the subgroups for the variables under consideration in the Korean language and Korean friendship.

Results of Portes's and Schauffler's study show that girls have a significantly greater propensity to retain the parental language than boys. They suggested that the result was "attributable to the greater seclusion of female youngsters in the home environment which exposes them to greater contact with parents."[15] Results of our survey of second-generation Korean adolescents also reveal that girls use their parental language more fluently and more frequently than boys. The respondents were asked how many hours their father and mother usually spent per week talking, playing, and/or watching TV with them. Male respondents reported that their fathers spent on average 5.7 hours per week while their mothers spent 8.0 hours. In contrast, female respondents said that their fathers spent 8.1 hours per week and their mothers 11.0 hours. The respondents were also asked to whom they talked to get help when they encountered a personal problem. Twenty-five

Table 4.5. T-Test Analyses of Group Differentials in Use of the Korean Language and Korean Friendship

	Korean Language				Korean Friendship			
	N	X bar	SD	SL	N	X bar	SD	SL
Sex								
Boys	97	12.8	2.9	P<0.01	99	6.2	2.7	N.S.
Girls	129	13.9	3.3		124	6.4	2.9	
Age								
Under 14	103	13.1	2.8	N.S.	102	5.2	2.5	P<0.000
15 or more	123	13.8	3.5		121	7.4	2.9	
Birthplace								
Korea	90	14.2	3.2	N.S.	102	5.2	2.5	N.S.
U.S. and third country	136	12.9	3.1		121	7.4	2.9	
Area of residence								
Queens	77	14.0	3.2	P<0.05	86	6.7	2.7	N.S.
Other areas	149	13.1	3.1		137	6.0	2.9	
Frequency of attending a Korean church								
Twice or more per week		14.7	3.2	P<0.05	50	7.2	2.9	P<0.05
Once a week or less		13.2	3.0		162	6.1	2.8	
Coresident with grandparent								
Yes		13.8	3.3	N.S.	41	6.2	3.0	N.S.
No		18.5	13.4					

percent of male respondents reported that they talked with their father, mother, or both in comparison to 34 percent of female respondents. These findings suggest that second-generation Korean girls spend more time and maintain closer relations with parents than Korean boys. Thus, our data, too, support the "contact hypothesis" proposed by Portes and Schauffler.

Table 4.5 shows that there is no gender difference in the level of Korean friendship. Considering that Korean American women have a higher intermarriage rate than men,[16] we expect a higher proportion of second-generation Korean female adolescents than their male counterparts to date non-Korean partners, especially white partners. But our data do not show any significant gender difference in the ethnic composition of dating partners. The preference of Korean women for white partners may occur later when they get into college.

It is interesting to see whether age has significant effects on second-generation Korean adolescents' ethnic attachment. Younger (fourteen years old and younger) and older adolescents (fifteen years old and over) do not differ significantly in the level of using the Korean language. Yet, the older group achieved a substantially higher score than the younger group in the Korean friendship index. This finding confirms the view, supported by data in other chapters of this book, that minority adolescents, including Asian Americans, become more and more conscious of their ethnic background and color as age progresses. Second-generation Korean high school students feel more comfortable with making Korean friends than their younger counterparts and maintain a higher level of social interactions with Korean friends because they become more conscious of their ethnic identity than they were before.

Our respondents consist of two different groups in terms of the place of birth: those born in Korea who immigrated to this country at the age of five or younger and those born in the United States or in a third country. Those Korean adolescents born in Korea are likely to have an advantage for preserving the Korean language over the others. Our data show that, indeed, is the case. However, the two groups do not have a significant difference in the scale of Korean friendship. Thus, the country of birth does not have significant effects on Korean American adolescents' friendship patterns as long as they immigrate to this country at an early enough age.

Second-generation children settled in an immigrant enclave are likely to have advantages for learning their parental language over those in suburban areas. Recent studies of Latino children support this hypothesis concerning the effects of residential clustering on language retention.[17] As noted in the introduction, Koreans in New York are highly concentrated in Flushing and several other Queens borough areas such as Woodside, Elmhurst, Bayside, and Little Neck. Second-generation Korean adolescents who live in these immigrant enclaves are likely to use the Korean language more fluently and more frequently than those in other areas. Our data show that those respondents who live in various Queens areas have a significantly higher score in use of the Korean language than those in other areas, supporting the "residential clustering" hypothesis. However, like birthplace, the area of residence does not have significant effects on Korean American adolescents' friendship patterns.

Korean immigrant churches facilitate second-generation Korean children's ethnic attachment by helping them learn the Korean language and customs and maintain social networks with coethnic friends.[18] Thus, second-generation Korean adolescents who regularly attend a Korean church are likely to show a higher level of ethnic attachment than others. Unfortunately, our data was not suitable for testing this hypothesis because almost all the respondents attended a Korean religious congregation every week. However, a large number of respondents (N = 51) attended a Korean church twice or more often per week, which makes it possible to divide the respondents into two groups in terms of frequency of attending a Korean church for a t-test analysis.

As shown in table 4.5, the respondents who attended a Korean church twice or more often per week have a substantially higher score in the scale of Korean language use and a moderately higher score in the scale of Korean friendship than the others. Korean American adolescents who go to a Korean church twice or more often participate in a Saturday Korean language school and/or an afterschool program, in addition to attending the regular service on Sunday. Therefore, it is quite natural that they use the Korean language more fluently and more frequently and have more close Korean friends than other Korean American adolescents.

Second-generation Korean adolescents who live with a grandparent are likely to have an advantage for learning the Korean language over others. Forty-two of the respondents (18 percent) were found to have one or more grandparents living together. However, the respondents who live with their grandparent are not better than the others in the use of the Korean language. Our data, which do not show how long the respondents lived with their grandparent, may not be suitable for testing the hypothesis concerning the effects of second-generation Korean adolescents' coresidence with a grandparent on their preservation of the parental language. We need longitudinal data to test the hypothesis in a satisfactory manner.

Conclusion

Our data show that second-generation Korean adolescents are far more fluent in English than in Korean and feel more comfortable speaking English with their Korean friends. Thus, in terms of their use of language they have achieved a high level of *cultural assimilation* and a low level of *cultural ethnic attachment*. However, they show a high level of social ethnic attachment, with about half of them having coethnics as their best, second best, or third best friend, or dating partner. Also, they show strong ethnic identity, with the vast majority choosing the label of "Korean" or "Korean American." It is important to note that few respondents—a much smaller proportion than samples of other second-generation groups—label themselves as "American." Thus, major findings from a survey of second-generation Korean adolescents support the theoretical view that although members of a minority group can achieve a high level of cultural assimilation, such cultural assimilation does not guarantee a similarly high level of social assimilation.[19]

We used t-test analyses to determine whether each of the six independent variables is significantly related to second-generation Korean adolescents' Korean language use and Korean friendship. Data analyses reveal that four of the six variables are highly correlated with respondents' use of the Korean language while only two of the variables are significantly related to Korean friendship. The female respondents are found to have a significantly higher score than their male counterparts in the index of Korean language use, supporting the "contact hypothesis." Data show that second-generation Korean adolescents' age is significantly related to their Korean friendship, but not to their use of the Korean language. Older respondents (fifteen years old and older) scored higher on the Korean friendship index than younger respondents. The Korean-born respondents (who immigrated at the age of five or younger) have a slight advantage for learning the Korean language than those who were born in the United States or in a third country. The respondents in a Korean enclave (Queens, New York City) are found to score higher in the Korean language use index than those in other areas, supporting the ethnic clustering hypothesis. Those who attend a Korean church more frequently are found to have a higher score in the Korean language use index than those who attend the church less frequently.

Because of a nonprobability sampling technique and unsatisfactory measurements, the findings have limitations in generalizability. Nevertheless, they provide a general picture about the retention of the Korean language, friendship, and ethnic identity among second-generation Korean adolescents in the New York area. The findings about Korean Americans' friendship patterns in particular are valuable because few other studies shed light on the friendship patterns of the "new second generation." But we like to emphasize that the major findings from this study are useful in understanding ethnic attachment patterns among Korean adolescents only in large Korean communities such as New York and Los Angeles. Second-generation Korean adolescents in smaller Korean communities are likely to show a lower level of ethnic attachment than our respondents drawn from New York.

Notes

1. Portes and Rumbaut, *Immigrant America*, 2d ed., chapters 6 and 7; Rumbaut and Cornelius, *California's Immigrant Children*.

2. A major survey study of the new second generation based at the Graduate Center of the City University of New York includes second-generation Chinese young adults in New York, as well as other second-generation young adults in the city. The investigators have completed data collection and have not published the results yet.

3. Strictly speaking, second-generation Koreans should include only U.S.-born Koreans with at least one foreign-born Korean parent. However, other researchers have used a broad definition of the "second generation." For example, in their survey study based on eighth- and ninth-grade students in Miami (1994), Alejandro Portes and Richard Schauffler defined the second generation as youth born in the United States with at least one foreign-born parent and children born abroad but who had lived in the United States for five years or more. See their article, "Language and the Second Generation: Bilingualism Yesterday and Today," *International Migration Review*, 28 (1994): 640–61.

4. Jeffrey Reitz, *The Survival of Ethnic Groups* (Toronto: McGraw Hill, 1980); Waters, *Ethnic Options*.

5. Portes and Schauffler, "Language and the Second Generation."

6. According to the 1990 U.S. Census, 93 percent of foreign-born Koreans five years old and over spoke a language other than English at home.

7. See Won Moo Hurh and Kwang Chung Kim, "Religious Participation of Korean Immigrants in the United States," *Journal of the Scientific Study of Religion*, 19 (1990): 19–34; Pyong Gap Min, "The Structure and Social Functions of Korean Immigrant Churches in the United States," *International Migration Review*, 26 (1992):1370–394.

8. According to a survey of Korean, Chinese, and Indian immigrants in Queens, New York City, conducted in 1997 and 1998, only 15 percent of randomly selected Korean respondents reported that they spoke English well or fluently, in comparison to 33 percent of Chinese respondents and 81 percent of Indian respondents.

9. Pyong Gap Min, "Korean Americans' Language Use," in *New Immigrants in the United States: Readings for Second Language Educators*, ed. Sandra Lee McKay and Sau-Ling Cynthia Wong (New York: Cambridge University Press, 2000), 306–32.

10. Sharon Lee and Marilyn Fernandez, "Trends in Asian American Racial/Ethnic Intermarriage: A Comparison of 1980 and 1990 Census Data," *Sociological Perspectives*, 41 (1998): 335.

11. Kibria, "The Construction of 'Asian American,'" 523–44; Harry Kitano, W. T. Yeung, L. Chai, and H. Hatanaka, "Asian American Interracial Marriage," *Journal of Marriage and the Family*, 16 (1989): 696–713.

12. In a survey of Korean, Chinese, and Indian immigrants in New York City, 15 percent of Korean respondents in comparison to 33 percent of Chinese respondents and 52 percent of Indian respondents reported that they had at least one black friend. See Pyong Gap Min, *Asian Ethnic Groups in New York* (New York: Columbia University Press, forthcoming).

13. Rumbaut, "The Crucible Within," 764.

14. Pyong Gap Min, "Cultural and Economic Boundaries of Korean Ethnicity," *Ethnic and Racial Studies*, 14 (1991): 225–41; Min, "Korean Americans' Language Use," 318.

15. Portes and Schauffler, "Language and the Second Generation," 655.

16. Harry Kitano and Lynn Kyung Chai, "Korean Interracial Marriage," *Marriage and Family Review*, 5 (1982): 35–48.

17. Portes and Schauffler, "Language and the Second Generation"; Rumbaut, "The Crucible Within."

18. Min, "The Structure and Social Functions of Korean Immigrant Churches."

19. Milton Gordon, *Assimilation in American Life: The Role of Race, Religion, and National Origin* (New York: Oxford University Press, 1964); Harry Kitano, *Japanese Americans: The Evolution of Subculture* (Englewood Cliffs, N.J.: Prentice Hall, 1976).

CHAPTER FIVE

FILIPINO AMERICAN YOUTH GANGS, "PARTY CULTURE," AND ETHNIC IDENTITY IN LOS ANGELES

Bangele D. Alsaybar

In the course of doing fieldwork among Filipino American youth gangs in Los Angeles, nothing intrigued and fascinated me more than the sight of the phrase "Pinoy Pride" tattooed across the bellies of some homeboys. At one of the more popular hangouts, the same phrase was written in bold letters at the top of a wall filled with posters depicting menacing symbols of terror and wickedness. I was reminded that decades back, youthful men in the fields of California had used the colloquial "Pinoy" as a term of reference and a symbol of Filipino identity.[1]

How would an anthropological ethnographer make sense out of a "conventional" symbol transposed onto a "deviant" context? Were these youth appropriating the same symbol of ethnic identity in ways that would seem inappropriate to conventional society? Focused rather narrowly on juvenile delinquency and crime, the literature on gangs in America reflects little interest in the construction of other types of identities,[2] suggesting that ethnic identity construction involves only "normal," conventional individuals—not socially abnormal humans like "gang members." More than once have I heard counselors and social workers at seminars declare that "when gang kids talk about 'Asian Pride' (or 'Filipino Pride,' for that matter), beware! What they're actually up to is more trouble, more violence!"

Field ethnography tells me that processes of ethnic identity construction, no less valid than those observed among so-called conventional groups, do occur in Filipino American "deviant" groups such as gangs. My exploration of the "gang" as a site for ethnic identity construction necessitates moving beyond traditional delinquency and crime discourses. I deconstruct popular notions of "gang" via combining a social constructionist "youth cultures" approach with a critical "anticriminology" stance exemplified in the writings of Stanley Cohen, Michel Foucault, and David Matza.[3] Concurring with Wulff,[4] I consider youth culture as not simply consisting of the spectacular, deviant, oppositional, or marginal groups; rather, it includes *all* young people, "problematic" or ordinary, mainstream or minority, lower class or middle class. Avoiding rigid dichotomization between "deviance" and "conventionality," this broadened conceptual framework allows for an analysis that goes beyond positivist programs that tend to unfairly criminalize or demonize youth. It looks at the leisure activities that occupy a significant portion of a youth's waking hours in pursuit of fun and excitement—not just the criminal and illegal activities that constitute only a minor portion of even the more hardcore gangs.

In the Filipino American community, gangs have played a significant role in the formation of a youth culture and provided a rare, albeit "deviant," vehicle for ethnic identity construction. Gangs and other youth groups interact in everyday life, bound together by participation in a social network cutting across ethnic, spatial, and class boundaries. This fascinating network revolves around the pursuit of fun and excitement, giving rise to what I call Filipino American "Party Culture," a complex of partying and other related festive and leisure activities. The groups that share Party Culture call themselves "crews," groups of friends and peers that hang out on a regular basis, bound together by a common passion or interest. Party crews and car crews make up the core of this network; smaller hip hop crews like break-dancers, graffiti artists, and all-female dance groups constitute a second layer of this network. A third outer layer is made up of college fraternities, sororities, and other campus-based Filipino American clubs and organizations.[5]

While exploring various ways by which ethnicity is constructed by Filipino American youths, this chapter specifically examines the role played by generation in the formation of youth groups and the nature of identity construction within them. Generational distinctiveness and similarity appear to be concretized in peer groups and age sets. Individual youths belonging to different generations, for instance, may belong to a "gang" or "crew," and in most cases, a generation (i.e., first or second) may predominate.

It appears that Philippine-born, first-generation youths, for example, constitute "gangs" that are virtual repositories of Filipino traditional culture, while "crews" dominated by 1.5-generation or native-born individuals tend to reflect much less connectedness to Philippine culture and may be more open to other cultural influences. In order to gain a clearer understanding of how generations figure in the deployment of strategies for ethnic identity construction, it becomes necessary to adopt a sociohistorical approach that highlights youth agency while relating group formation to changing demographic, social, and cultural conditions. What processes of ethnic identity formation are manifested? What indigenous as well as U.S. sociocultural elements have been utilized, and under what sociohistorical conditions related to immigration have these youths constructed their identities?

Unlike conventional (structuralist) perspectives that tend to view youth as passive entities shaped by external forces and treat youth as "uncompleted adults" in the process of incorporation into parent society, a "youth cultures" approach grants greater autonomy to youth as active agents in their own right. It is a dynamic framework that offers the benefit of a combined social network and processual (sociohistorical) analysis. It opens a window to the fusion as well as opposition between generations as they interact through time and space in an ongoing process of culture-making and identity construction.

Prior to the 1960s, before the arrival of huge waves of migration from the Philippines, there was no visible Filipino American youth culture in Los Angeles. Immigration quotas were generally small and restrictive; the early Filipino laborers were barred from bringing their wives with them, and harsh antimiscegenation laws prevented men from intermarrying with white women. In 1930, Filipino men outnumbered Filipino women by a ratio of approximately 23:1.[6] Sustained immigration based on family reunification has radically changed the picture: 1990 census data specific to Los Angeles County show that out of 223,276 Filipinos, 23 percent (a little over 50,000) fall within the older children and youth age brackets (ten to twenty-four).[7] Although California-wide data reveals that the foreign-born gradually outpaced the U.S.-born during the 1970s and 1980s, a UCLA demographer, Paul Ong,[8] projects the U.S.-born ultimately outnumbering the foreign-born by the year 2000.

It appears that while researchers are currently breaking new ground in examining processes of identity construction among Filipino American youth, it is the youth readily accessible—such as students in institutional settings (i.e., UC campuses)—that are being studied.[9]

This chapter presents data (primarily in the form of ethnographic notes and tape recorded life histories) derived from field observation and participation in nonschool, ongoing social life of Filipino American gangs and other youth groups bound together in a "Party Culture" network. The "field," for me, included gang hangouts and places of fun and leisure—the social world out there—regularly visited by gang members, such as bowling alleys, parks (for initiations and picnics), cemeteries (for funerals of slain homeboys), malls, residential garages turned into dance floors by party crews, nightclubs, and illegal street races as well as legal races at an established speedway.[10]

The Barkada and Youth Origins of the Filipino American Community in L.A.

Transplanted social (structural) and cultural institutions provide resources for ethnic identity construction. One such institution brought by Filipino immigrants to America is the *barkada*, the indigenous peer grouping suffused by an egalitarian orientation emphasizing mutual caring, loyalty, and friendship that often tends to run deeper than blood relationships. While not confined to men (women and gays form *barkadas* too), it is widely visible as a brotherhood, male-bonding, and masculinity-constructing institution.[11] The *barkada* is one of the primary groups within which early socialization of the Filipino takes place. A well-known Filipino anthropologist, F. Landa Jocano, argues that along with the family and kin group, the *barkada* experience initially shapes "the personality of the individual and equips him with values for adult participation in community activities before any other agency or institution in the environment can affect his social development and psychological growth."[12]

Although *barkada* can be negatively charged and identified with deviance, largely because prison gangs and street corner groups of rowdy and misbehaving youths are called *barkada* too, a *barkada* can be either conventional or deviant. As used in the social science literature, the word "gang" denotes an individual who has been clearly categorized and labeled as a deviant, an "other" who is prejudged to be different, dangerous, and threatening to conventional society. In contrast, *barkada* as used in Philippine society is perhaps less prone to a stigmatizing and labeling characteristic of the Western concept of "gang" and is more accepting of a wider latitude of behaviors ranging from "conventional" to "bad" or "deviant." Also, *barkada* cohorting is not confined to the time of adolescence. It is not uncommon for Filipinos to carry on lifelong *barkada* relationships.

The need for, and pursuit of, brotherhood that lies at the *barkada*'s core appears to be no different from that which has given rise to the plethora of confraternities, religious cults, and movements, and hundreds of Greek-letter fraternities that flourish in Philippine colleges, universities, and even high schools. The idea of brotherhood is a powerful organizing principle in Philippine culture, society, and history. The Katipunan, a secret society that sparked the revolution against Spain, was a brotherhood that reflected a creative fusion or blending of indigenous millenarian/messianic ritual and organizational structure with symbolic elements borrowed from Free Masonry.[13]

This indigenous propensity for brotherhood was transplanted to America, undergoing modification in response to local conditions and expressing itself through the formation of fraternal organizations and various youth groups from gangs to car crews and party crews, and more recently through Filipino American fraternities on southern California campuses.[14] It seems clear to me that in contrast to the discourse of the larger society and its control culture concretized in "gang," *barkada* offers an "emic" and more culturally appropriate framework for comprehending processes of Filipino American youth identity constructions.[15]

The history of Filipino migration to the United States has been clearly favorable to the rise of male *barkadas* and their transformation into gangs and other forms of youth groups. The earliest Filipino migrants were youthful males in their late teens recruited to work in the farms of California and canneries of Alaska.[16] Because Filipino laborers were not allowed to bring their wives with them, and harsh antimiscegenation laws prohibited them from marrying white women, the early Filipino communities were virtual bachelor societies. Oral histories derived from "First Wave" Filipinos point to the existence of youthful male *barkadas* during the 1920s and 1930s.[17]

This Filipino male cohort frequented taxi dance halls and pool houses.[18] In their search for relaxation and escape from the drudgery of manual labor, they were often forced to defend themselves against men of other ethnicities. Far from being "gangs" in the contemporary usage, these groups banded together based on town or regional identity, age cohort, and common interests. They named their cliques after their towns or regions of birth in the Philippines.[19]

Racial prejudice prevented Filipinos from residing in more upscale neighborhoods, forcing them to settle in poorer Latino neighborhoods.[20] The precursor to Temple Street gang, widely known by its *placa*, "TST," was reportedly cofounded by Filipino and Mexican youths during the late 1920s or the early 1930s.[21] This indicates that young Filipino men were cohorting with Latino men. Carey McWilliams notes that during the infamous Zoot Suit riots of 1942, Filipinos were among those beaten up and mistaken for *pachucos* by irate, off-duty white sailors. [22] If Filipino youths had fraternized with Mexican American youths and even became members of precursors to barrio gangs, then those Filipinos mistaken for *pachucos* were not merely wearing zoot suits to make a fashion statement but were most likely "Filipino *pachucos*."

The Post-1965 Era: The Rise of the All-Filipino Barkada/Gang

Los Angeles is reputedly the prime destination point for post-1965 Filipino immigration to the United States;[23] the massive influx brought significant implications for *barkada* and youth cultural transformations. The professional and well-educated immigrants brought their wives and children with them, thus enlarging the youth mass base and setting the stage for the development of a visible youth culture. Settled family life became the norm. Compared to the time of the bachelor societies of earlier decades that saw Filipino youths merge with Latino groups, the post-1965 era saw the emergence of sizeable, all-Filipino American *barkadas* and other groups such as car racers and party crews.

"Satanas," the most feared and oldest of Filipino American gangs, started out as a conventional *barkada* that was a car club too. *Veteranos* recall that in 1972 they came regularly to the Filipino-town area during the weekends to play basketball and kick back together.[24] What made this *barkada* distinct from other groups was its preoccupation with Volkswagen Beetles. The weekend get-together was a chance to show off their modified engines, car stereos, magnesium alloy rims, and long-distance two-way radios. On some weekends they would drive to the high desert where one of the boy's parents owned a ranch.

As this car club became more and more visible, Latino gangs such as 18th Street, Diamond, and Echo Park began "hitting them up": challenging them by way of throwing the question, "Where're you from?" "We were a car club but apparently, we were being mistaken for a gang; when the harassment and provocations intensified, we starting fighting back," recalls one *veterano*. This pattern of being provoked into fights with Latino gangs led the *barkada* to seek the help of toughies in the Filipino community, such as those who belonged to the Temple and other street gangs. A small Filipino clique called "13 PI" was already known in the local street world, with some members carrying indigenous monikers like *Palos* (eel) and *Ipis* (cockroach).

Another *veterano* described this situation of powerlessness and vulnerability to the Latinos, lords of the streets:

> During the seventies and early eighties, Filipinos were nothing. We were oppressed by the Mexicans. We were like second class. Because the Mexicans were the majority, we Filipinos didn't want to make trouble. But at the same time we didn't want to be pushed around. That's why we became united, there was a common enemy. When we saw a Pinoy in need we did not hesitate to help. During those days we didn't have nice cars, so when we took the bus we became easy targets at the bus stops. *Cholos* would drive by in their low riders and attack us.

Within this perceived situation of ethnic antagonism directed against them, the need for protection against gangs of other ethnicities, primarily Latino, appears to have engendered the formation and rapid growth of Satanas. But even before Satanas came into being, there had been Filipinos who joined Mexican gangs. Some *veteranos* said that they had joined Mexican gangs because the latter reigned supreme, and the "If you can't lick 'em, join 'em" mentality prevailed. Some had joined Latino gangs "out of disgust and frustration over the inability of Filipinos to do something about the power of the Latinos."

During the mid-1970s, a steady stream of Filipino immigrants kept coming in; Filipino grade schoolers were slowly but steadily becoming visible in such inner-city schools as Marshall, King Jr. High, Belmont, and Virgil. Schools played a vital role in consolidating immigrant Filipino youths and creating ethnic group consciousness. Furthermore, *barkadas*, which grew out of neighborhood play groups, became reinforced by a common school identity. Thus, in addition to the streets and malls, schools became a venue for Latino antagonistic actions against Filipino youths.

Satanas during its peak in the late 1970s reportedly had as many as five hundred youths claiming membership.[25] Organizationally, Satanas is a coalition of various age sets and cliques located in various parts of L.A. County, with the founding L.A. clique acting as the traditional base. Of thirty homeboys I became friends with in the course of fieldwork, I intensively interviewed a total of twenty, drawn from each of the five age cohorts (from the 1970s through the early 1990s). Eleven had fathers who were professionals such as engineers, lawyers, and accountants, and independent businessmen. One homeboy's father was a Philippine airforce pilot. At least eight had mothers who had four-year college degrees while others had at least high school diplomas.

Half of these respondents had parents who had separated (or had gotten divorced in the United States). The other half had parents still living together, although some respondents told of wayward fathers (i.e., alcoholic, wife-beater, and womanizer). Seven of the ten whose parents were separated said that the separation had occurred in the Philippines, prior to coming to America; seven voluntarily told me that back in the Philippines, they were already considered "problem kids." Four informants said that they had early high school fraternity involvements in Manila; none had ever joined a street gang. The majority (fifteen) can be considered at least "middle class" or better, while five appear to be economically deprived. Not one of the twenty informants had finished college, but four had completed two years of junior college. At least nine finished high school, and seven are either dropouts or truants. Ten of the older homeboys are currently employed; two are computer operators, four are bank clerks, one is a health care worker, two are in the army, and one is a messenger for a telecommunications company.

Satanas is made up of Philippine-born and native-born (second-generation) males. From its founding in 1972 to around the mid-1980s, the membership had been overwhelmingly Philippine-born (around 90 percent), with about 10 percent being American-born. After the mid-1980s the gang continued to be largely Philippine-born, but the new recruits had come to America at a much younger age; some were toddlers when they came here; others were of preschool age. They belong to the "1.5 generation," in between, neither the first nor the second generation. Some could still understand Tagalog, a few could speak it and carry on a conversation. But they have vague recollections of the country of birth, and many of the cultural traditions seem strange to them. This group shares an identity problem with the American-born homeboys. Those who joined the gang in the 1970s tended to be children of farm workers, retired armed forces servicemen, and the vanguard of the early post-1965 wave of immigrants. Those who joined in the late 1980s and early 1990s are children of immigrants who came mostly in the late 1970s and early 1980s.

From second-generation homeboys, I learned that they joined Satanas not simply to identify with a group and feel a sense of belonging—a great part of it was the need to belong to a group that was *Filipino* or *Pinoy*. Seeing a big group of Filipino boys together made it much more attractive to join the group and feel a sense of "Pinoy Pride." Solow, for instance, said that up to the age of thirteen, he hardly saw Filipino youths in his school; thus, he hung out with Chicanos. But when he transferred to a school where there were many Filipino youths, "that's when I started hanging out with my kind . . . and then I joined Satanas," he said. Inca said that he joined Satanas because he wanted to learn more about his departed father's cultural heritage. He says that what he learned about Filipino culture from his first-generation homeboys was just about as much and about the "same stuff" as he learned from his family. Aside from *Ilocano* (a major language in the North Philippines) that he acquired from home, he learned to speak some Tagalog from Satanas.

Philippine-born homeboys who came in their mid-adolescent years tended to paint a picture of harmonious relationships with the American-born and 1.5 generation. But others saw it differently. Inca said that like him, many other second-generation homeboys persevered and learned much about Filipino culture, but there were bound to be differences in the way different generations saw reality. "Knowing that I had lived here longer than anyone of them who had just arrived, there were going to be differences," he said. Bomber and Raider, both 1.5 generation, confirmed the existence of generational conflicts within the group. Said Bomber: "The Tagalog speakers formed a separate group. They couldn't relate to the people that spoke English. They tried to dominate, they'd talk shit, you know. That's why I didn't kick back with them." Raider referred to the newly arrived as "FOBs" ("fresh-off-the-boat"). He also had the impression that these "FOBs" were more interested in girls than anything else. Inca and Aztec, both sons of pioneering Filipino farm workers, felt similarly left out. "Simply because I couldn't speak Tagalog, I got left out of a lot of stuff. . . . And you know, that kind of hurt, because you got a guy who's trying to do something for the homeboys. The culture clash kind of slapped me in the face, because it wasn't the way I thought it would be," said Inca as Aztec nodded in agreement.

But all the generations found themselves united when faced by common threats posed by enemy Hispanic and Filipino groups. "When you gangbang, or if you were in danger of being attacked by enemies, everybody was down for you. Everything was suicidal, you know. . . . We didn't care . . . all we do is like . . . whatever happens, happens," Raider said. Pride in the Filipino kept them together under the Satanas umbrella.

Law enforcement (Los Angeles County Sheriff) estimates some fifty to sixty Filipino gangs in L.A. County.[26] Based on my own fieldwork, however, there are only four or five major gang groups and many smaller cliques that are either allied or "cliqued up" in some way with the major groups. I see two dominant gang models in the Filipino American community: the "urban type," exemplified by the Satanas, and the "suburban" type, exemplified by the "BNG" (*Bahala Na Gang*). Satanas grew out of the inner city; its homeboys lived initially in predominantly Latino neighborhoods, thus getting exposed to Latino culture. It is not surprising, therefore, that Satanas has borrowed heavily from the Latino *Cholo* tradition. Their dress style, hair, and other symbolic expressions like graffiti are *Cholo*-like. The rough conditions of the inner city also forced them to adopt behaviors that have adaptive survival values, such as fighting and other aggressive ways.

Satanas homeboys come from the entire socioeconomic range, from poor to middle or upper-middle class, but their families (often professional parents) came in the 1970s and settled in inner-city areas like the mid-Wilshire and Temple districts. In contrast, the BNG originated in suburbia during the 1980s. They are viewed as "richer and more well off" than Satanas homeboys. They settled in upscale neighborhoods like Hancock Park in Los Angeles and the Hawthorne/Torrance area in the South Bay. This is reflected in the way they dressed themselves—unlike the *Choloized* Satanas, they wore GQ-style clothes and drove late-model Japanese cars. They experienced little of the inner-city conditions familiar to the Satanas, but they were no less prepared to engage them in violent wars. Satanas *veteranos* claim that their BNG rivals used their superior material resources to buy guns and other high-powered weapons. But suburban *barkadas* are known more for partying, fun-seeking, and girl-hunting than fighting—a reputation that they bristle at. The Satanas fighting machine was honed by years of fighting some of the deadliest inner-city Latino gangs.[27]

The Pinoy gang is not criminogenic or organized expressly for crime, as media, law enforcement, and social workers sometimes tend to portray. I note that time spent in doing crime and other illegal activities takes only a small portion (at most 10 percent) of their waking hours. The Filipino American gang spends most of its time hanging out together in pursuit of fun and excitement and engaging in conventional leisure pursuits. Partying and nightclubbing, street racing, watching action movies (usually gangster movies), bowling, fishing, and going to theme parks like Magic Mountain or Raging Waters are among the preferred recreational activities. The Filipino gang is hardly "street" in the true sense; whether urban or suburban, the favorite hang-outs are not street corners or vacant lots but places of fun and amusement like malls, pool halls, bowling alleys, nightclubs, and movie houses.

Partying is a way of life for Filipino American homeboys and homegirls.[28] Through the gang and youth culture network, everyone seems to know when and where the next party will be held, especially on weekends. The Satanas are interested in obtaining information on parties being planned by rival gangs; in this regard, girls (especially the "ganghoppers") are the prime sources of information. During times past, gate crashing was a way of expressing supremacy over all other groups. In fact, Satanas reserved the "right" to attend without formal invitation all parties held within the Filipinotown area; *veteranos* of the early 1980s said that, "People pretty much recognized our claim to the area and opened the gates for us, out of respect, maybe even fear."

Biboy recounted how they would barge into a party and the DJ would announce: "'Ladies and gentlemen, the Satanas are here!' All of us would shout in unison, 'We're number one, Satanas!' When they see us coming, 'Okay, ladies and gentlemen, Satanas in the house!' The crowd would go, huu, huu, huu! Then the *bebots* (girls) would start, 'There they are, let's dance with them!'"

Party Culture and the Rise of the Filipino American Club Scene

Although leisure pursuits and fun-seeking have always been the focal point of the Filipino American *barkada*, the rise of Party Culture can be traced back to the mid-1980s when the youth scene was much less diverse and gangs were the dominant and highly visible type of group. In a community seemingly lacking in role models for the youth, one DJ recalls that the Filipino homeboys (especially the Satanas) looked cool and attractive because they had the proud look and stance of bad asses, drove fast imports, and had the company of the prettiest females in the neighborhood.[29] Back then, either being in a gang or being cliqued up with one was the "in" thing. House parties were vulnerable to drive-by shootings and the early flyer parties staged in hotels in downtown Los Angeles were at times abruptly ended by gang fighting on the dance floor.

In tandem with enterprising promoters (these pioneering youths were just in their mid-teens), youthful Filipino DJs played a central role in creating a Filipino club scene in Los Angeles. Achieving this feat is attributable, to no insignificant degree, to getting cliqued up with the gangs (performing gigs for them on a more or less regular basis and in the process, being identified with them) and riding on the popularity of gang-associated hip hop culture. Since gangs treated the party scene as some kind of turf that they lorded over (and they were among the most avid of party-goers), gang members were among the early youth entrepreneurs who saw the business potential in flyer parties.[30] But the biggest and most successful promotion crews realized early on that in order to bring the Filipino parties to the established nightclubs, the outbreaks of gang-instigated violence on the dance floor, in the ticket lines, or in the parking lot after the dance had to be curbed. A safe environment had to be created for party-goers. They accomplished this by imposing tighter security measures (at great financial cost) and waging an aggressive "fun-without-violence" type of campaign among their ranks. Meanwhile, the production crews that failed to secure their parties lost their crowds and their businesses, and quickly faded into oblivion.

After a "crazy" decade in the 1980s that saw the gang as the dominant youth grouping (a phenomenon that appears to have peaked in the early 1990s), gangs in the Filipino American community seem to have started diminishing in popularity and appeal by the years 1992–1993. Significantly, this appears coincident with FBI reports of progressively diminishing crime rates during the last seven years. According to a recent *Los Angeles Times* report, "Law enforcement experts credited a variety of factors, including a booming economy and declining unemployment, greater attention to community-based policing, more prison beds and tougher sentencing in some areas through measures such as California's 'three strikes' law."[31]

While not disputing the impact of an improving economy and effective law enforcement on decreasing crime rates nationwide, a more accurate picture might emerge if the internal dynamics of youth culture and the role of youth as intending agents are taken into consideration. Why are the "crews" seemingly "in," while the "gangs" are diminishing in appeal as vehicles for identity construction? I attribute the changed situation in the 1990s primarily to the emergence of alternatives to gangs and the opportunities for nonviolent competition offered in the club and car scenes (competitions at car shows, races, break dancing, and DJ battles, etc.). Moreover, the appropriation of gang aesthetics by the commercialized mainstream pop music industry has "decriminalized" gang culture while at the same time commodified it for consumption in conventional society. The novelty of the gang appears to be wearing out, since one can adopt its aesthetics (i.e., dress, music, lingo) by being a car racer, a break-dancer, or a party crew member. Youths have simply gotten tired of all the killings and violent incidents; as one male youth put it, "I can still make a name for myself, have fun, and meet lots of girls without gangbanging." I credit the safer youth scene today to the efforts of leading Filipino American production crews in curbing violence on the dance floor; these DJs and promoters are virtual icons and significant role models to thousands of youths. They illustrate the way youth are capable of self-policing their ranks, shaping a nonviolent culture, and encouraging legitimate moneymaking and artistic excellence.

Within the last four years, the proliferation of party crews (there are reportedly around fifty production [party] crews in L.A. County today, ranging in membership from under ten to around fifty) and literally hundreds of car crews (varying in membership from ten to more than a hundred) merging into Party Culture reflecting both a Filipino American and trans-Asian youth lifestyle has provided alternatives to joining gangs. Compared to groups in the 1970s and 1980s, crews are largely second and 1.5 generation and much more multiethnic in composition, reflecting the demographic composition of suburban communities with large Asian populations (like the San Gabriel Valley).

The growing Filipino American club scene in Los Angeles has spawned incipient capitalists, giving rise to youthful business enterprises. No longer just a place to have fun and meet new people, the party scene has become a strategic site for business networking and moneymaking as youthful entrepreneurs take advantage of the large regular crowd (from two hundred to two thousand, depending upon the production crew holding the party). Record companies come to promote their latest releases, stickers, and T-shirts. Youth magazines, like *Flip* (a variety magazine devoted to the Filipino American youth scene) and *RPM*, come to write about the club scene, take pictures, and distribute free copies of their latest issues. Youthful clothing entrepreneurs, like "Tribong Pinoy" (Pilipino Tribe), promote their line of wear bearing indigenous ethnic designs. If one of the older and bigger production crews reportedly grosses close to half a million dollars a year, the combined income of the forty or more production/party crews in the Filipino American community must constitute a multimillion-dollar industry.

Differing Strategies for Ethnic Identity Construction

The gang, the dominant youth grouping in the Filipino American community from the 1970s through early 1990s, was predominantly made up of immigrants. Its basic strategy for ethnic identity construction was "Philippines-oriented," with an ideology based on "Pinoy Pride." Historically, "Pinoy Pride" arose in direct response to the collective "hurt pride" felt by immigrant youths being insulted with racial slurs, called names, and beat up by marauding Latino *Cholos*.

Filipino homeboys often resort to stereotyping to promote the idea of Pinoy superiority, whether it be fighting, morality, love making, intelligence, or even hygiene. For example, Solow said, "The dressing, like that, we can tell between a Filipino and a Mexican . . . and the look. You can tell a beaner, a wetback. We look fucking neat, a Filipino *Cholo!*" Ascribing values to their own ethnicity,[32] another homeboy said, "We take care of our homeboys. We keep them. We don't leave them out in the street like fucking baseheads out there, man. We talk to them, 'Hey, man, straighten out,' you know. We put them on the hotseat."

The *barkada* functions as a disseminator and preserver of indigenous Filipino culture. For instance, Tagalog and the street lingo of Manila are widely spoken; some homeboys born and raised in non-Tagalog-speaking regions of the Philippines, in fact, learned to speak Tagalog through membership in groups like Satanas. Homeboys also observe and participate in many traditional festivities such as Christmas midnight masses, child baptisms, and other community events. The Satanas is known for using the premises of a well-known Filipino American community center as a regular hangout. In fact, there were times when homeboys engaged in politics by actively supporting some candidates for the local community organization (i.e., campaigning for their candidate, transporting relatives and friends to the polling place).

Veteranos or older homeboys teach "Pinoy Pride" to the younger ones. At one huge birthday party, I saw a *veterano* sharing what he knew about Filipino toughness and bravery with a group of younger recruits. "Do you guys know why the .45 caliber revolver was invented?" asked the *veterano*.

> In the early part of this century, when the Americans were trying to pacify the countrysides, American soldiers found out that they could not put away Filipino Muslim fighters armed with sharp machetes and other bladed weapons. Even as they kept firing, these Pinoy Muslim fighters refused to fall; they kept charging at them. The Americans were then forced to invent a more powerful handgun capable of downing these brave Filipino fighters.

Hebdige argued that "style" is a social marker used by a subculture to denote its distinctiveness from others.[33] The Satanas reflect an ability to create styles of their own by combining indigenous elements with elements borrowed from other cultural traditions. The original cohort had been touched by the Filipino "hippie" counterculture called "Jefrox," which emerged in Manila during the late 1960s and early 1970s. Jefrox was popularly associated with loud rock music, drugs, long hair, and bell-bottomed jeans. The dress style of the second cohort (mid- to late 1970s) was a cross between Jefrox and *Cholo;*[34] they brushed up the hair and wore nets and bandanas; they also wore sandals and started wearing baggies and loose shirts.

Some preferred wearing heavily starched khakis with the creases well pressed out. This kind of khaki outfit was commonly used by pioneering *manongs* (farm workers) of the 1930s. Wearing khaki was a symbolic expression of their unity with the traditions of the early Filipinos in California. In the 1980s and early 1990s the homeboys had become distinctly "Filipino *Cholos*" in dress style, hand signs, tattoos, and graffiti. Satanas prefer oversized baggy pants (black as night), white T-shirts, and pendletons. The more muscular boys often wear tank tops to display their bulging muscles.

The seeming decline of "Philippines-oriented" gangs dominated by Philippine-born youth and the rise of second-generation partying and auto racing[35] points to generational differences in strategies for ethnic and racial identity construction. As exemplified by the Satanas, ethnic identity construction was primarily in direct response to the experience of initially settling in inner-city, Latino neighborhoods and being harassed and attacked by *Cholo* youths. They came into direct contact with *Cholo* culture, out of which they appropriated elements for the construction of a "Filipino *Cholo*" identity.

In contrast, there was much less direct contact with *Cholo* gang culture in the experience of second-generation Filipino American youths growing up in more upscale and affluent suburban neighborhoods. And by the time of the 1990s, gang aesthetics had been appropriated by the mainstream popular industry; with the rise of the Filipino American and Asian American club scenes, the second generation began receiving a modified kind of gang aesthetic (or cultural style) via the medium of popular music and culture, particularly African American hip hop. I consider the current "gang style" adopted by contemporary car and party crews as largely drawn from mainstream popular culture, specifically hip hop, which has become pervasive. Both males and females take great pains dressing themselves up in brand-name gear such as Tommy Hilfiger and Nautica identified with the hip hop crowd; boys wear baggies and oversized shirts; girls wear hoochie-style shorts and tank tops. Popular gang argot seems universal (addressing each other as "homies" or "homegirls" and using expressions like "hit up" and "being down for the hood" are commonplace). Gang style is so much "in" that it is often difficult to differentiate between "gang" and "nongang" based on dress style alone.

Dominated by the second generation, today's crews aspire for multiple and overlapping identities (not only Filipino but also "Asian"), in contrast to the immigrant-led and Philippine-born gangs of the 1970s and 1980s that vigorously promoted "Pinoy Pride" alone. Party crew names, for instance, such as "Legend," "Raw," "Vibe," and so on, the names that reflect an aspiration for fun and entertainment, are devoid of ethnic symbolism. Car crew names, such as "Zoom," "Jetspeed," "Kosoku," and "Kioken," reflect their mixed Asian and other ethnicity memberships and hint at the development of a more "trans-Asian" type of identity. Contrast this with the names of Filipino American gangs of the 1970s and 1980s such as "MP" ("*Mabuhay ang Pinoy*" or "Long Live, the Filipino!"), "Pinoy Real" ("PR," meaning "pure Filipino"), and "LVM" (Luzon, Visayas, and Mindanao, the three main island groups in the Philippines); the names reveal an aspiration for constructing an identity within the parameters of traditional Filipino notions of social space.

The second generation's openness to creating an identity and lifestyle based on the appropriation of mainstream popular music genres like hip hop and Anglo American technological symbols like cars and drag racing appears to be distinct from a more politicized "Filipino American" cultural ideology (associated with community activists) that would construct an identity based on the appropriation of indigenous symbols and values, and the inculcation of Filipino cultural heritage (through folk dancing, Filipino festivals, cultural evenings, etc.).[36]

Conclusion

It has never been my intention to valorize or glorify the criminality and antisocial behaviors often associated with gangs. But what I have presented is a dimension of gang and youth culture that has rarely been explored. Only by field immersion did I discover the significance of leisure in Filipino American gang life and the way the pursuit of fun and excitement binds gangs and crews in a Party Culture network.

This chapter has examined the role played by generation in the formation of youth groups in the Filipino American community and the nature of identity construction. Three main time periods are significant, with a particular type of grouping and generation being dominant in each time period. During the early 1920s and 1930s, the prototypical *barkada* frequenting taxi dance halls was the dominant type. From 1965 to around 1992, the gang was dominant, while from 1992–1993 to the present, the crew appears to have displaced the gang as the preeminent group. I argue that the Filipino American gang, largely but not strictly monoethnic, with its ideology of "Pinoy Pride," was the dominant youth grouping during the 1965–1992 period, because it was overwhelmingly Philippine born (first generation) in membership. That was also the time period when massive waves of migration saw the Philippine-born population outpace the U.S.-born.

On the other hand, the crew seems to have replaced the gang as the preeminent grouping in the 1990s, largely because the second generation (U.S.-born and 1.5 generation) has grown in numbers and now appears to dominate the various types of groups. It appears, therefore, that due to generational differences, the gang and the crew represent two different but related phenomena; each reflects varying strategies or orientations for constructing identities—one Philippine born, the other U.S. born.

Philippine-born gang members, for instance, reflect a greater connectedness to Filipino culture and history than U.S.-born party crew or car crew youths, who seem to be more attuned to mainstream popular culture currents like hip hop. However, this seeming divergence actually contributes to a kind of dynamic "convergence" in the Party Culture network, where youths of different generations interact and engage in an ongoing process of creating a Filipino American youth culture. In the space of this youth culture, they construct multiple and fluid identities: Youths are able to draw from the "Pinoy Pride" ideology that drove the pioneering gangs to the trans-Asian and incipient capitalist ideology that drives budding entrepreneurs in the club and car scenes.

Notes

This chapter is a revised and expanded version of a paper originally read at the American Anthropological Association meetings in November 1997 in Washington, D.C. I am grateful to professors Pyong Gap Min, Kyeyoung Park, and Karen Brodkin for giving me encouragement and constructive comments.

1. See Donald Takaki, *Strangers From a Different Shore* (Boston: Little, Brown, and Co., 1989) 315. Cordova, *Filipinos: Forgotten Asian Americans*, (Dubuque, Iowa: Kendall/Hunt Publishing Company, 1983) 38.

2. Formation of "street" identity, largely viewed as a phenomenon determined by poverty and conditions of material disadvantage, appears to be the focus of sociological structuralist gang researchers. See, for example, W. B. Miller, "Lower Class Culture as a Generating Milieu of Gang Delinquency," *Journal of Social Issues*, 14:3 (1958): 5–19; Richard Cloward and Lloyd Ohlin, *Delinquency and Opportunity: A Theory of Delinquent Gangs* (New York: Free Press, 1960); Richard Cloward and Lloyd Ohlin, *Delinquent Boys: The Culture of the Gang* (Glencoe, N.Y.: Free Press, 1960). In the 1980s and 1990s, a newer type of structuralism that further refined the causal relationship between gangs and poverty has gained ascendancy, inspired by W. J. Wilson's theory of the underclass. The new structural interpretation basically views gangs as a by-product of conditions (such as deindustrialization and changes in the U.S. labor market) that give rise to, and perpetuate, a permanent underclass in inner cities and barrios. See Joan Moore, *Going Down to the Barrio* (Philadelphia: Temple University Press, 1991); and John Hagedorn, *People and Folks: Gangs, Crime, and the Underclass in a Rustbelt City* (Chicago: Lakeview, 1988). For a critique of structuralist and underclass approaches, see Martin Sanchez Jankowski, *Islands in the Street: Gangs and American Urban Society* (Berkeley: University of California Press, 1991). Street identity is only one among other identities that are constructed in gangs, including gender and ethnicity.

3. See Stanley Cohen, *Against Criminology* (New Brunswick: Transaction Publishers 1992); Stanley Cohen, *Visions of Social Control* (Cambridge: Polity Press, 1985); Stanley Cohen, *Folk Devils and Moral Panics* (London: MacGibbon and Kee, 1972); Michel Foucault, *Discipline and Punish: The Birth of the Prison* (New York: Vintage, 1979); David Matza, *Delinquency and Drift* (New York: John Wiley and Sons, 1964); David Matza, *Becoming Deviant* (Englewood Cliffs, N.J.: Prentice-Hall, 1969). See also Michael Brake, *Comparative Youth Culture* (London: Routledge and Kegan Paul, 1985); and Jack Katz, *Seductions of Crime: Moral and Sensual Attractions of Doing Evil* (New York: Basic, 1988).

4. See Helena Wulff, "Introducing Youth Culture in Its Own Right: The State of the Art and New Possibilities," in *Youth Cultures: A Cross-Cultural Perspective*, ed. Vered Amit-Talai and Helena Wulff (London: Routledge, 1995), 1–18.

5. See Bangele D. Alsaybar, forthcoming Ph.D. dissertation, "Constructing Deviance: Filipino American Youth Gangs and Party Culture in Los Angeles," (University of California, Los Angeles, Department of Anthropology).

6. Pauline Agbayani-Siewert and Linda Revilla, "Filipino Americans," in *Asian Americans: Contemporary Trends and Issues*, ed. Pyong Gap Min (Thousand Oaks, Calif.: Sage, 1995), 155.

7. A compilation of Search To Involve Pilipino Americans (SIPA) attributed to the following sources: Los Angeles 1994: State of the County Data Book (United Way of Los Angeles, 1995); and Asian Pacific Factfinder: Los Angeles County.

8. Paul Ong, *California's Asian Population: Past Trends and Projections for the Year 2000* (Los Angeles: Graduate School of Architecture and Urban Planning and Asian American Studies Center, UCLA, May 1989).

9. See Diane Wolf, "Family Secrets: Transnational Struggles among Children of Filipino Immigrants," *Sociological Perspectives*, 40: 3 (1997): 457–82; Yen L. Espiritu, "The Intersection of Race, Ethnicity, and Class: The Multiple Identities of Second Generation Filipinos," *Identities* 1: 2–3 (1994) 249–73. Utilizing youth focus groups, Wolf explores some issues and problems confronting youth such as educational ambivalence, teen suicide, and parent-children communications. She suggests that colonialism, transnational dilemmas, and contradictions within the family underlie the problems besetting Filipino American youth. Via individual interviews with college students, Espiritu noted that children of professional immigrants from the Philippines reflect fluid, multiple, and overlapping identities. She makes the observation that the ethnicity of second-generation Filipino Americans remains "largely symbolic," pegged tenuously to food and family closeness experienced at get-togethers and periodic family reunions. She argues that as children of middle-class, acculturated parents, "they have grown up largely without assigned roles or groups that anchor ethnicity. The majority do not live in an ethnic neighborhood, attend school with other Filipino children, or belong to Filipino organizations."

10. I conducted intensive fieldwork on the Satanas (Tagalog word for "Satan"), the oldest and best-known Filipino American gang in Los Angeles during the early 1990s. The outcome was my master's thesis in Asian American Studies, "Satanas: Ethnography of a Filipino American Street Brotherhood in Los Angeles" (University of California, Los Angeles, 1993). I established initial field contacts while working as a gang outreach worker for Search to Involve Pilipino Americans, a social service agency in Los Angeles.

11. Jean Paul Dumont, "The Visayan Male Barkada: Manly Behavior and Male Identity in a Philippine Island" (typescript personally sent by author, 1994).

12. F. Landa Jocano, *Management by Culture* (Quezon City, Philippines: Punlad Press, 1990), 27.

13. See Reynaldo Ileto, *Pasyon and Revolution* (Quezon City, Philippines: Ateneo De Manila University, 1979).

14. One of the more interesting developments in the Filipino American youth culture scene is the emergence of Pinoy college fraternities in southern California campuses. From Grace Borrero's unpublished paper at UCLA ("Shedding Some Light on the Dark Boys," 1997), we learn about "Theta Delta Beta" (TDB), once a party crew and basketball crew turned college fraternity. A "parody of the Greek system," the founders of TDB reportedly decried the "segregatedness" of Greek-letter frats on campus.

15. "Gang," to me, is a term of control; it reflects the perspective of law enforcement and racist culture, given the "moral panic" over immigrants and gangs that swept Los Angeles in the late 1980s. See John Huey-Long Song and John Dombrink, "'Good Guys' and Bad Guys: Media, Asians, and the Framing of a Criminal Event," *Amerasia Journal* , 22 (1996): 25–45; and Mike Davis, *City of Quartz* (London: Verso, 1990); Michael Omi and Howard Winant, *Racial Formation in the United States from the 1960s to the 1990s* (New York: Routledge, 1994). "Gang" has become a code word for "outsider" or "alien" in racist discourse condensing images of race, crime, and youth. I regard "gang" and "crew" as social constructs emergent in specific time periods and as types of *barkada*. See David Theo Goldberg, *Racist Culture* (Cambridge, Mass.: Blackwell, 1994)

16. See Takaki, *Strangers From a Different Shore.*

17. Royal Morales, "Pilipino Americans: Youth Gang and Delinquency," unpublished manuscript, n.d.

18. Two excellent articles on Filipino men and taxi dance halls of the 1920s are Rhacel Parrenas, "'White Trash' Meets the 'Little Brown Monkeys': the Taxi Dance Hall as a Site of Interracial and Gender Alliances between White Working Class Women and Filipino Immigrant Men in the 1920s and 30s," *Amerasia Journal*, 24: 2 (1998): 115–34; Linda E. Maram, "Brown Hordes in McIntosh Suits: Filipinos, Taxi Dance Halls, and Performing the Immigrant Body in Los Angeles, 1930s–1940s," in *Generations of Youth: Youth Cultures and History in Twentieth Century America*, ed. Joe Austin and Michael Nevin Williard (New York: New York University Press, 1998), 118–35.

19. Morales, "Pilipino Americans: Youth Gang and Delinquency."

20. See Valentin R. Aquino, "The Filipino Community in Los Angeles," (Masters thesis, University of Southern California, 1952); he provides interesting information on the spatial/ecological distribution of Filipinos in L.A. before the 1950s.

21. As for Filipino men hanging out with Latino men, the noted gang expert and anthropologist James Diego Vigil recalled that during

his adolescent years, he had met Filipino youths who were members of Latino gangs in the neighborhood where he grew up (Professor Vigil told me after his job talk at the UCLA Anthropology department in 1992).

22. Carey McWilliams, *North From Mexico* (New York: Greenwood, 1968), 248. One of my *veterano* informants in Satanas keeps an heirloom of sorts: a zoot suit which his father used to wear. His father, he said, used to hang out with Latino zoot suiters.

23. According to U.S. Census data, there were only 12,122 Filipinos in Los Angeles in 1960. By 1970, only 5 years after passage of the milestone Immigration and Reform Act of 1965, the count was 33,459, an almost threefold increase. In 1980, there were 100,040, an increase over the 1970 count of 199 percent. The 1990 Census shows a count of 223,276, an increase of 123.2 percent over the 1980 count. Los Angeles County is home to the largest Filipino community outside the Philippine archipelago.

24. *Veterano* is a term for members of older cohorts. *Peewees* are the recruits or new members aged thirteen to fifteen. Boys in their early twenties are *jr. vets*. Those in their mid-twenties are *Veteranos*. *O.G.s* or *originals* are the founders.

25. In the early 1990s, however, membership drastically dwindled, largely due to the rise of car crews and party crews (the emerging Party Culture network), police actions, incarcerations of errant homeboys, and flight to the Philippines of homeboys evading arrest and prosecution.

26. See District Attorney's Office, *Gangs, Crime, and Violence in Los Angeles* (Los Angeles: District Attorney's Office, May 1992).

27. "BNG" (*Bahala Na Gang*, from the Tagalog expression "*bahala na!*" or "come what may!") and Satanas were locked in bitter rivalry during most of the 1980s and early 1990s. Although the material disparities were not that great, magnified socioeconomic differences and the drive for supremacy in the Filipino American community appear to be at the bottom of their rivalry and the cycle of violence that characterized their relationship. Some of the more serious crimes, for which Satanas homeboys were incarcerated, include murder and attempted murder committed against rival Latino gang members and other Filipino gangs. Among younger members, GTA (Grand Theft Auto) and illegal possession of drugs (especially marijuana) are the common crimes. Even the most notorious Pinoy gangs, however, are not noted for engaging in large-scale drug-dealing and other forms of illegal moneymaking, unlike organized Asian crime syndicates and gangs.

28. There are female cliques tied to male gangs; however, most of these so-called girl gangs are not independent groups but are usually

the girlfriends of homeboys. Much has been noted about the "invisibility" of girls in male gang studies. While not intending to perpetuate gender bias, this chapter is limited to the male *barkada*/gang (I address gender construction issues in my forthcoming dissertation).

29. DJ "Duwendz" (Jose Buktaw) at a PANA (Philippine American Network and Advocacy) conference workshop on youth, April 1996.

30. I am indebted to Isaiah Dacio (famed "DJ Icy Ice") for educating me in Party Culture history and introducing me to the world of disc jockeying, and to David Gonzales, chief promoter and brains behind the phenomenal success of Legend Entertainment, for illuminating me on the business angle of partying and promoting. "Flyer parties" are called as such because parties at established clubs are announced or advertised through colorfully designed flyers containing specific information about the coming event. Big production groups often disseminate thousands of flyers (by mail or direct handouts) for each dance event.

31. *Los Angeles Times*, "Crime Rates Continue Record Seven-Year Plunge," May 17, 1999.

32. "Ascribing values to the group" is one of the ways in which individuals construct ethnicity, according to Waters, *Ethnic Options*, 134.

33. Dick Hebdige, *Subculture* (London: Methuen, 1979).

34. In his book, *Barrio Gangs* (Austin: University of Texas Press, 1988), James Diego Vigil provides an authoritative description of "Cholo" style.

35. See Michael Karl Witzel and Kent Bash, *Cruisin': Car Culture in America* (Osceola, Wis.: Motorbooks International, 1997) for an insightful account of car culture as an American teenage socializing tradition.

36. One of the more lively points of debate in the Filipino American youth scene today is a seeming clash between an "ideology of fun and socializing"—the dominant ethos of Party Culture—and a more politicized "Filipino American ideology" identified with academia, the Asian American movement, and a small but militant hip hop underground. Adherents of the former claim to be "future-oriented," in contrast to what they perceive to be a "backward-looking" program of the latter group. The underground is said to be critical of Filipino American hip hop party culture for "selling out" and ignoring social/political issues and concerns such as racism, women's oppression, and inner-city poverty.

CHAPTER SIX

FORMATION OF ETHNIC AND RACIAL IDENTITIES: NARRATIVES BY ASIAN AMERICAN PROFESSIONALS

Pyong Gap Min and Rose Kim

Immigrants from Third World countries began streaming into the United States in the late 1960s. More than thirty years have passed since their arrival, and the children of those immigrants have come of age. Many have completed college and entered the job market. They are represented in a number of professional fields, such as politics, journalism, and the fine arts—arenas that have been typically inaccessible to their immigrant parents because of language and cultural barriers.

Social scientists, especially immigrant scholars belonging to the immigrant groups under investigation, started researching post-1965 immigrants shortly after the contemporary mass migration began.[1] In the late 1980s, researchers began studying the "new second generation." A number of articles and several books focusing on the second generation have been published.[2]

An important issue regarding the adaptation patterns of the second generation is their level of ethnic attachment, as characterized by their retention of ethnic culture, participation in ethnic networks, and ethnic identity. Given this, it is no wonder that most of the studies focusing on second-generation Asian Americans have examined the issues directly or indirectly related to one or more dimensions of ethnic attachment.[3]

These studies have limitations in understanding Asian-Americans' patterns of ethnic attachment because they are based on survey or ethnographic data, with high school students usually used as the respondents or informants. High school samples are not suitable for examining the respondents' or informants' social relations, including their affiliations with ethnic organizations and dating patterns. Moreover, studies based on high school samples have further limitations in examining ethnic or pan-ethnic identity because as shown in two other chapters of this volume, one by Yen Espiritu and the other by Hung Thai, ethnic or pan-ethnic identity is often suppressed in early years but emerges in young adulthood. In addition, the studies cited above have limitations in illuminating information about pattern of pan-Asian ethnicity because as case studies of one or two Asian ethnic groups they do not provide comparative perspectives.

To overcome these limitations, we have conducted a study of Asian Americans' ethnic attachment using personal narratives by fifteen young Asian American professionals. Personal narratives may be more effective than personal interviews for analyzing the process of the change in ethnic identity over one's life course.[4] A few books have examined ethnic identity and related issues using personal narratives.[5] This chapter intends to examine Asian Americans' ethnicity through narratives written by fifteen young Asian American professionals. It examines all three dimensions of Asian Americans' ethnicity, that is, retention of ethnic culture, participation in ethnic networks, and ethnic identity, focusing on their ethnic and pan-ethnic identities.

How Were the Fifteen Essays Written?

Selection of the Essayists

We identified fifteen young Asian American professionals who were children of post-1965 immigrants. We selected them partly because they were willing to write about their lives and the issues that they faced growing up as Asian Americans. One coauthor of this study is a second-generation Asian American professional. She identified eight essayists in New York and Los Angeles through her personal and professional connections. The other coauthor is an immigrant sociologist. He selected the other seven essayists, based on recommendations from colleagues in Los Angeles and New York.

Three essayists are immigrants who completed high school in their native country. Seven are 1.5-generation Asian Americans who were born in their home countries and immigrated to the United States between the ages of two and twelve.[6] The remaining five essayists are second-generation Asian Americans, born and raised in the United States. We selected the contributors partly because they met our criteria, as far as balancing ethnic groups, gender, and occupations. The contributors represented seven different ethnic groups: Chinese, Japanese, Korean, Filipino, Vietnamese, Indian, and Bangladeshi. They ranged in age from twenty-six to forty-nine at the time of writing their essays, but the vast majority were in their early to middle thirties. They represented a variety of professions: the comptroller of a small, private college; a social worker; an assistant district attorney; a medical doctor; a political aide; two professors; and an actor. We originally requested essays from seven men and eight women, to maintain a gender balance. However, two men dropped out at the last minute and were replaced with women. As a result, women contributors wrote two-thirds of the essays.

There are significant class differences in ethnic identity and life experiences among members of the same ethnic group.[7] Since we could not examine class differences with only fifteen contributors, we decided to focus on young Asian American professionals who had achieved a moderate degree of professional success in the mainstream economy. The essayists came from middle- and upper-middle-class families and graduated from prestigious or at least above-average universities. By focusing on these Asian American professionals, we do not intend to imply that most Asian Americans graduate from prestigious universities and hold professional occupations. However, the percentage of Asian Americans represented in prestigious public and private colleges and universities is much greater than their population size, and most of such graduates eventually enter professional occupations.[8] Yet we do not know what barriers highly educated Asian American professionals encounter in the workplace. Furthermore, researchers have not examined whether highly educated second-generation Asian Americans have lost much of their ethnic cultural traditions and ethnic networks through incorporating into the white middle class. By selecting professionals, we can answer these questions.

The Construction of the Essays

Although each essay was intended to be an autobiography, we knew it would be impossible to cover one's life within fifteen or so pages. So we asked the writers to focus on one or more of the following issues related to ethnic and pan-ethnic attachments: (1) experiences of prejudice and discrimination; (2) retention of ethnic culture; (3) ethnic versus nonethnic friendships; and (4) ethnic and pan-ethnic identities. We asked them to discuss these issues in connection with their experiences of growing up at home, at school, and/or on the job. We gave the contributors detailed guidelines as to what particular questions they needed to answer in order to cover each of the above topics.

As already pointed out, many native-born Asian Americans consider themselves American when they are children, but increasingly adopt their ethnic identity as they grow older. We asked the contributors to discuss such changes, if any. Recently, feminist scholars have emphasized the intersection of race, class, and gender as analytic categories for understanding the disadvantages and powerlessness experienced by low-class minority women.[9] Researchers have indicated 1.5- and second-generation Asian American women go through qualitatively different experiences from their male counterparts, particularly inside their parental home.[10] We expected the female contributors to be highly critical of their parents' unequal marital relations and conservative gender socialization practices based on the patriarchal ideology brought with them from their home countries. We asked the respondents to comment on these two points.

Some contributors considered ethnic and pan-Asian identities a far more important issue than experiences of discrimination, whereas others had more to say about their family lives. Thus not all contributors devoted equal space to each topic. We encouraged the contributors to introduce any other topic that was personally meaningful in their life experiences as Asian Americans. We edited the essays and, in most cases, asked the contributors to revise particular paragraphs and/or add more information on a particular topic to address the four major issues. Most of the essays were written in 1995 and revised in 1996. We have used pseudonyms to protect the anonymity of the essayists.

Expectations Based on Current Theories and Data

Experiences with Prejudice and Discrimination

Asian immigrants were victims of severe prejudice and stereotyping in the nineteenth and early twentieth centuries.[11] The Chinese Exclusion Act and other anti-Asian laws at the end of the nineteenth and early twentieth centuries were partly consequences of the stereotypes and prejudices held by the majority of Americans against Asian immigrants. The success of many U.S.-born Chinese and Japanese Americans and the migration of a large number of professional Asian immigrants since 1965 have led to changes in how the majority of Americans perceive Asian Americans; Asians are viewed more positively as high achievers who earn academic and professional success. However, despite the "model minority" image, Asian Americans are still subjected to many negative stereotypes.[12] The age-old perception of Asian Americans as perpetual foreigners who are unassimilable still embarrasses many Asian Americans. Though third- and fourth-generation Asian ethnics have lost their cultural traditions almost completely and feel comfortable forming friendships mainly with white Americans, Mia Tuan reveals,[13] these multigeneration Asian ethnics suffer the same stereotyping of Asian foreignness as do first-generation immigrants and their children.

Asian immigrants generally have severe labor market disadvantages compared to white Americans. Statistical analyses of Asian Americans' earnings indicate that Asian immigrants, men in particular, earn far less than U.S.-born white Americans with comparable educational levels.[14] The same studies show that U.S.-born Asian Americans are not much disadvantaged in their earnings compared to white Americans. But they are underrepresented in managerial positions[15] and encounter "the glass ceiling" problem when they try to move up to high-ranking, well-paid positions.[16]

Asian immigrant children with language barriers, like other immigrant children, encounter prejudice and racial harassment by white and black students.[17] Even U.S.-born Asian American students who are fluent in English cannot avoid rejection, prejudice, and racial violence from white peers because of their color;

they often experience discriminatory treatment, even by white teachers.[18]

Retention of Ethnic Culture

Classical assimilationists proposed a zero sum model of acculturation, in which the acculturation of immigrants and their children involved the gradual replacement of their ethnic culture with American culture.[19] From this perspective, the children of low-class immigrants who have grown up in an immigrant enclave, while lacking fluency in English, are more likely to retain their language and culture than others. In contrast, children from middle-class and professional families who have grown up in a white middle-class neighborhood are expected to be highly assimilated into American culture, with little retention of their ethnic cultural traditions. Thus, the classical assimilation theory leads us to believe that our highly educated professional essayists will have achieved a high level of acculturation, replacing their ethnic language and culture with English and American culture.

However, research on the "new second generation" during recent years suggests that many of these professional essayists may maintain strong bilingual and bicultural orientations. The children of contemporary immigrants, including Asian immigrants, have advantages over the children of earlier immigrants in retaining their cultural traditions because of several factors.[20] Two structural factors deserve attention here. First, technological advances in communication, air transportation, and the media enable contemporary immigrants and their children to maintain transnational networks with their home country.[21] Second, since the early 1970s, the federal and local governments and educational institutions have changed policies toward minority groups and minority students from Anglo conformity to cultural pluralism, which has helped the children of contemporary immigrants to maintain their ethnic language and culture.[22]

Recent empirical studies indicate that the children of contemporary immigrants are highly assimilated into American culture and that they prefer using English rather than their ethnic language when communicating with friends.[23] But they also show that 1.5-generation high school students are usually bilingual and that a significant proportion of second-generation students are bilingual.[24] As noted above, transnational ties and multicultural policy help immigrant families of all class backgrounds to transmit their language and culture to their children. Yet, middle-class and professional immigrants with more resources can take greater advantage of these resources and are better able to take advantage of contemporary technological advances and multicultural policy more effectively to teach their children ethnic language and culture.[25] Many well-to-do Asian professional and business parents send their children to their home country regularly for an ethnic education. Given their class advantages for preserving their ethnic heritage, many of our essayists may be strongly bicultural.

Ethnic versus Nonethnic Friendships

There is no question that our contributors as young Asian American professionals have achieved a high level of cultural assimilation. The question is whether they have achieved a comparable level of social assimilation. Milton Gordon suggested that members of a minority group could achieve a high level of cultural assimilation, but that such cultural assimilation does not guarantee a high level of social assimilation because the latter depended much upon the level of their acceptance by members of the dominant group.[26] This phenomenon of a high degree of cultural assimilation, combined with a lack of significant social assimilation, was observed not only among African Americans, but also among earlier Jewish and Japanese Americans.[27] It is interesting to see whether second-generation Asian Americans will follow the pattern suggested by Gordon.

The major findings from several studies indicate that second-generation Asian Americans generally prefer coethnic friendships to nonethnic friendships.[28] Yet, they also suggest that second-generation Asian Americans maintain frequent social interaction with white Americans. For example, in a survey of second-generation Korean junior and senior high school students in New York, 57 percent of the respondents indicated a Korean as their closest friend and the same proportion chose a Korean as their dating partner.[29] However, the majority of the respondents indicated a white person as one of their three closest friends, and 31 percent chose a white person as their dating partner. Because of their high educational and occupational levels, the fifteen Asian-American professionals in our research project were expected to maintain a higher level of friendship with white Americans than the Korean high school respondents in the above study.

Ethnic and Pan-ethnic Identities

Despite the general public's tendency to lump all Asian groups together, each Asian group has its own language, religion, and unique cultural traditions. Second-generation Asian American children who live with their immigrant parents in their formative years are exposed to their parental language, religion, and other aspects of their ethnic and subethnic cultures at home. These cultural elements practiced at home and in the ethnic community can be an important basis for second-generation Asian Americans' ethnic identity. Therefore, we expect our essayists to have strong ethnic identities largely based on salient aspects of their ethnic and subethnic cultures.

Second-generation Asian Americans do not usually live in an ethnic enclave and find their occupations in the general economy rather than in the ethnic economy. Their residential and occupational assimilation may make them feel comfortable and lose their ethnic identity. Yet other structural factors force them to accept their ethnic or pan-Asian identity. Of all structural factors, the general perception of Asian Americans as foreigners or at least as less-than-full American citizens probably has the most significant effect on their ethnic and racial identities. For third- and fourth-generation white ethnics, who are accepted as full American citizens, ethnic identity is a matter of personal choice to meet their search for a community.[30] However, being ethnic is a societal expectation for third- and fourth-generation Japanese and Chinese Americans, no matter how far removed they are from their immigrant roots or how different they are from their foreign-born counterparts.[31]

Structural factors related to their adjustments to the host society may have stronger effects on second-generation Asian Americans' pan-Asian racial identity than on their ethnic identity. Governments and schools lump together all groups that originate from the Asian continent and the Pacific Islands when compiling data for policy and resource allocation purposes. Most Americans also have difficulty in distinguishing members of various Asian groups, despite some observable physical differences. Most Americans refer to Koreans and Vietnamese as "Chinese." White and black Americans have physically attacked Asian Americans on the basis of mistaken ethnic identifications. In 1982, for example, two white men beat to death Vincent Chin, a Chinese American whom they mistook for a Japanese. Accordingly, all Asian Americans need to make a broad pan-Asian coalition to protect their interests in social services, education, politics, and other areas.[32] Some scholars have argued that the pan-Asian racial formation will be an important feature of Asian American experiences in the post Civil Rights era.[33]

Analyses of the Essays

Experiences with Prejudice and Discrimination

As expected, the 1.5- and second-generation essayists experienced prejudice and rejection by white and black peers when they were school children. Most were school children in the late 1960s and 1970s when Asian Americans were rare, especially in the predominantly middle- and upper-middle-class white schools that many of them attended. Outwardly different from the rest, they were physically and verbally abused by their classmates. The experiences were painful and unsettling.

Albert, a U.S.-born Indian American, now a doctor, described the abuses he suffered in elementary school:

> My classmates were so ignorant that they mistook me for a Native American. They accused me of doing "rain dances" and said "how" to me, lifting up their hands. I even endured physical violence. One time, several kids decided to gang up on me for no reason.

William, a U.S.-born Chinese American, now a law student and formerly a political aide, was harassed verbally and physically by his classmates at a dominantly white school in Queens, New York. His fellow students spat on him, barred him from eating lunch with them, and taunted him by mimicking the "choppy" English spoken by Asian characters on films. William finally felt accepted by his classmates after he enrolled in the Stuyvesant High School of Science in Manhattan, a prestigious public high school where 40 percent of the student body was Asian. He was even elected president of the student body.

Other essayists who were not verbally or physically assaulted often felt alienated from their classmates. Michelle, a Korean American psychologist who immigrated when she was eight, mastered English and behaved like an all-American teenager, but her white classmates still subjected her to "humiliating questions," such as, "Where are you from?" and "What do you eat at home?" Steven, a Korean American attorney who immigrated at ten, said that at his predominantly white parochial school "approaching white girls was difficult because I was not among the school's elite."

Many essayists anticipated college as a chance to make a fresh start. It also provided a break from their parents and family home, often the strongest ties to their ethnicity. College generally proved to be a more tolerant and cosmopolitan environment, and none of the contributors described discriminatory experiences while there. Samod, a U.S.-born Indian American who worked as a public schools advocate, described feeling initially annoyed at an African American professor who invited her to a meeting for students of color, but later realized that she shared a bond with them because of her "nonwhite status." For many of the contributors, the college environment helped to strengthen their ethnic and pan-Asian identities, as is discussed further in the next section.

Nearly all essayists are keenly aware that people of color, including Asian Americans, are subject to discrimination in the United States. Yet only two essayists, both first-generation immigrants, said that they suffered racial prejudice in their careers. Some 1.5- and second-generation contributors explicitly said that they had not encountered discriminatory treatment in the workplace. In fact, their ethnicity may have been beneficial, as in the case of Nicole, a U.S.-born Korean American writer, who entered journalism through a minority recruitment program at the *Los Angeles Times*. This lack of discriminatory experiences may be due partly to the fact that most contributors are still in the early stages of their professional careers; once they have reached certain levels, they are likely to encounter barriers to their career mobility, that is, the so-called glass ceiling problem. Unfortunately, none of the 1.5- and second-generation contributors has had a career long enough to test this hypothesis.

Michael, a U.S.-born Filipino American actor, discussed the disadvantages of Asian Americans in the acting profession, although he did not specify any personal experience of discrimination in the workplace. While a greater awareness of cultural diversity may have created more artistic roles for Asian Americans, the latter often remain shallow or stereotyped. Michael, who was cast in *Space: Above & Beyond*, a science fiction series of a futuristic Marine Corps squadron, described his discomfort in playing Lt. Paul Wang, a cowardly soldier who betrayed his comrades.

> Whenever I see Asians in military uniform, I cannot help but recall common images of Asians from the Vietnam War and World War II. They were "yellow-bellied cowards" who took the lives of loyal Americans. They were treacherous and crafty, impossible to gauge. Wang could be seen as all of these stereotypes, I thought.

The rarity of color-blind casting limits the roles available to Asian Americans and has led Michael to consider other avenues, such as writing or developing his own projects.

Of the three first-generation immigrants, however, two discussed job-related discrimination in the United States. Beth, a Vietnamese immigrant who fled Saigon after it fell to the communists in 1975 and who is now the comptroller of a small, liberal arts college, said she felt "unfairly passed over" for promotion to become a vice president. Meena, an Indian immigrant who was a consumer economics professor, described the academic environment as white and male-dominated, complaining that her white colleagues believed that her minority status was the main reason why she was offered a faculty position. These two women may have been more likely to experience discrimination in their career trajectories because of the longer length of their careers. Yet, compared to the other contributors, they also seem to be at a greater disadvantage because of their imperfect English pronunciation and lack of job information networks. Interestingly, although Albert did not comment on his own experiences of discrimination in the workplace, he did emphasize that his Indian-born parents had encountered anti-Asian and anti-Indian discrimination in their careers.

Strong, Bicultural Experiences

Our review of the essays indicates that, although as children the contributors resisted learning their ethnic languages and cultures, they showed an increasing interest in them as they grew older. As expected from the literature review, most of the contributors, as young adults, were highly bicultural. According to the majority of accounts, the contributors' parents made great efforts to transmit their native language, customs, and values to their children. William, a native-born Chinese American, attended Saturday language schools in the 1970s, when such schools were rare. Diana's mother started a Sunday morning language class at home to teach her Bengali. Albert, a native-born Indian American, visited his parents' homeland when he was ten.

Despite their parents' efforts, the contributors resisted their ethnic culture, preferring to identify themselves as Americans when they were children. Their resistance stemmed from the pressure to be "normal" and to blend into predominantly white communities that were virtually free of Asians or recent immigrants. Nicole said she was ashamed of her parents' broken English when they visited her in school. Suzuko, a television news producer, said that until her mother reminded her, she had entirely forgotten a childhood episode of locking herself in the bedroom after school to protest against attending Japanese language school.

Two contributors, however, Michael and Fuji, both native-born Americans of Filipino descent, said that their parents encouraged them to assimilate. When Michael's brother asked his parents to address him only in English in front of his white friends, his parents complied without objection. Fuji said he pursued a variety of different sports in high school to combat the stereotype of a "nerdy" Asian.

Many contributors looked forward to college as an opportunity to escape from the demands of their parents' cultural expectations. For 1.5- and second-generation immigrants, parents are often the strongest link to their ethnicity.[34] Ironically, many essayists developed an interest and pride in their ethnic subculture at college. Michael said that his arrival at Brown University marked the first time he had seen a significant number of Asian Americans. He described the evolution of his racial identity.

"Growing up, I considered myself to be an 'American' and unconsciously avoided all things 'Asian.' Later I explored and grew proud of my Asian identity." Although Suzuko resisted attending a Japanese language school as a child, she followed her father's advice and went to Japan for college and spent seven years there, obtaining a college degree and starting a career in television production that she later transplanted to the United States. In high school, Samod often clashed with her father over his efforts to instill pride in her Indian heritage. But, upon entering college, she began to develop a great interest in Indian history and culture and spent two years in India to learn more.

The switch from striving to blend into the mainstream culture to adopting their ethnic culture was influenced by many factors. First, Asian Americans were more visible in the college environment, often composing a significant proportion of the student body. Second, the college environment was much more multicultural and cosmopolitan. Many of the colleges attended by the essayists included Asian language and Asian area study courses that represented their Asian subculture. The availability of such courses was closely related, as previously noted, to the expansion of multicultural studies in the United States ever since the early 1970s. Finally, and most important, the interest in their ethnic heritage as they matured had much to do with the psychological process of coming to terms with their own ethnic and racial identities. This issue is discussed in great detail later.

The contributors generally grew to appreciate their bicultural heritage. They viewed their ethnic values, such as a strong work ethic, respect for scholarly achievements, and esteem for elders, as positive additions to their lives. Nicole said that as a child she had resented her parents' prohibitions against television, but, as an adult, she had decided she would impose the same restrictions on her own children. Steven said that the strong work ethic he learned from his parents gave him an edge over his predominantly white colleagues at the district attorney's office. Jean, a counselor for foreign students at a college, said that she trained her children to show respect to their elders by the traditional Filipino custom of *mano*, placing the right palm of an elder's right hand against the younger person's forehead.

Yet the contributors were harsh in criticizing other aspects of their ethnic cultures. As expected, all women—whether immigrant or second generation—were extremely critical of the more patriarchal traditions practiced in Asian ethnic communities and Asian cultures. The first-generation women tended to be more vociferous than the second generation in their criticism of the double standards associated with Asian patriarchal practices; they clearly felt that gender role divisions thwarted their careers and professional ambitions. Interestingly, Julie, a dietician and a first-generation immigrant, entitled her essay, "Reaching the Glass Ceiling—at Home." The title establishes the issue of gender roles at home as the central theme of her essay. Born and raised in an upper-class Chinese family, Julie was an eager student who embraced learning more about the world. After getting married, however, she settled into a job as an administrative dietician and raised two sons. In her forties, when she wanted a more intellectually challenging job and considered going to law school, her husband dismissed her ambitions as ridiculous. He regarded raising children and keeping a home as a woman's primary duties. Julie sees her husband and children as major factors restricting her life choices; she feels that her husband's lack of understanding and her own sense of being trapped in a domestic role have put a strain on their marriage. Meena, a first-generation Indian immigrant and now a professor, meanwhile, extensively criticized arranged marriages, sexual double standards, and other patriarchal customs in the Indian immigrant community and in India.

While the first-generation women tended to realize the existence of sexual double standards as they grew older, it was different for 1.5- and second-generation women. Nicole said "oppression of women" was her initial, most salient impression of Korean culture as a child. Growing up, she and her sister were sent into the kitchen to prepare food for guests, whereas her two older brothers were allowed to sit with the adults in the living room. Michelle said that she was more attracted to white men than to Korean men, partly because of her disapproval of the oppressive, patriarchal practices of Korean culture. She noted that Korean American men were more likely than Korean American women to favor the traditional gender roles because the *status quo* benefited men. Michelle, a college professor, said that the strong, patriarchal nature of Korean culture and the generally passive role of women hindered the development of skills needed to succeed in the white, male-dominated academic culture.

The contributors also criticized the authoritarian structure of the ethnic family. Steven felt that his lack of social skills stemmed from the Korean cultural patterns that prevailed in his family:

> We rarely talked with one another. Dinners often lasted less than fifteen minutes since we never uttered an unnecessary word. In traditional Korean society, a child was considered virtuous if he or she was silent and obedient to his or her parents.

Steven, who was paralyzed through a car accident, also criticized Korean culture for failing to accommodate or recognize those with physical handicaps. Once regarded as a valuable member and future leader of his church, he became an object of pity—"treated more like an infant than as a man"—after the accident. His experiences were traumatic, as reflected by the title of his essay, "A Handicapped Korean in America." Because of the uneasy reception he received, Steven stopped going to church and avoided interacting with other Koreans.

High Social Assimilation

In their precollege years, the second- and 1.5-generation essayists suffered an inferiority complex about being Asian and the children of immigrants. Many shunned their ethnic culture and sought to blend into the white mainstream culture, forming friendships with children who were white or Jewish. This tendency was partly due to their living in predominantly white neighborhoods and attending predominantly white schools where coethnics and other Asian Americans were rare. Their inclination to gravitate toward whites was also the function of the social marginalization of Asian Americans and Asian culture at the time they grew up.

Though Nicole described feeling socially isolated at the virtually all-white junior high school to which she was bussed, she later shunned her classmates at the predominantly Asian and Latino high school she attended. She ruminated on her rejection of her classmates:

> Many years later I recognized these feelings as being the possible result of living in a society where Asian Americans were not regarded as the mainstream. When I read about the concept of "internalized racism" (i.e., the replication of racist

prototypes within one's own mind), I was also able finally to come to terms with my past, conflicted feelings.

William also described shunning his fellow Asian Americans in elementary school and, to a lesser extent, in high school. He said he resented how classmates at his predominantly white parochial school romantically paired him with a Chinese immigrant girl who did not speak English fluently, just because they were of the same race. He avoided interacting with the girl at school, and was only willing to help her with her homework over the telephone. In high school, William deliberately avoided joining Asian American and Chinese American clubs.

In college, the essayists tended to develop pride in their ethnic and/or pan-Asian identities. Coethnics and other Asian Americans were more common on college campuses. Asian American student organizations and academic courses that explored Asian culture were also available. Michelle, who associated entirely with white friends in elementary and high schools, said she tried to divide her time equally between white and Korean friends in college. William, meanwhile, served as editor of a student magazine on Chinese American issues at Harvard.

However, other essayists continued a preference for white friends even in college, rarely associating with members of their ethnic group or other Asian Americans. In her freshman year at the University of Chicago, Nicole, a Korean American, formed friendships mostly with whites and "consciously and unconsciously avoided associating with East Asians, particularly Korean Americans." Samod said that she "moved comfortably" into the Anglo American social circle in her college dining room. As an Indian American, she "felt little connection with the handful of Asian students, who were mostly East Asian and culturally different from me." Diana, another South Asian, also described feeling that she had little in common with the East Asian and East Asian Americans who dominated the Asian student organizations.

Seven of the twelve essayists born or raised in the United States discussed their dating experiences. Their comments, as well as our discussions with those who chose not to write about their dating experiences, strongly suggest that highly educated, second-generation Asian American professionals tend to prefer whites as dating and marital partners. All seven contributors who discussed their dating experiences were either married or engaged at the time of their essays. Four had white spouses or partners. Of the five contributors who chose not to discuss their dating experiences, three were in serious relationships with white partners.

The four female contributors with white spouses seem to have chosen them partly because they expected them to be more egalitarian than coethnic men. Diana said that Bengali men often criticized her as being "too aggressive" or "very Americanized." Most of the Bengali men with whom she had grown up returned to India for their brides. Asian American men, in comparison to Asian American women, are more likely to marry women from their mother countries.[35] Michelle, a 1.5-generation Korean American, has a Korean American husband, but said that she was attracted to white men because of her resentment toward Korean patriarchal culture. Without her parents' "don't marry a non-Korean" script, she might have ended up marrying a white man, she wrote.

Though Asian American men are more likely than Asian American women to marry coethnics or other Asians,[36] even male essayists expressed a preference for white women. Fuji, a second-generation Filipino American, said his current wife and first wife, as well as most of his dating partners, were white. Albert is married to a fellow Indian American, but dated mostly non-Indians in college. Two other male contributors were intimately involved with white women. As two contributors noted, their selection of white dating partners was largely the function of an absence of Asians. Ten or fifteen years ago, the number of Asian Americans in colleges and in the workplace was much lower than today. Now, Asian Americans can find more coethnic and other Asian American partners. Between 1980 and 1990, the overall intermarriage rate of Asian Americans, particularly the rate of their intermarriage with white partners, decreased significantly, while the rate of their Asian–Asian marriages increased significantly.[37] However, the prevalence of white partners reflects more than the difficulty of finding coethnic or Asian American partners. The prevalence of younger-generation Asian Americans' dating and intermarriages with white partners also means that well-assimilated second- and 1.5-generation Asian Americans are generally well received by whites.

Finally, it is noteworthy that some of the female contributors married or engaged to white men were strongly bicultural. For example, Suzuko completed college in Japan and worked there a few years before returning to the United States. Samod and Diana both spent at least a year in India after graduating from college. Both women describe themselves as culturally and psychologically ethnic, and said that their husbands acknowledged their bicultural background and binational identity. This finding conflicts with the classical assimilation model that assumed that intermarried minority members would be highly assimilated into the mainstream and, in turn, weakly tied to the ethnic group culturally, socially, and psychologically.[38] Although the women are acculturated into the white mainstream culture as highly educated professionals, they are also strongly attached to their ethnic subculture and binational in their loyalty and identity. An emphasis on multiculturalism and fluid national boundaries in the transnational, postmodernist age has enabled these younger-generation Asian American professionals to maintain bicultural backgrounds and binational identities. The same forces apparently have led white Americans to accept Asian American partners who have strong ethnic attachments.

Struggling for Ethnic and Racial Identity

The essayists' struggle to come to terms with their ethnic and racial identities is the most significant aspect of the experiences captured in the fifteen personal narratives. The process of claiming their ethnicity often unfolded over years and involved tremendous pain and inner conflict. While two of the three first-generation, immigrant essayists discussed how prejudice and discrimination had affected their career mobility in the United States, none referred to the psychological turmoil involved in the formation of their ethnic identities. In contrast, most second- and 1.5-generation essayists devoted much space to this struggle; in fact, this struggle lay at the core of several essays.

The 1.5- and second-generation essayists were raised in homes where their parents spoke their native language, ate their native food, and practiced their native customs; yet outside the home, their culture was marginalized and largely invisible. Those of Filipino, Korean, Indian, Vietnamese, and Bangladeshi descent, representing countries with a more recent immigration history, apparently experienced a greater sense of invisibility than those who were Japanese or Chinese; during the 1960s and 1970s, most Americans associated Asians with China and Japan. As a result, most essayists developed a negative self-image and attempted to reject their ethnic culture and their nonwhite physical characteristics. They tried to be white and associated with white students.

Yet, as they grew older, they realized that they could not dismiss their differences, particularly their nonwhite physical differences. Growing up, they became increasingly aware that, regardless of their efforts, they would not be accepted as completely "American." This realization led them to develop their bicultural and nonwhite ethnic and racial backgrounds. Although the acceptance of their ethnic and racial backgrounds initially was painful, they grew more comfortable and confident with their ethnic identity over time. Recalling the moment she observed how physically different she appeared from her classmates in a school hallway mirror, Michelle describes the painful, but positive transformation of her ethnic identity:

> This incident served as a catalyst for painful soul searching and marked the beginning of an inner journey toward greater self-acceptance. Until that point, my struggle with ethnic identity and the denial of my Korean-ness had been largely unconscious, but I began to see that the cost of my denial was too high a price. I accepted the reality of my biculturality, that I was inevitably both Korean and American, and that I had a unique opportunity to learn from both cultures, rather than rejecting one for the other. For the first time since that moment in the second grade when I wished that I was a blond-haired girl with the last name Smith, I began to see my bicultural experience as a blessing and an opportunity rather than a curse.

The formation of ethnic and racial identities greatly influenced the essayists' academic interests and career choices. Though several of the essayists were pressured by their parents to study medicine or law, they turned to the social sciences, humanities, and the arts in their struggle to define their ethnic identity. Samod abandoned her plan to go to medical school and took courses in Asian studies. Diana spent a year studying painting at a university near Calcutta to learn more about her roots.

Michelle, meanwhile, wrote, "My overriding motivation to pursue a career in psychology is directly related to my bicultural experiences." She said she wanted to focus on bridging the gap between first- and second-generation Koreans. Cathy's decision to volunteer at a refugee service agency in Denver and her graduate training in social work were similarly related to the formation of her ethnic and racial identity as a Vietnamese and Asian American.

The essayists have varying degrees of racial identity. Whereas their ethnic identity is related closely to the ethnic subculture practiced in their parents' home and in their parents' home country, their racial identity stems from the consciousness of their nonwhite status in a white-dominant society. To state it alternately, their racial identity is related closely to the perception that nonwhites are not fully accepted in American society. Their nonwhite racial identity is expressed as either pan-Asian or Third World (people of color). Throughout his essay, Michael used the terms "Asian American identity" and "Asian Americans," without ever referring to Filipino American identity or Filipino Americans; this suggests a strong Asian American identity, but a weak ethnic identity. Two Korean Americans, Michelle and Nicole, and one Chinese American, William, have a moderate level of pan-Asian identity, but their culturally based ethnic identity is much stronger. Michelle, Nicole, and William also had close friends of other East Asian backgrounds and are affiliated with pan-Asian organizations.

Samod and Diana, both of South Asian descent, said they felt little affinity with East Asians, such as Chinese, Korean, or Japanese Americans. Samod seemed to find a more common ground with African Americans than with East Asians. Giving up her dream of becoming a medical doctor, she chose to work for a predominantly black school district in New Jersey. Her identity as a person of color developed partly through the realization that South Asians were discriminated against and subject to racial violence because of their skin color in ways similar to African Americans. "Even with their economic privilege, Indians remain dark-skinned and vulnerable to the vagaries of cultural and ethnic discrimination," she wrote. Her identification as a person of color was also influenced by the history of British colonization in India. Remember that the technique of nonvio-

lence employed by Mahatma Gandhi in the Indian independence movement against the British colonial government was
later adopted by civil rights leader Martin Luther King Jr.
William and Nicole also expressed some kinship with African
Americans and Latinos because of their nonwhite status. After
graduating from college, William created a conflict resolution
program for African American and Latino students in Harlem.
Nicole, meanwhile, as a teenager, participated in NAACP-led
marches for school desegregation and worked to improve conditions for migrant farm workers through the United Farm
Workers organized by Cesar Chavez.

The absence of Asian role models also fostered identification
with other minorities. Samod said she was greatly influenced by
the writings of Toni Morrison, the Nobel Prize–winning author
who has written in rich detail about black experiences in the
United States. Nicole and William also mentioned black and
Latino role models. William wrote: "Growing up, I did not have
any Asian American role models aside from my parents. In the
ridicule and prejudice that I fought in grade school, I turned instead to African Americans like Medgar Evers and Martin
Luther King Jr., and Latinos like Cesar Chavez for strength and
guidance."

The fact that highly successful Asian American professionals
identify with African Americans and Latinos and adopt a moderate level of racial identification as a person of color goes
against our expectations. Asian immigrants are generally prejudiced against African Americans and have a tendency to align
with whites in a white–black biracial dichotomy. Yet several of
the second-generation essayists identify more with African
Americans and Latinos than with whites. Although only a small
proportion of second-generation Asian Americans may claim a
Third World racial identity, it is significant and represents the
real possibility of a "rainbow coalition."

Most of the women have varying degrees of gender identity,
in addition to their ethnic and racial identities.[39] The combina-
tion of these three identities—ethnic, racial, and gender—significantly affects the women's worldview, political identity, and
overall behavior and attitudes. The women realize that their parents' home country is far more patriarchal than the United
States, and this alone is a sufficient reason why they cannot live

there permanently. Yet they are also aware that women have disadvantages compared to men in the United States as well. Thus, for the women essayists, their gender identity is tied inseparably to their ethnic and racial identities, making them feel doubly handicapped as minority members and women in a white, male-dominated society. Samod clearly expressed this Third-World, feminist political ideology in her essay:

> With this growing awareness of my invisibility, I became much more insistent on being taken on my own terms, as a woman and as an Indian. My friendship with women became much more important to me, and became a space in which to explore my sense of gender identity. This political identity created a lot of conflict with Clay. It became increasingly difficult to understand each other across the enormous differences between how we looked at the world, as men and women, as Anglo-American and Indian-American, as white and non-white.

Although most essayists born or raised in the United States did not feel fully accepted by American society, they felt more comfortable living in the United States than in their parents' home country or in another foreign country. Interestingly, many essayists grew more conscious of their American identity while travelling abroad. During her visit to India, Samod said she "became more conscious for the first time of how truly American I am." Diana recollected that "in Japan, I found myself identifying as an American more than I had done before." Cathy, too, realized the American side of her identity while teaching English in Japan.

Conclusion

The central themes that emerge in the fifteen personal narratives cannot be applied to young Asian Americans as a whole because the number of essays is too small and the authors of the essays are all highly educated Asian American professionals. Nevertheless, the essays provide important theoretical and practical implications for understanding the ethnicity of newly emerging 1.5- and second-generation Asian American professionals in general and the formation of their ethnic and racial identities in particular. The major findings from the essays are especially important, because no previous study has examined in detail various aspects of ethnicity on the part of 1.5- and second-generation Asian Americans who are children of post-1965 Asian immigrants.

As expected, the personal narratives reveal that Asian immigrant professionals have more disadvantages in the labor market and more uncomfortable job experiences than their American-born counterparts. But what is not clear is whether well-educated and highly acculturated 1.5- and second-generation Asian American professionals encounter the "glass ceiling" problem in their career mobility because of their race. That none of the 1.5- and second-generation essayists discussed specific experiences of discrimination in the labor market may be due to the fact that they are still in the early stages of their careers. They may encounter the glass ceiling problem as they reach higher levels. We need a further study that examines labor market experiences of Asian American professionals by generation through personal interviews with a large number of cases.

Given available information now, the essayists' experiences with unwelcome remarks and physical harassment in their pre-college school years are not surprising. Yet due to the model minority image, policy makers, teachers, and even parents seem to be unaware of the harsh experiences that academically successful Asian American children suffer. By virtue of the phenomenal increase in the Asian American population and increasing emphasis on multicultural education, Asian American school children today may have experiences that are more positive and rewarding than most of the essayists. Yet, as noted in the literature review, many Asian immigrant children and even native-born Asian American children still encounter rejection and physical harassment from white and black students.

All the essayists born and raised in the United States attended prestigious universities and attained careers in the mainstream economy. According to classical assimilation theory, these younger Asian American professionals should be acculturated into the mainstream American culture, without retaining much of their ethnic subculture. However, many essayists were characterized by strong, bicultural experiences. The development of strong bicultural orientations was assisted by the multicultural and cosmopolitan environment of American colleges, as well as the transnational ties maintained with their parents' home countries. This seems to support the view that post-1965 immigrants, whether Asian or not, have advantages over earlier white immigrants in transmitting their cultural traditions to their children.[40]

Milton Gordon suggested that acculturation is a precondition for social assimilation.[41] However, the analyses suggest that acculturation, in the sense of replacing their ethnic culture with American culture, is not a precondition for social assimilation. Despite their strong bicultural experiences, the essayists feel comfortable being friends with and dating white partners. Not only the female, but also the male essayists dated more white partners than coethnics or Asian Americans. However, even more noteworthy is the fact that the essayists did not have to relinquish their ethnic culture as a precondition for dating or marrying white partners. The three female essayists with the strongest bicultural experiences, in fact, are married to white partners. Given that over 40 percent of American-born Asian Americans engage in intermarriages and two-thirds of them intermarry white partners,[42] it is not surprising that the 1.5- and second-generation essayists feel comfortable making friends with and dating white partners. However, the finding of the intermarried essayists maintaining strong ethnic attachment is significant because researchers have long tended to consider minority members' intermarriage with white partners as a sign of their one-sided assimilation into a white culture and white society.

The findings that most 1.5- and second-generation essayists experienced psychological conflicts in the process of forming their ethnic identity is interesting, but not unexpected based on available knowledge. More significant findings from the essays are related to pan-Asian and Third World racial identities. The 1.5- and second-generation essayists holding varying degrees of pan-Asian identity were expected from the bulk of literature on pan-Asian identity and solidarity reviewed at the beginning of this chapter. However, the essays provide important clues to pan-Asian ethnicity, not apparent in the existing pan-Asian literature. Focusing on the structural sources of pan-Asian ethnicity, such as racial lumping and anti-Asian violence, researchers have generally emphasized pan-Asian solidarity in general, without specifying which particular Asian groups are mostly likely to band together. The essays indicate that Chinese, Japanese, and Korean Americans, who share similar cultural and physical characteristics, maintain more frequent social contacts. Many South Asians, however, seem to feel more kinship with African Americans and Latinos than with these East Asian ethnics because of their darker skin color and their colonial past.[43]

Not only South Asian Americans, but also some East Asian Americans feel moderate levels of kinship with African Americans and Latinos. They do so partly because they are sensitive to the racial discrimination encountered by nonwhite minority groups in the United States and partly because these minority communities provide role models in fighting white racism. In their socioeconomic status, Asian Americans are far more similar to white Americans than to African Americans and Latinos. Moreover, as previously noted, Asian immigrants feel far more in common with white Americans than with African Americans and Latinos and are highly prejudiced against African Americans. Thus, the increase in the Asian immigrant population seems to contribute to a racial division of American society into black and nonblack populations.[44] However, the fact that many of our contributors feel kinship with African Americans and Latinos suggests that a large proportion of U.S.-born Asian Americans may participate in a broad minority coalition to protect common interests against the white population.

The patterns of Asian American professionals' pan-Asian and Third World racial identities that emerge from the essays are interesting and plausible. Yet, fifteen autobiographical essays do not provide conclusive evidence for our generalizations. To test these hypotheses, we need further studies that involve personal interviews with a large number of informants.

Notes

1. Herbert Gans, "Toward a Reconciliation of 'Assimilation' and 'Pluralism': The Interplay of Acculturation and Ethnic Retention," *International Migration Review*, 31 (1997): 875–92.

2. Gibson, *Accommodation without Assimilation*; Gans, "Second-Generation Decline," 179–92; Charles Hirschman, Philip Kasinitz, and Josh DeWind, *The Handbook of International Migration: The American*

Experience (New York: Russell Sage Foundation, 2000); Kibria, "The Construction of 'Asian American': Reflections on Intermarriage and Ethnic Identity among Second-Generation Chinese and Korean Americans." *Ethnic and Racial Studies* 20 (1999): 523–44. Portes and Zhou, "The New Second Generation," 76–94; Rumbaut and Cornelius, *California's Immigrant Children*; Zhou and Bankston, *Growing Up American*.

3. Espiritu, *Asian American Panethnicity*; Espiritu, "The Intersection of Race, Ethnicity and Class," 251; Kibria, "The Construction of 'Asian American'"; Nazli Kibria, "College and Notions of 'Asian American': Second-Generation Chinese and Korean Americans Negotiate Race and Identity," *Amerasia Journal*, 25 (1999): 29–52.

4. We can get information about the change in ethnic identity over different life stages through personal interviews by asking retrospective questions. But the informant usually would have difficulty responding quickly to the question of how his or her ethnic identity has changed in the course of his or her life. In a personal narrative, one can describe the change more accurately because he or she has enough time to reflect on it.

5. Thomas Dublin, ed., *Becoming American, Becoming Ethnic: College Students Explore Their* Roots (Philadelphia: Temple University Press, 1996); Maria Hong, ed., *Growing Up Asian American: Stories of Childhood, Adolescence and Coming of Age in America, from the 1800s to the 1990s by 32 Asian American Writers* (New York: Avon Books, 1993); Jeffrey Rubin-Dorsky and Shelly Fisher Fishkin, eds., *People of the Book: Thirty Scholars Reflect on Their Jewish Identity* (Madison: University of Wisconsin Press, 1996).

6. Using a broad definition, some researchers include in the second generation those children born abroad who came to the United States at the age of twelve or before. But most researchers make a distinction between the second and 1.5 generations to separate U.S.-born children from those who came to the United States before they reached adolescence. See Gans, "Second-Generation Decline"; Portes and Zhou, "The New Second Generation"; Ruben Rumbaut, "The Agony of Exile: A Study of the Migration and Adaptation of Indochinese Refugee Adults and Children," in *Refugee Children: Theory, Research, and Services*, ed. Frederick L. Ahearn and Jean Athey (Baltimore, Md.: Johns Hopkins University Press, 1991), 53–91.

7. Gordon, *Assimilation in American Life*, 40–54; Portes and Rumbaut, *Immigrant America: A Portrait*, 2d ed., 222–25.

8. According to a current population survey conducted in March 1997, 42 percent of Asian Americans twenty-five years old and over completed a college education in comparison to 24 percent of the U.S. population. For those twenty-five to thirty-four years old, 49 percent of

Asian Americans completed a college education compared to 27 percent of the U.S. population. See U.S. Bureau of the Census, "Selected Population Characteristics of the Population by Race: March 1997" [http://www.bls.census.gov/cps/pub/1997/int_race.htm].

9. Margaret Anderson and Patricia Hill Collins, eds., *Race, Class, and Gender*, 4th ed. (Belmont, Calif.: Wadsworth, 2001); Patricia Hill Collins, *Black Feminist Thought: Knowledge, Consciousness, and the Politics of Empowerment* (New York: Routledge and Chapman, 1990).

10. Pyong Gap Min, *Changes and Conflicts: Korean Immigrant Families in New York* (Boston: Allyn and Bacon, 1998), chapter 5; Wolf, "Family Secrets," 457–82.

11. Hurh and Kim, "The 'Success' Image of Asian Americans," 512–36.

12. Espiritu, *Asian American Women and Men*; Lowe, *Immigrant Acts*; Mia Tuan, *Forever Foreigners or Honorary Whites? The Asian Ethnic Experience Today* (New Brunswick, N.J.: Rutgers University Press, 1999).

13. Tuan, *Forever Foreigners or Honorary Whites?*

14. Hurh and Kim, "The 'Success' Image of Asian Americans,"; Min Zhou and Yoshinori Kamo, "An Analysis of Earnings Patterns for Chinese, Japanese, and Non-Hispanic Whites in the United States," *Sociological Quarterly*, 35 (1994): 581–602.

15. Joyce Tang, "The Career Attainment of Caucasian and Asian Engineers," *Sociological Quarterly*, 34 (1993): 467–96.

16. Harriet Orcutt Dunleep and Sheth Sanders, "Discrimination at the Top: American-Born Asian and White Men," *Industrial Relations*, 31 (1992): 416–32.

17. John Wilshire Carrera, *New Voices: Immigrant Students in U.S. Public Schools* (Boston: National Coalition of Advocates for Students, 1988); Gibson, *Accommodation without Assimilation*; U.S. Commission on Civil Rights, *Civil Rights Issues Facing Asian Americans in the 1990s* (Washington, D.C.: U.S. Government Printing Office, 1992), 88–99.

18. U.S. Commission on Civil Rights, *Civil Rights Issues Facing Asian Americans in the 1990s*.

19. S. G. Cole and M. Cole, *Minorities and American Promise* (New York: Harper, 1954); Gordon, *Assimilation in American Life*; W. Lloyd Warner and Leo Srole, *The Social Systems of American Ethnic Groups* (New Haven, Conn.: Yale University Press, 1945), 285–86.

20. Massey, "The New Immigration and Ethnicity in the United States," 631–52; Min, "A Comparison of Post-1965 and Turn-of-the-Century Immigrants," 65–94.

21. Linda Basch, Nina Glick-Schiller, and Christina Szanton-Blanc, eds., *Nations Unbound: Transnational Projects, Postcolonial Predicaments, and Deterritorialized Nations* (New York: Gordon and Breach Science,

1994); Nancy Foner, "What's New about Transnationalism? New York Immigrants Today and at the Turn of the Century," *Diaspora*, 6 (1997), 355–75; Michel Laguerre, *Diasporic Citizenship: Haitian Americans in Transnational America* (New York: St. Martin's Press, 1998); Nina Glick-Schiller, Linda Basch, and Christina Szanton-Blanc, *Toward a Transnational Perspective on Migration: Race, Class, Ethnicity, and Nationalism Reconsidered* (New York: New York Academy of Science, 1994).

22. David Theo Goldberg, *Multiculturalism: A Critical Reader* (Cambridge, Mass.: Basil Blackwell, 1994).

23. Joanne Hong and Pyong Gap Min, "Ethnic Attachment among Second-Generation Korean Adolescents," *Amerasia Journal*, 25 (1999): 165–80; Pyong Gap Min and Youna Choi, "Ethnic Attachment among Korean-American High School Students," *Korea Journal of Population and Development*, 22 (1993): 167–79; Portes and Schauffler, "Language and the Second Generation," 640–61; Portes and Rumbaut, *Immigrant America: A Portrait*, 2d ed., chapter 6; Rumbaut, "The Crucible Within," 748–94.

24. Rumbaut, "The Crucible Within."

25. Portes and Zhou, "The New Second Generation"; Portes and Rumbaut, *Immigrant America: A Portrait*, 2d ed., 222–25.

26. Gordon, *Assimilation in American Life*.

27. Kitano, *Japanese Americans: The Evolution of a Subculture*; Erich Rosenthal, "Acculturation without Assimilation," *American Journal of Sociology*, 55 (1960): 275–88.

28. Min and Choi, "Ethnic Attachment among Korean-American High School Students"; Kibria, "The Construction of 'Asian American'"; Thai, "Splitting Things in Half Is White."

29. Hong and Min, "Ethnic Attachment among Second-Generation Korean Adolescents."

30. Waters, *Ethnic Options*.

31. Tuan, *Forever Foreigners or Honorary Whites?*

32. Espiritu, *Asian American Panethnicity*.

33. Omi and Winant, *Racial Formation in the United States*; Dana Takagi, "Post-Civil Rights Politics and Asian-American Identity: Admissions and Higher Education," in *Race*, ed. Steven Gregory and Roger Sanjek (New Brunswick, N.J.: Rutgers University Press, 1994), 229–42.

34. Gans, "Second-Generation Decline."

35. Pyong Gap Min, "Korean Immigrants' Marital Patterns and Marital Adjustment," in *Family Ethnicity: Strengths in Diversity*, ed. Hariette McAdoo (Newbury Park, Calif.: Sage, 1993), 185–204.

36. Lee and Fernandez, "Trends in Asian American Racial/Ethnic Intermarriage," 323–42.

37. Larry Hajime Shinagawa and Yong Gin Pang, "Asian American Panethnicity and Intermarriage," *Amerasia Journal*, 22 (1996): 127–52.

38. Gordon, *Assimilation in American Life*; Lieberson and Waters, *From Many Strands*.

39. Men, too, have a less salient but significant gender identity. However, none of the five male contributors discussed his gender identity. This may have been due partly to the fact that, unlike the women, we did not ask them to do so.

40. Massey, "The New Immigration and Ethnicity in the United States"; Min, "A Comparison of Post-1965 and Turn-of-the-Century Immigrants."

41. Gordon, *Assimilation in American Life*.

42. Lee and Fernandez, "Trends in Asian American Racial/Ethnic Intermarriage."

43. For further information about South Asians being apart from other Asian Americans, especially from East Asians, see Nazli Kibria, "Not Asian, Black or White: Reflections on South Asian Racial Identity," *Amerasia Journal*, 22 (1996): 77–88; Lavina Dhingra Shankar and Rajini Srikanth, eds., *A Part, Yet Apart: South Asians in Asian America* (Philadelphia: Temple University Press, 1998).

44. Herbert Gans, "The Possibility of a New Racial Hierarchy in the Twenty-First-Century United States," in *The Cultural Territories of Race: Black and White Boundaries*, ed. Michele Lamont (Chicago: University of Chicago Press, 1998).

CHAPTER SEVEN

COLLEGE AND NOTIONS OF "ASIAN AMERICANS": SECOND-GENERATION CHINESE AMERICANS AND KOREAN AMERICANS

Nazli Kibria

The traditional college years, the late teens through the mid-twenties, are years of extraordinary maturation and growth. These are years when many young people leave home and meet very different kinds of people often for the first time, come upon previously unheard of ideas, and have the opportunity, and indeed, the task, of defining for themselves and for others who they are—what they think, the values they hold, and their place in a world beyond the one in which they grow up.[1]

As evident to even perhaps the most casual observer, Asian American students respond in highly varied ways to the challenges and opportunities for self-exploration that are offered by the complex racial environment of contemporary U.S. college campuses. Drawing on materials from a qualitative study of postcollege second-generation Chinese and Korean Americans, in this chapter I explore negotiations of race and identity during the college years, focusing on the development of approaches to the "Asian American" concept, in particular its meaning and significance as a basis of affiliation and community. My analyses focus on those persons who had for the most part, not been involved in pan-Asian organizations and activities during college. While pan-Asian organizations are present on most college campuses today, many Asian American students do not participate or become affiliated with them.

While the institutional and political development of the Asian American concept has been extensively studied, we know far less about how the rank and file of those who are widely viewed as "Asian American" understand and respond to this notion. That is, the "public "dimensions of pan-Asian ethnicity have been more extensively studied than its "private" aspects.[2] This is particularly so when it comes to the large segment of Asian Americans who are generally detached or uninvolved in pan-Asian activity, networks, or organizations. Yet, an exploration of the experiences of such persons can provide important insights into the opportunities and constraints that surround the development of a pan-Asian coalition and community.

Race, Asian Americans, and the Post–Civil Rights Campus

The post–civil rights college campus is one in which issues of race have been prominent. The decades since the 1960s have seen a rise in the numbers of racial minority students attending college.[3] While this increase has not been uniform across types of institutions or affected minority groups equally, it is nonetheless one that has transformed the overall racial composition of the college population. Drawing on a 1991 report issued by the American Council on Education, Paul Loeb notes that "students of color presently number 1 out of 6 at four-year colleges and 1 out of 5 if you count two-year community colleges."[4] Asian American students have been an important part of this development. According to Shirley Hune and Kenyon Chan, in 1994 Asian Pacific Americans constituted 4.8 percent of those obtaining bachelor's degrees.[5] Between 1984 and 1995, the numbers of Asian Pacific Americans enrolled in higher education institutions rose 104.5 percent, with comparable figures of 5.1 percent for whites, 37 percent for African Americans, and 104.4 percent for Hispanics. Students of Asian origin have also been an important part of the growth in the foreign student population on U.S. college campuses.[6]

Reflecting this rise in minority student presence, the college campus has been an important arena for larger societal debates on questions of racial equity and integration. Issues of race, for example, have been at the core of controversies over curriculum and course content as well as faculty hiring and student admissions policies. These controversies appear as "hot buttons" in a campus environment that some describe as highly polarized along racial lines.[7] There are, for example, disturbing reports of widespread harassment and violence against minority students.[8] After describing the hostilities experienced by black students following the acquittal of O.J. Simpson, a verdict that was viewed by blacks and whites in sharply divergent ways, a 1995 *New York Times* article concludes: "The overall picture of racial relations on campus is one that seems to get more brittle as time goes by."[9] Racial polarization among students is also suggested by what has been described as "balkanization." That is, in ways that violate the expectations of integration, some observe that the current trend is for students to engage in social activities that are divided along racial lines. Whether it is in terms of the campus organizations that they join or those with whom they spend their spare time, students stick to their own racial groups:

> A quick glance at the local eateries on campus is more suggestive of segregation than integration. Blacks sit with blacks, whites sit with whites, Asians sit with Asians, each group clustered at separate tables.[10]

Asian Americans have been positioned within these currents of racial controversy in complex and at times seemingly contradictory ways. Particularly important here has been the image of Asians as a "model minority," a group that is culturally predisposed to socioeconomic achievements. In educational settings, this stereotype is tied to the assumption that Asians are good students, an idea that is supported by several general indicators of high academic performance among Asian American students.[11] As analyzed by Dana Takagi, the example of Asian Americans as a minority group that is successful through merit has thus often been used to support arguments in favor of ending affirmative action in college admissions. As a result of this perception, Asian Americans are less likely to experience the label of "undeserving" that is often applied to minority students. In other words, while black and Latino students may be resented and condemned for having reputedly been admitted due to preferential policies and not merit, the same charge is less likely to be made of Asian American students, given their reputation for academic excellence. Among the potential consequences of this positioning are tensions and feelings of distance between Asian American and other racial minority students, as well as their differing attitudes on such issues as affirmative action.[12] Related to this is the possibility of greater uncertainty among Asian American students in comparison to those of other minority groups about the prevalence of racism on college campuses.

However, the construction of Asian Americans as "meritorious" does not mean that they have been immune from racial hostility on college campuses. The reputation of Asians for academic achievement means that they are not only applauded but also feared and resented. In selective colleges and universities for example, the significant presence of Asian-origin students has elicited hostility, in ways that echo the hysterical fears of a "yellow invasion" that marked the environment in which laws to halt Asian immigration were enacted in the late nineteenth and early twentieth centuries. Anxieties about an "Asian takeover" are reflected in informal student cultures in the appearance of such phrases as "Made in Taiwan" to refer to UCLA. Asian students are also resented for generating competition in the struggle for grades. They are the "damned curve raisers," making the academic game more difficult for everyone else. In short then, racial hostility toward Asian-origin students often takes as an explicit focus the problems created for others by their academic achievement.

Besides these broad racial currents, there are also the racialized images of the "typical Asian student" that are a part of contemporary campus life. For Asian American students, these images are an important part of the context within which negotiations of identity take place. While quite varied in certain respects, these images affirm an understanding of "Asianness" as embodying qualities or traits that are deeply contradictory to U.S. culture's emphasis on individuality. More generally, there is an affirmation of the "foreignness" of Asians, or their location outside of what is prototypically "American."

The reputation of Asians as academic achievers is tied to the popular image of Asian students as "nerdy"—extremely studious, serious, shy, mathematically inclined, and lacking in social skills and outside interests. The "Asian nerd" embodies qualities that are fundamentally antithetical to individuality. There is a routine, or a machinelike quality to academic achievements here, as highlighted by the charge that Asian students are "good but not exceptional."[13] In other words, while competent in a routine sense, Asian students lack the edge of individual spark and creativity that could lead them into exceptional achievement. The idea of "foreignness" is also deeply embedded in this image. The deficient social skills, passivity, and orientation toward math and technical subjects that are part of the image suggest a certain lack of comfort and familiarity with the norms and expectations of U.S. culture.

In recent years, there has developed another seemingly contradictory Asian student image, one that, while perhaps specifically associated with foreign students from Asia, affects Asian Americans as well. This is the image of the frivolous and well-to-do Asian student who is "cliquey" and focused on parties and conspicuous consumption. Folded into this image are other popular stereotypes of Asian cultural behavior. This includes the idea of Asians as group oriented, driven by the dictates of conformity to group life. Thus, the party-oriented Asian student is obsessed with the display of material goods (e.g., clothes, cars) that will gain him or her status within the clique. The particular markers that are part of this status game can be viewed as further affirmations of the foreign status and nature of Asian students. That is, in their character and substance, the makers (e.g., a particular style of clothing) are seen as off cue or not in sync with what is "culturally American." Also embedded in this image is the association of Asian culture with gender traditionalism. That is, the Asian cliques are marked by a culture of gender traditionalism that supports male dominance and enforces separate standards for men's and women's behavior. In essence, these notions affirm "foreignness"; the Asian-origin student is an outsider to what is "American."

For many Asian Americans, college is a time when they first come to seriously consider the notion of "Asian American" and its relationship to themselves. Here it is important to bear in mind that college students have been critical of the history and development of the Asian American movement. The movement was organized on college campuses in the 1960s by young U.S.-born Asian American activists who were inspired by the civil rights struggles of the time.[14] The founders of the movement defined an ideology of pan-Asianism that has continued to provide a basic framework for the organization and activities of pan-Asian American groups. In essence, "Asian American" is defined here as a signifier of a strategic political community, one that is driven by the shared racial interests of persons of Asian origin in the United States as well as a larger struggle against racism.[15]

Among the legacies of this history is the widespread presence on campuses of pan-Asian student associations that aim to bring together students of varied Asian ethnic origin for political and social events. Some colleges and universities have also developed courses and programs in Asian American studies and student centers devoted to Asian Americans. For Asian-origin students, such forums offer an opportunity to explore the concept of "Asian American" and become exposed to the ideology of pan-Asianism, often for the first time in their lives. For those students who choose to do so, perspectives on "Asian American" are likely to be shaped in important ways by this ideology.

The development of Asian American institutions and forums on college campuses has been supported by the rising numbers of Asian American students. It has also been encouraged more generally by the prominence of racial issues on campuses as described earlier. Asian American groups and organizations have been part of the discourse and debate that surrounds these issues. Ironically, however, the potential for strengthened pan-Asian organization has also coincided with increasing questions and concerns about the limited involvement of Asian American students in pan-Asian groups. Often cited here is the growing ethnic and generational heterogeneity of the Asian American population. In the 1960s, the Asian-origin college population was largely U.S.-born and of Japanese or Chinese origin. Reflecting the demographic shift experienced by the Asian American population since the immigration reforms of 1965, today, however, it includes many first-generation persons as well as students from a wide range of Asian ethnic backgrounds. These developments can make the possibility of organizing along ethnic lines (e.g., Chinese American, Korean American) both more feasible and attractive than pan-Asian activity. This is particularly so for first-generation students for whom ethnic loyalties and a sense of connection to the historically rooted conflicts and enmities between Asian societies are likely to be sharper than that among U.S.-born Asians.

Even, however, for those students who remain distant from pan-Asian activity, the college years are likely to be a time of encounters with the Asian American concept and reflection about what it means for identity and community. For one thing, regardless of whether or not one chooses to be involved, pan-

Asian groups and organizations are a visible part of campus life. It is also the case that the notion of "Asian American" has become an established part of the discourse that surrounds racial issues in the contemporary United States. Thus, while an Asian-origin student may very well avoid pan-Asian activities on campus, she or he is nonetheless likely to confront the idea of "Asian American" in some fashion.

Methods

The materials presented here are drawn from sixty-four in-depth interviews with Chinese Americans and Korean Americans in the Los Angeles and Boston areas. The study was limited to 1.5- and second-generation Chinese and Korean Americans between the ages of twenty-one and forty. I define this group to include those who are the children of immigrants and have been born and/or raised in the United States since the age of twelve or earlier. Interviewees were asked to talk about the role and meaning of their racial and ethnic affiliations in such life spheres as work, family, and neighborhood over the life course. The interviews, which lasted from one-and-a-half to four hours, were tape recorded and later transcribed. Informants were initially located through the membership lists and referrals of a variety of churches, professional and social clubs, and college and university alumni associations. The sample was expanded through "snowballing," whereby informants were asked for referrals to others who fit the criteria for inclusion in the study.

In terms of family of origin, the social background of the sample was varied. Some, for example, had grown up in working-class or small business families while others were from professional upper-middle-class homes. However, the majority of the sample was college educated. Fifty-five of the sixty-four informants had bachelor's degrees from four-year colleges or universities, and in some cases, graduate and professional degrees as well. Of these fifty-five persons, twenty-three had attended public institutions (i.e., state/city colleges and universities), while thirty-two had been to private ones. Two of the others interviewed had obtained two-year associate's degrees from community colleges. Of the remaining informants, two had never attended college and five had attended but had left before completing their undergraduate degrees. The sample included persons who had attended college in the period ranging from 1975 to 1995, with a large number clustered in the 1980s.

A wide range of specific colleges and universities was represented in the experiences of the sample. Although concentrated on the East and West coasts, there was also diversity in the regional location of the institutions. These variations are important given the tremendous differences in racial environments across institutions. For example, institutions differ in the relative numbers of minority students, and more specifically of students of Chinese, Korean, and other Asian origins. Related to this are the variations across institutions with respect to policy on issues of race and multiculturalism. Reflecting these variations, those of my informants who had attended college in the 1980s and 1990s and in California were most likely to have found themselves on campuses with a significant Asian American student presence as well as Asian American studies programs and centers. As I have mentioned, my analyses here focus on the segment of informants who indicated a lack of involvement in pan-Asian organizations during their college years. This segment constituted a majority of forty-one out of the sample of sixty-four persons.

Identity Negotiations and Perspectives on "Asian American"

The second-generation Chinese and Korean Americans' accounts of their college years revealed different perspectives on "Asian American." In what follows I explore these perspectives, focusing on the processes—the events, circumstances, decisions, and negotiations—that surround them. While the narratives tended to be dominated by one perspective over another, it was also the case that they often appeared in shifting and overlapping ways in the accounts of individuals

The "Comfort" of Asian American Friendships

Among the accounts of social life during the college years were those that involved the development of a primary friendship network composed mainly of Asian Americans of varied ethnicities, usually of Japanese, Chinese, and Korean origin. For some, this development was one that overlapped with participation in organized pan-Asian groups and events on campus. My focus here, however, is on the experiences of those who remained uninvolved in such activities, despite an Asian American social circle.

Few informants spoke of their Asian American social circle as the outcome of a highly conscious decision or choice. Instead, the immediate response most often offered was that it had "just happened." In their view, underlying this "natural" course of events were the special ties of Asians. These derived from the commonalties of race and culture among Asians, and the shared experiences and personal histories implied by them. That is, because Asians had a shared racial identity in the United States, they had all experienced certain things—being racially labeled and lumped together as "Asian," and being stereotyped as "nerdy," "foreign," and so forth. Related to this, there was the shared experience of feeling the sting of rejection from others, particularly from whites. It was also felt that Asian Americans shared common experiences that derived from the values that had been a part of their upbringing—an emphasis on education, family, and work. In short, the conception of "Asian American" embedded in this account was that of a community of a shared worldview or understanding, stemming from the commonalities of race and culture. Given all this, it was not surprising that friendships with Asian Americans had "just happened."

Wai Han, a Chinese American, had attended a state college in California in the mid-1980s. In speaking of how her college friendship circle had been primarily Asian American, she refers at first to being extremely busy with the pressures of both classes and jobs. Friendships with others required some active effort, in contrast to those with Asian Americans that developed in natural, almost organic fashion. She felt that there was a greater sense of social ease and receptivity among Asian Americans:

> I was working and didn't have a lot of time. I lived at home part of the time. My friends were from classes. They were all Asian. I mean not just Chinese, but Korean, Japanese. It wasn't planned, it just happened. I've noticed that Asians are more receptive to me in terms of friendships.

Rather than something that had "just happened," for George, a Korean American, a pan-Asian social circle had developed in active response to the college environment. George spoke of how he had found white students at an Ivy League University he had attended in the 1970s to be standoffish and unreceptive to him. In contrast, relationships with Asian American students were easy and comfortable. He felt this was in part because of family backgrounds that had been marked by the common values of education and family:

> I found myself mainly with Asian American friends. In fact there were three of us who were really close and they used to call us the "Three Musketeers." Interestingly, one guy was Chinese American, the other was Japanese American, and of course, I was Korean American. Maybe it's because _____ University is such an old, conservative, and white place. But we felt more comfortable with each other. I found a lot of the students snobbish, unfriendly. Asian Americans tend to have more in common, you know. They have similar views on education and family. Similar family experiences like pressure from parents to do well when you're growing up.

As suggested by George's words, the negotiation of Asian stereotypes was part of his involvement in an Asian American friendship network. For George, the "Asian nerd" stereotype was part of a general environment of hostility toward racial minorities, one that only strengthened the bonds of his Asian American friends. The stereotype then, contributed to his understanding of "Asian American" as a community of solidarity against racism. But there were also other ways in which the stereotypes were negotiated and incorporated into notions of "Asian American." Several informants with pan-Asian friendship networks spoke of how the stereotypes of Asian students as "nerdy" and party-oriented were more applicable to the Chinese or Korean groups on campus. This was, they felt, because of the large numbers of first-generation as well as foreign student Chinese and Koreans that were part of these ethnically bounded groups. Creating a pan-Asian friendship network was a means to differentiate oneself from these groups and, by extension, the stereotypes and connotations that were a part of them. This was because those who were a part of pan-Asian friendship networks tended to be second- or later generation Asian Americans. Meg, for example, spoke of avoiding the Chinese crowds on campus even as she "hung out" with Asian Americans. A Chinese American, she had attended a private university in California in the early 1990s:

> I've thought about this before. I think it could have been good for me to have had a variety of friends. But psychologically . . . I didn't feel comfortable around Caucasians. I felt more in control of the situation when I was with other Asians. There's a common background there with Asians. The other day my friends and I were talking about how whenever we got together, we always asked each other about how our parents were, how the family was, that kind of thing. And how that just wouldn't be a normal topic of conversation for whites. Also, all our growing-up experiences were the same . . . you can't date until this age, or your parents disapprove of you dating this type. We all understood that. My girlfriends especially. (What was the ethnic background of your friends? Were they Chinese, or . . .) Oh no. It was real mixed. There was like a Chinese student crowd, and there was the CSA (Chinese Student Association). I guess I could have been involved but I felt a lot more comfortable with Asians. A lot of the Chinese crowd was not very Americanized. They're very different from me. More into the group thing, the material thing. You know, parties and stuff. I wouldn't fit in.

Meg's words highlight the ways in which consciousness of generational divisions was often an important aspect of understandings of "Asian American" among these informants. But the variable of generation was asserted not simply to achieve distance from the Asian stereotypes. It was, more generally, implicated in efforts to construct a more nuanced and selective understanding of the special ties of Asians. That is, discussion of the greater comfort and ease of relationships with Asians was punctuated with comments about how these were more likely to be felt with some Asians and not others. Sandra, for example, viewed the second-generation experience—that of growing up in the United States as a child of Asian immigrants—to be a vital aspect of the shared personal history and worldview of Asian Americans. A Korean American, Sandra had attended a private women's college in the mid 1980s. It is important to note that the

working-class Asian immigrant history that she invokes is homogenizing of the realities of socioeconomic diversity among
contemporary Asian immigrants:

> I would say the whole immigrant experience really brought us
> closer together. It's like they know what it's like to have par-
> ents who do not speak the language fluently, who are handi-
> capped . . . culturally and verbally. And they know what it's
> like to see their parents working seven days a week and in
> these often dangerous settings or very kind of blue-collar work
> like dry cleaning. So I think that common experience ties us to-
> gether.

Although in far more muted or less explicit ways, informants
also recognized differences of Asian ethnic background in their
discussion of the natural ties of Asian Americans. Due to similarities in physical characteristics as well as overlaps of history
and culture, especially a tradition of Confucianism, this bond
was far more pronounced among persons of East Asian descent.
This point was made by George, a Korean American. As described earlier, George's closest friends in college had been Chinese American and Japanese American:

> Of all the Asian groups, Koreans, Japanese, and Chinese have
> the most in common. (In what way?) Everybody gets mixed
> up; they can't tell us apart. (That doesn't happen to a Viet-
> namese or a Filipino?) It can happen, but it's less likely, espe-
> cially if you're talking about Asians looking at each other. It's
> much easier I think to tell a Korean from a Filipino person than
> Chinese. It's also that there are common roots for Koreans,
> Japanese, and Chinese if you go way back. Like our writing is
> from the same family. And the cultures are based on Confu-
> cianism.

What I have described above are accounts of the college years
that are marked by a sense of identification with "Asian American" as an affiliation, despite noninvolvement with organized
pan-Asian activity. This lack of involvement was reflected in important ways in the understandings of "Asian American" articulated here. While race and racism were widely acknowledged
as part of the special bond of Asians, these ideas did not always
translate into recognition of the shared political interests of

Asian Americans or a conception of Asian American as signifying a strategic political community. Also differentiating these perspectives from the ideology of pan-Asianism is the idea of a pan-Asian culture, in particular the shared Asian values of family and education. Mindful of the realities of diversity among Asian Americans, the Asian American movement has been critical of efforts to construct "Asian American" as a cultural community.

There was an elasticity to the notion of pan-Asian community articulated here. That is, while informants spoke of these bonds as encompassing Asian Americans in general, they also at times made distinctions. As I have described, generational divisions, especially those between immigrant and second-generation persons, were a particularly prominent distinction. For the second-generation Chinese and Korean Americans, "Asian American community" emerged out of a central experience and identification with the United States, one that those who had not grown up elsewhere did not fundamentally share.

"Asian American" as an Artificial Construct

Some of the second-generation Chinese and Korean Americans spoke of their college social life with reference to a friendship circle that was primarily Chinese American or Korean American. Participation in Chinese or Korean organizations on campus could be part of these accounts, but not necessarily so. This pattern of ethnically oriented social involvements, somewhat more prevalent among the Korean Americans than Chinese Americans,[16] meant that perspectives on "Asian American" were forged here in contrast and often in opposition to understandings of Chinese or Korean American as a basis of identity and community—a construct that was artificial and externally imposed, masking the more natural ties and solidarity of specific ethnic groups, such as Chinese or Koreans. For some, the activities of pan-Asian organizations on campus only highlighted the contrived character of Asian American community. For a variety of reasons, they felt distant from the political agenda of these organizations and did not see their interests and ideas to be represented by them.

While in some accounts, a pattern of friendships with fellow ethnics was continuous with social life before college, for others it was something new. In the latter case, informants often spoke of how college had for them been a time of exploring and coming to terms with their Chinese or Korean identity. The presence on campus of significant numbers of Chinese and Korean Americans both allowed and encouraged such explorations. Often mentioned here was the experience of encountering for the first time fellow ethnics who were U.S.-born/raised and who thus contradicted the Asian stereotypes. That is, they were not "nerdy," "foreign," or "traditional" in their attitudes toward men and women. Thus, as in the case of the earlier accounts, negotiations or identity were marked by the Asian stereotypes and the use of generation to achieve distance from them. We see this in the account of Susan, a Korean American who had attended a state college in California in the early 1980s:

When I started going to _____ I was really anti-Korean because I thought all Korean men or boys were really chauvinistic and domineering like my dad. Or really wimpy or nerdy. And I didn't really have respect for Korean girls because my sense was they didn't have any ambition in life. They just wanted to marry right and to gossip about clothes, boys, that type of thing. They weren't conscious about other things that were going on. I don't know where I got this idea but I was really dissatisfied with Korean women. So I had this stereotype of Korean women and I used to tell myself "I'm not going to hang out with Koreans when I get to college because they're so narrow-minded and they only speak Korean and they don't assimilate." But then once I got there I met Koreans and they encouraged me to join their Korean student organizations and stuff. I realized that it was kind of a bonding that almost comes natural. I think I realized my identity and I also realized that not all the Korean kids fit the stereotype. There were Korean kids just like me who grew up in predominantly white neighborhoods, and had a lot of white friends. They weren't all nerdy or chauvinistic. We could relate to whites really well. (So your friends in college were mainly Korean American?) Yeah, I mean there were so many Korean Americans there that I didn't need to go beyond that. I mean I had a lot of friends. I did have some Chinese and Japanese friends I met through a pre-law Asian students group. But still, with Koreans it's different, I feel like there's a natural attraction.

In Susan's account, the meaning and significance of friendships across Asian groups is assessed in contradistinction to Korean ones. In comparison, intra-Asian bonds come up short, appearing weak and insignificant. For Jeff, a Korean American who had attended a private university in the Northeast in the early 1990s, intra-Asian ties were not only weak in comparison to ethnic ones but also had an aura of falsity about them. For him, the transition to a primarily Korean American social circle had taken place during college. It had been triggered by a growing sense of discomfort and alienation from the predominantly white social groups around which he had initially organized his social life. Also important to note is that Jeff's perspective on racial issues had been deeply affected by the 1992 Los Angeles riots, during which his parents' small business had been seriously damaged:

> I would say that the first time that I started feeling a close bond with Koreans was in college. It's funny because when I started in my freshmen year, I joined a white fraternity and I was fairly active. I didn't really participate in any of the Korean functions and I guess the Koreans called me whitewashed. Then I had a good friend who was part of that Korean clique. By my second year, I kind of assimilated into the Korean crowd. (What happened with the fraternity?) I was less and less involved. I was one out of three Asians in a very large organization, and it felt strange. It was subtle, but I don't think I was accepted. So my friends were pretty much Korean in college and it's been that way since then. I find it's more comfortable. (Is that also the case with Asian Americans from other groups? Do you have other Asian friends?) No, not really. I mean I had acquaintances in college who were Chinese, that kind of thing. I can't say I had more in common with them than whites or blacks or whatever. It's a mistake to think there's any real bond going on there. We speak different languages, have different perspectives.
>
> I was in college during the riots. I remember reading right after the riots about how the Chinese and Japanese communities in L.A. were just . . . unfazed. I mean, it didn't concern them—it was a Korean problem. You know, I just don't see that there's too much in common going on there. Why do we have to go around pretending that Asian Americans are the same?

The resentment felt by Jeff about what was felt to be the pretense of Asian American unity was echoed by several informants.

Some referred to encounters with pan-Asian groups and activities in which the fiction of Asian American community was made sharply visible to them. This was the case for Terry, a Chinese American who had attended a state college in California in the early 1980s. Unlike the accounts described so far, for Terry a pattern of Chinese American friendships was not new, but something with which she had grown up, having been raised in the Chinatown areas of San Francisco and Los Angeles. Terry draws on her exposure to an Asian American student organization and its internal tensions as a point of contrast for highlighting the cultural and other similarities of Chinese in comparison to Asians in general. It is of note that she also qualifies this notion of a natural Chinese bond by recognizing generational divisions among Chinese, and demarcating her sense of ethnic affinity to American-born Chinese in particular:

> Most of my friends were Chinese, I felt more comfortable socially with Chinese. (How about Asian friends, I mean from other Asian groups?) I did have some Asian friends in college who were not Chinese. At first, I went to the Asian students association. But it was very political. One group would say: We're not getting represented, we want a voice. I couldn't get into it, I couldn't see the point. I find it less stressful with Chinese; I'm talking mainly American-born Chinese. We have the same history, we grew up with the same superstitions, foods.

Several informants echoed the general sense of discomfort voiced by Terry about the pan-Asian organizations on campus. Some complained of the "radical" political agenda of the pan-Asian groups. Their own sense of dissonance and distance from the progressive politics of Asian American groups only confirmed the fake, contrived character of "Asian American" as a basis of identity and community. We see this in the words of Bill, a Chinese American who had attended a private university in California in the early 1980s. Bill had found the progressive political agenda of the pan-Asian groups on campus to be unconvincing and in fact distasteful. While he was not very interested in the Chinese student groups, either, in the latter half of has college career he found himself with a "Chinese clique." Besides connoting a certain economic glamour, Chinese ties were natural and primordial—rooted in blood:

In college I stayed away from Chinese for a long time. I mean I didn't go looking for Chinese. The Chinese Students Association was not very interesting to me. Neither were the Asian student groups. They were too crazy. Always spouting off about oppression. I really think this whole Asian thing is over-played. In the last couple of years I got into a Chinese clique. It was a change—I'd spent all this time avoiding Chinese. And then it seemed kind of exciting. China is such a booming area economically. I felt kind of drawn to it. I think it's like they say, being Chinese is in your blood.

The pattern of ethnic social involvements described above was one that provided the social context for an understanding of "Asian American" as peripheral if not false or artificial as a ba-sis of identity and community. It was a community of fellow Chinese and Korean Americans rather than a pan-Asian American one that provided the means for coping with the social challenges of college life. As was true of the understandings described in the previous section, here, too, talk of the "natural" bond of Chinese and Koreans was constantly punctuated with qualifications, in particular that of the distinction between immigrant and second-generation persons.

"Asian American" as Stifling to Individuality

The last accounts that I turn to are distinguished by a lack of connection to Asian, Chinese, or Korean American communities on campus. Some informants (especially those who went to college before the 1980s) explained this absence with reference to a lack of opportunity, or the presence of very small numbers of fellow ethnics or Asian Americans on campus. More often though, what was related was an active rejection of the available opportunities to make these connections. "Asian American" was understood here as a force that stood in opposition to individuality and the exercising of freedom and choice with respect to affiliation and identity. This was so in two ways. First, Asian American communities were seen to collectively embody qualities and traits that were antithetical to individualism. These included the stereotypical qualities of clannishness, group conformity, and gender traditionalism. Second, individuality was challenged by the very fact of prescribed membership. That is, the fact that one was expected to belong to Asian American group(s), regardless of how one felt about it, was stifling. As we will see, informants experienced this expectation of belonging as emanating not just from non-Asians but also from within the Asian American communities on campus.

For Gordon, a Chinese American, the expectations of Asian friendship were particularly troubling. Students of Asian-origin on campus responded to his refusals to join them by labeling him as "banana"—someone striving to be white and denying his true heritage. The significance of this expectation as well as his discomfiture about it were only compounded by the reaction of his white friends who teased him about belonging to the "Asian crowd." Thus the dynamics of these expectations, along with his negative impressions (e.g., close minded, serious) of the Asian student groups meant that the very idea of Asian American community made him feel claustrophobic:

> It was very strange at _____ University because that was the first time that I was surrounded by other Asian people. And it was kind of funny, but I felt uncomfortable with it. (How did it make you feel uncomfortable?) I never really looked at myself as Asian. Well, I never really looked at myself as anything, you know growing up in this white suburb. When I got there, I was solicited to join the Korean club and the Chinese club and the Asian club. But I had never grouped myself as Asian or Chinese or anything like that. And so it was just something new. I met a lot of them and it really turned me off. It's the closed-mindedness to the point where they kind of shun out other people. It's kind of mean to say, but I didn't enjoy being with them. They were not very fun. They were very serious. (Were these people mainly Asian immigrants? Or were they raised here?) Both, I didn't see a huge difference there. I would get a lot of flak, from both sides. The Asian group, they would give me a hard time . . . hey, why aren't you hanging out with us? Are you a "banana"? My friends (white) would kid around about it, and ask me why I wasn't hanging out with the Asians. They were joking, they knew I wouldn't fit in with the Asians.

As suggested by Gordon's response to my question about differences between immigrant and U.S.-born Asian students, distinctions among Asians did not figure heavily in his understandings of Asian American community. What becomes clear here is

the quality of fluidity that surrounds the stereotypes, in particular their shifting ability to apply to both pan-Asian boundaries
and the ones contained within them. We see this in the words of
Ben, who like many others voiced a sense of repulsion to the
"cliquey" and conformist character of Asian campus communities. He begins by speaking of his experience with Korean students, but then slips into talking about Asians in general. Ben had
attended a private university in the Northeast for a year in the
early 1990s, before dropping out and joining the armed services:

> Those Korean guys came up to me and said, why aren't you
> hanging out with us? Why aren't you part of the gang, the Ko-
> rean posse? I was thinking, are we still in high school? A
> Korean posse? Is this for real? It was too stifling, I didn't want
> to be part of some group. I think it's important for people to be
> themselves. You always see these Asian people in a group,
> everything's a group.

For women in particular, an aversion to "traditional," male-
dominant gender roles often marked their accounts of why they
had steered clear of the Asian, Chinese, or Korean communities
on campus. This was suggested by Katherine, a Korean American who had attended a private university in the Northeast in
the early to mid-1980s. Katherine begins by speaking specifically
of her experiences with the Korean Students Association, but
then moves on to Asians in general. What she felt to be the male
chauvinism of the Asian men, along with the general emphasis
on group activity, led her to stay away from the Asian groups:

> I had a really broad group of friends. We had a rooming group
> of ten women and we looked like the United Nations. Puerto Ri-
> can, Japanese American, a woman from Seattle, two black
> women from the South. I did find though that I couldn't hang
> out with Koreans who were in Korean groups; that wouldn't
> work for me. I went to the Korean Student Association meetings
> and I felt like they were pointless. The men pretty much led the
> meetings. Basically I really like Asian women and I don't really
> get along with Asian men. There are few Asian men who are
> willing to let down all preconceptions about women, I've even
> seen that with a lot of really liberal, well-educated Asian guys.
> And I seem to break a lot of stereotypes about Asian women. In
> any case, the whole group thing drove me nuts.

While Katherine's concerns about gender traditionalism focused on the behavior of Asian men, for Jane they centered around impressions of the women who were part of the Chinese student groups on campus. According to her, not only were the women deferential to men but also frivolous in nature, focused on ostentatious material displays. As a student from a modest financial background, Jane was particularly offended by these displays. A Chinese American, she had attended a private university in California in the early 1980s:

> I was working and going to school at the same time. I had a scholarship and I felt a lot of pressure to do well. You know I had basically gone to an inner-city school, and I don't think the academic standards had been too high. I had to work really hard to get good grades. I was on scholarship, but financially it was still not easy. So socially I wasn't all that active, until about my third year. My close friends were people I met in class. Pretty much Caucasian. (Did you join any Asian or Chinese student groups?) No. I did have a Chinese friend who dragged me to a couple of meetings and a dance organized by a Chinese group. It was a real turnoff. I was almost offended in some ways. It was a big status thing, expensive clothes, cars. And I didn't like the whole male-female dynamic. It was too much like the delicate Asian flower waiting for the man to sweep her off her feet.

Men informants, too, voiced complaints about an excessive "party focus," particularly in relation to the Chinese and Korean groups and organizations on campus. Thus Sung, a Korean American, spoke of being turned off by the "drinking club" atmosphere of the Korean Students Association on campus. He also felt no sense of connection to the Asian American organizations on campus. He did not agree with the fundamental political agenda of the organizations and felt a lack of space for dialogue within them. All of this only enhanced his association of the idea of Asian American affiliation with conformity and the restriction of free choice. Of note is his comment that his friends were a diverse group, a point often made by informants in the course of affirming through contrast the cliquish and conformist character of the Asian groups. Diversity in friendships thus becomes a kind of proof of individuality and the ability to make choices apart from groups:

My friends in school were really just a motley crew, and that was something I really liked. I wasn't interested in the Korean Students Association, which was a social thing. I mean it was like a drinking club, a place to find a future wife, that kind of thing. It was like a fraternity. (How about Asian American groups?) I went to a couple of Asian American meetings my first year but the agenda that they had just didn't sit well with me. I mean I couldn't get all that interested in what they had to say. They were very much oriented toward trying to frame the Asian American experience using language or way of describing things that is similar to civil rights. There was no room for disagreement, dialogue. You know I thought it was a kind of stretch. African Americans have been screwed in this country for a long time. Whereas Asians have generally been treated better.

The accounts of the informants so far are dominated by negative impressions and reactions to Asian student groups on campus. A somewhat different perspective was provided by Connie, a Chinese American who had attended state college in California in the late 1970s–early 1980s. Having grown up in a largely Chinese neighborhood, she saw college as an opportunity to meet people from other groups. She felt that her college experiences had taught her to feel comfortable with different kinds of people. Thus while for her, Asian American community did not have the kinds of negative connotations that it did for the other informants described here, it was nonetheless associated with limitations, a restriction on individual choice. Once again, a racially diverse friendship network is associated with free choice in contrast to the constraints of an Asian or a Chinese social circle:

As soon as I got there, I found myself in an Asian clique. These Asian persons that I didn't know came up and invited me to sit with them in the dining hall. And every night we'd eat together and there would be this long table of about twenty Asian Americans . . . Japanese, Chinese. And then I decided, what's going on here, I want to meet some other kinds of people. So after my first year I kind of expanded, joined some different groups and met other people. I had some white friends for the first time in my life, and I had Hispanic friends. (How did you feel with the other, the non-Asian friends that you made? Did you feel accepted?) Oh yes, absolutely. I think it was really important for me, because I started to feel more comfortable with other people.

To summarize, the perspective described here is one in which "Asian American" is understood as stifling, claustrophobic, and contradictory in an essential sense to individuality. Popular stereotypes of Asian culture clearly play an important role in shaping and giving form to such understandings. Also important was the sense of pressure felt by informants to belong to pan-Asian Chinese or Korean communities on campus. Resisting these pressures was a means to affirm one's individuality.

Conclusion

This chapter highlights the diversity of social patterns and experiences among second-generation Chinese and Korean Americans during their college years. This diversity is not surprising, given the range of backgrounds, resources and specific college contexts involved. At the same time, my materials also suggest some ways in which experiences are shaped by a common racial context. These include racialized constructions of persons of Asian descent as "foreign," as captured by popular stereotypes of the "typical Asian student." These stereotypes entered into the identity negotiations of my informants in powerful yet varied ways, affirming different understandings of "Asian American." For some, it provided the basis for an understanding of Asian American as a community of solidarity while for others it was an affiliation that violated identity choice. Moving across these variations was a common response—a tendency to deflect the stereotypes onto immigrant or foreign national Asians. My findings thus highlight the ways in which these stereotypes contribute to and play on immigrant versus later generation fissures in Asian American communities.

Those who are the focus of this chapter were disengaged from pan-Asian student organizations and activities during their college years. Many specific explanations were offered for this absence of connection, ranging from a lack of time and energy to invest in extracurricular activities to disagreement with the progressive politics of the organizations. The lack of engagement was perhaps most striking among those who expressed a sense of pan-Asian connection and identification. As I have discussed, the understanding of Asian American community here was both less political (at least in the explicit sense) and more focused on issues of culture than that offered by the ideology of pan-Asian-ism. Some of these informants described themselves as "apoliti-cal" while others did not find the political agenda of Asian American organizations to be of much relevance and interest. While quite tentative and diffuse in nature, a process of ethni-cization of "Asian American" is suggested here. That is, there are hints of a transformation, one by which "Asian American" is seen by those who are encompassed by it as not simply an ex-ternally imposed category but a signifier of community, a shared culture and history. In invoking a pan-Asian culture, this process of ethnicization drew on ideas embedded in the model minority stereotype—in particular the presumed Asian emphasis on edu-cation and family. Also noteworthy were the ways in which dis-tinctions of immigrant versus later generation and East Asian versus "other Asian" were used to demarcate the boundaries of pan-Asian American community.

But while some of the second-generation Chinese and Korean American identified "Asian American" as a natural basis of com-munity, most rejected it as a significant basis for affiliation and identity. For some it signified an effort to impose an artificial and fake social and political unity. Yet for others "Asian American" signified a restriction on individuality. These rejections capture the contradictions that are part of the notion of Asian American. That is, while "Asian American" has come on the one hand to signify a political strategy of empowerment, it also remains for persons of Asian descent a homogenizing and externally im-posed category.

Notes

Thanks to Linell Yugawa for helping me to think through my ideas about the college experiences of Asian Americans. Also thanks to Karen Pyke for her careful feedback.

1. Ruth Sidel, *Battling Bias: The Struggle for Identity and Community on College Campuses* (New York: Penguin, 1994), 12.

2. For a discussion of the distinctions between "public" and "private" ethnicity, see Philip Kasinitz, *Caribbean New York: Black Immigrants and the Politics of Race* (Ithaca, N.Y.: Cornell University Press, 1992).

3. See Dana Y. Takagi, *The Retreat from Race: Asian American Admissions and Racial Politics* (New Brunswick, N.J.: Rutgers University Press, 1992) and Shirley Hune and Kenyon S. Chan, "Special Focus: Asian Pacific American Demographic and Educational Trends," in *Minorities in Higher Education*, ed. D. Carter and R. Wilson (Washington, D.C.: American Council on Higher Education, 1997), 1–63. Minority enrollment rose from 6.4 in 1960 to 13.8 percent in 1977. In 1995, 11.7 percent of those obtaining bachelor's degrees were minority students, and 16.8 percent in 1994.

4. Paul R. Loeb, *Generation at the Crossroads: Apathy and Action on the American Campus* (New Brunswick, N.J.: Rutgers University Press, 1994), 190.

5. According to Hune and Chan, in 1995 60 percent of Asian Pacific Americans attending college were enrolled at four-year institutions, 80 percent were in public institutions ("Special Focus: Asian Pacific American Demographic and Educational Trends," 51).

6. See Sidel, *Battling Bias*, 42. Asians have constituted about half of the foreign student population.

7. See Diversity Project, *An Interim Report to the Chancellor* (Berkeley: Institute for the Study of Social Change, 1989), 22.

8. Sidel, *Battling Bias*, 7–8.

9. Peter Applebome, "Nation's Campuses Confront an Expanding Racial Divide," *The New York Times*, October 25, 1995.

10. Takagi, *The Retreat from Race*, 145.

11. For example, Hune and Chan report better preparation and higher expectations of going to college for Asian Pacific Americans than other racial-ethnic groups ("Special Focus: Asian Pacific American Demographic and Educational Trends," 51).

12. According to the 1991 Diversity Report from the University of California at Berkeley, Asian American students made several cases in which black and Chicano/Latino students had been assessed as undeserving but had received admission through preferences. The report also cites survey results showing sharp discrepancies between the support of affirmative action between Asian American and other minority students. Thus 12.1 percent of Asian American students surveyed said that they "definitely" agreed with the underrepresented ethnic minority policy. This was in contrast to 61.5 percent of blacks, 40.6 percent of Chicanos, 40.2 percent of Latinos, and 35.7 percent of Native Americans.

13. Deborah Woo, "The 'Overrepresentation' of Asian Americans: Red Herrings and Yellow Perils," in *Race and Ethnic Conflict*, ed. Fred Pincus and Howard Ehrlich (Boulder, Colo.: Westview Press, 1994), 314–26.

14. Espiritu, *Asian American Panethnicity*.

15. Kibria, "The Construction of 'Asian American,'" 523–44.

16. Possible explanations for this discrepancy include the greater heterogeneity of the Chinese American population in comparison to Korean Americans, in terms of nationality, class, and generation.

CHAPTER EIGHT

SECOND-GENERATION ASIAN AMERICAN IDENTITY: CLUES FROM THE ASIAN ETHNIC EXPERIENCE

Mia Tuan

You know, I'm tired of the Kristi Yamaguchis and the Michelle Kwans! They're not American . . . when I look at a box of Wheaties, I don't want to see eyes that are slanted and Oriental and almond shaped. I want to see American eyes looking at me.[1]

—Bill Handel, popular morning DJ for KFI-AM, one of the nation's most listened to talk radio stations.

"American Beats Kwan"

—MSNBC's erroneous headline after figure skater Tara Lipinski beat Michelle Kwan for the Gold medal during the 1998 Winter Olympics. Both women are Americans.

In my work with third-generation and later Asian Americans (hereafter referred to as Asian ethnics) certain features have emerged that I have argued contribute to their shared experience as longtime Americans of Asian ancestry. The most striking of these centers around the struggles they face in overcoming the perception that all Asians, irrespective of generational status, are foreigners in this country. From this false assumption, numerous consequences have emerged. One of these centers around questions they face from others over whether they are "Asian enough" in the way they conduct themselves or their lifestyles. In their interactions with non-Asians, they must contend with the expectations of others who believe they should be closer to their ethnic roots than their American ones. Meanwhile, their interactions with and observations of Asian immigrants reveal just how much they differ from their foreign-born counterparts.

Many Asian ethnics are aware that Asian immigrants look upon them as watered down, "less than" versions of themselves.[2]

At the same time, they also face resistance to being seen as "real" Americans as captured by the excerpts above. Even prior to the spate of recent immigration, Asian ethnics struggled to be recognized as authentically American with legitimate places in this society.[3] The World War II internment of over 110,000 Japanese Americans, two-thirds of whom were American born, stands as the embodiment of this disregard and blurring of national and ethnic identities.[4] Thus, while the current influx of Asian immigrants has reinforced the notion that all Asians are foreigners, the tendency to see Asian ethnics as conditional citizens has a long-standing history.

Given the tremendous growth in Asian immigration over the past few decades, the seeds for future generations of Asian ethnics have been planted. As their generational elders, the experiences of current Asian ethnics provide important clues to what the future may hold for these up and comers. Naturally, questions of "cultural authenticity" are more pronounced the farther one is removed from the immigrant generation. But as several contributors in this book have shown, members of the 1.5 and second generations are already actively struggling to make sense of what it means to be racially Asian, ethnically Korean, Vietnamese, and so on, and nationally American in terms of their personal identity and cultural practices and beliefs.[5] How current Asian ethnics are negotiating these concerns may offer the future 1.5 and second generations insights and models for how they wish to address some of these issues.

In this chapter I explore the "authenticity dilemma" confronting Asian ethnics today and discuss how they negotiate a social terrain where others define them as neither *real* Americans nor *real* Asians. However, they have not passively accepted either of these "less than" labels. On the contrary, I argue that Asian ethnics have and continue to actively struggle against the stereotypical labels others impose on them. As part of their resistance, many dismiss the essentialism inherent in the belief that ethnic authenticity lies solely in practicing particular cultural traditions or rigidly upholding the same values as those held in the motherland. Furthermore, they insist that uniquely Chinese American, Japanese American, and even Asian American cultures have developed in this country and it is within these hyphenated spaces where their true authenticity lies.

Methodology

To explore the authenticity dilemma confronting Asian ethnics, I draw from interviews gathered for a larger study I conducted on the middle-class Asian ethnic experience. Between 1994 and 1995, I led a research team in interviewing ninety-five third-, fourth-, and fifth-generation Chinese and Japanese ethnics living in northern and southern California in order to: (1) determine the content, meaning, and salience of ethnicity in their lives; (2) explore the extent to which they felt that ethnicity was an optional rather than imposed facet of their identities; and (3) examine the role played by race in shaping life experiences.[6] All the participants are well educated and from urban areas; many are white-collar professionals in fields such as medicine/health, banking, law, engineering, publishing, computer technology, education, finance, insurance, and real estate. Others were housewives, small business owners, students, and a few artists. The youngest participants were in their early twenties while the oldest were well into their seventies. Forty-eight participants are of Japanese ancestry, three of mixed Chinese-Japanese heritage, and the remaining forty-four are of Chinese ancestry.

The fact that this study was conducted in California is of special significance. Ever since Chinese were first brought in to labor in mines and railroads, California has remained the state with the largest concentration of Asian Americans.[7] It is also a particularly appropriate place for studying native-born Chinese and Japanese Americans; 42 percent of the nation's native-born Chinese and 36 percent of native-born Japanese reside there.

Clearly, California is a rich and essential site for studying the Asian American experience. Strangely though, whether their numbers and long history have promoted greater social acceptance or the reverse—greater hostility—is not at all clear. Asian ethnics in California have the most substantive reasons to feel part of the mainstream and subsequently to feel that ethnicity is an optional part of their identity. After all, they have been present in the state since the mid-1800s, are well integrated into its social fabric, and may be found in all occupational fields. Further, California is the primary receiving state for Asian immigrants, a situation that may actually reinforce a sense of ethnic identity among Asian ethnics.

In addition, the general climate toward immigrants, both legal and illegal, is decidedly less hospitable today. With California's governor Pete Wilson stirring up tensions, increased hostilities come as no surprise. Asian ethnics who are mistaken for Asian immigrants have received some of this negativity.[8] Possibly, such cases of mistaken identity may cause Asian ethnics to question their own levels of acceptance by the mainstream. Subsequently, because of perceived social exclusion, ethnicity may become more salient for them.

Findings

"I'm not your typical American when people think American." — Not American Enough

According to classic assimilation scholars such as Robert Park[9] and Milton Gordon,[10] ethnicity's salience in people's lives declines with each passing generation, a prediction based on years of researching the white ethnic experience. Today, identifying along ethnic lines and pursuing an ethnically embedded lifestyle have largely become optional facets of life for white ethnics.[11] As Richard Alba[12] argues, identity choices for white ethnics today can be capriciously based on nothing more than a "sense that it is nicer to be an X, rather than a Y."

Of course, this state of affairs did not take place overnight. European immigrants who poured into the country in the early part of the twentieth century suffered greatly at the hands of nativists who looked upon their cultures as backward and threatening to the American way of life.[13] Nativists demanded that newcomers shed their language, rituals, and practices in exchange for an all-encompassing American identity and access to the privileges associated with that status. Clearly these immigrants paid a heavy price, but the very success with which their descendants have become one of "us" has reinforced this country's belief in its ability to assimilate and embrace diverse peoples.[14]

As longtime Americans who are not part of the racial norm, Asian ethnics face a markedly more circumscribed set of identity options. How they choose to identify is not solely a private affair as it is for white ethnics. They experience real pressures to identify in ethnic or racial terms because these remain salient markers to others. Most identify in hyphenated terms as Chinese American, Japanese American, and, increasingly, Asian American. Cathy Leong,[15] who identifies as Asian American, explained her choice:

> For myself I have more Japanese, Korean, Filipino friends, just through work and the people we associate with, you know, my coworkers and stuff like that. So I think there's more of an emphasis on Asian American.

As more individuals come to think of themselves as members of a general family of Asian Americans and associate accordingly, they are more likely to embrace the pan-ethnic label to describe themselves. Since the bulk of her friends are other Asians, Cathy feels more comfortable reinforcing the racial bond while downplaying ethnic differences.

Emily Woo, who also identifies as an Asian American, does so because it encompasses both her Chinese and Japanese roots:

> Q: How do you identify yourself?
> A: That's a really hard question actually. I guess as an Asian American. I don't consider myself just Japanese, just Chinese. I don't consider myself just American. I don't know. I kinda like terminology like Asian American and African American because it's kinda messy . . . By blood, I'm Chinese and Japanese. By culture, I don't know if I am so much of either. I don't know. . . . Mom would always tell me I used to get confused growing up. "How can I be Japanese and Chinese and American?" "Well, you are half Japanese, half Chinese, and all American."

For Emily, identifying along racial lines as an Asian American eliminates the cumbersome task of acknowledging both components of her ancestry, a strategy white ethnics of mixed ethnic ancestry also utilize.[16] Her rationale provides a glimpse into how future generations of mixed ethnic ancestry Asians may possibly identify.

Tony Lam, also of Chinese and Japanese ancestry, prefers to call himself an American Asian. As the son of a career soldier and a veteran himself, he chooses to emphasize his patriotism to this country by asserting his American identity first. And yet, Tony also expressed great frustration over what could be characterized as a societal "blindspot" to the role Asian Americans have played in defending this country:

> Q: How do you identify yourself?
> A: American Asian. . . . I saw that parade in '92 on Hollywood Boulevard and they had veterans marching down. (pause) I tell you which group was missing. Asian. There was not one Chinese, Japanese, Filipino, Korean, Pacific Islander in uniform. Now I know they served. (pause) It's either the fault of those people who plan that parade or the fault due to a lack of vigilance for an Asian veterans organization by not insisting on it (pause) through all that hard times. I still persist that I'm an American but I'm not going to deny that I'm Asian because first thing they're not going to let me do it. I still got to (pause) about Asian culture whether I like it or not. . . . You see, Caucasians must understand that they (pause) put that on us and we must learn to confront people who say those kinds of things so we should say things like, "No I don't know that, I hope you know your French food. Or, he's Scottish (pause) look, look, what are you? Okay, Armenian. Tell me about Armenian stuff. We should put that on them. I think it's fair, they got to get a taste of what they did or how dumb they sound or who's truly American. Yeah, I am American and then Asian.

Tony considers himself to be a loyal American who risked his life to defend his country. The sad irony, however, is that there are others who do not consider the United States to be his country. Even if he chose to identify solely as an American, he believes "they," presumably white Americans, would not legitimate his choice—"They're not going to let me do it."

Others also spoke about the pressures they experience to identify in ethnic or racial terms. Ted Uyematsu:

> Q: How about identifying as just a plain old American?
> A: Yeah I would, but you know (pause) there's (pause) but then again you have to realize that I'm not your typical American when people think American. In your mind you don't see a whole blooded Japanese guy you know. They conjure up some blond headed dude that (pause) but I would have no problem seeing myself but I think it would confuse certain people if I were to say that.

Ted demonstrates a clear understanding of what the typical American male presumably looks like—and he does not even come close. Subsequently, while he has no qualms calling himself an American Ted believes others might take issue with him since he believes white ethnics feel, to use Herbert Blumer's[17] terminology, a sense of "proprietary" claim to the term. As such, he was unsure how his usage of the term would be received.

Others were even more direct in stating how inappropriate *in other people's eyes* it would be if they were to identify as Americans without any nationality hyphenation. Rick Wubara describes why he identifies as Japanese American:

I don't think I can be just American just for the fact that I look different from the typical American, white. (Why not just Japanese then?) Because I definitely am Americanized, an American raised in America. And I don't always agree with what Japanese, Japan stands for.

"I look different from the typical American." "I'm not your typical American." Statements such as these vividly convey the dilemma Asian ethnics, as racialized ethnics, face. They have learned by watching how others respond to them that they are viewed as outsiders to this society. Despite being longtime Americans they are not perceived as such since they do not fit the image of what a "real" American looks like.[18] This, I believe, is the key difference separating the white ethnic from the Asian ethnic experience. While white ethnics must actively assert their ethnic uniqueness if they wish this to feature prominently in their interactions with others, Asian ethnics are assumed to be foreign unless proven otherwise.

"They still look at the Chinese as foreigners" — The Realization of Difference.

No one ever asks a Polish American after the first generation why they don't speak Polish or are they ashamed of being Polish because they don't speak Polish. But (they will say) that you're ashamed of being Chinese, or you don't understand Chinese culture because you don't speak Chinese. But no one ever asks that of anybody else. I mean if your grandparents speak French, and you still cook coq au vin, but no one ever demands that you also know how to speak French. And no one ever asks you, where did you come from.

The frustration Carol Wong experiences is hard to miss in this passage. She believes there is a double standard in operation. While white ethnics are free to discard their ethnic links and merge with the American mainstream after the first generation, Asian ethnics do not have this option; an assumption of foreign- ness stubbornly clings to them irrespective of generational status.

Carol was not alone in her way of thinking. Others concurred with her assessment of the status difference between Asians and whites. Based on their experiences with prejudice, discrimination, and stereotyping they understand that the public is unable or un- willing to distinguish between Asian ethnics and immigrants. That these respondents, residents of such diverse and cosmopoli- tan areas as Los Angeles and San Francisco, still feel this way is telling. Subsequently, they believe their status in this society is vulnerable to changing social, political, and economic conditions beyond their personal control.[19] For instance, the majority agree their lives would be affected not only if the United States were to go to war with their country of origin but if war were declared on any Asian country since "whites or blacks can't tell the difference between Asian Americans and Asians." Carol Wong again:

> When there was all the whoop-to-do about Japan and all the businesses that Japan owns and all the property that Japan owns in this country, (while) England, Canada and the Nether- lands own a whole lot more individually than Japan ever did. But it was this thing of the Pacific horde. And of course Amer- ican car companies screwed up and they had to blame it on someone else.

References to Japan and Middle Eastern "bashing" as well as the wartime internment of Japanese Americans were frequently made to substantiate their views. And while not everybody be- lieved that a mass internment sanctioned by the federal govern- ment could happen again, most agreed that hostilities from the general citizenry were likely. Friends and coworkers who knew them as individuals probably would not act differently, but strangers and nativists certainly would. As Jonathan Tse put it, "They'd see us as being evil and they'd start, it's just like what they do with the Middle East and the Soviet Union. They would all look down on us."

We see this with the recent Asian campaign finance scandal involving questionable campaign donations made to the Democratic National Committee as well. That the possible wrongdoing of a handful of Asians and Asian Americans has cast a shadow over all Asian American donors is an all too familiar scenario. Contributors with the misfortune of having an Asian or Asian sounding last name have had to endure intrusive questions concerning their citizenship status and other highly personal matters. As Daphne Kwok, Executive Director for the Organization of Chinese-Americans put it, "Wouldn't a more neutral approach be to investigate all contributions over $5,000 and not just those targeting the APA community?"

Would the lives of white ethnics be affected if war were declared on their country or countries of origin? Most believed no. Morrison Hum, who was required to wear a badge identifying himself as Chinese during World War II, looked to the past to substantiate his opinion:

Q: If the United States were to go to war with Europe . . .
A: Probably not, because they are considered white. I don't believe so. Like the Germans. (pause) But you stand out because you are colored. It would make you feel bad too. Feel ashamed of your native country. "Whiteness," once again, is equated with being American; "Asianness" is not.

And because it is not, questions regarding the Asian ethnics' loyalty to this country are raised. This was the case during World War II and many of the Asian ethnics believe this is still the case today. Daphne Kitano:

Q: If the United States were to go to war with Europe . . .
A: No, because it didn't really happen to Germans in World War II and they were our enemies and the Italians were our enemy and it didn't happen to them, you know, which leads me to believe the obvious that it was just on the basis of color of your skin. If you weren't white and you were Japanese and even though you were American you were still the enemy. . . . I still feel there's some trend that the media is generating about how Japanese are taking over the United States

or buying out everything, which is totally not the real case. They're not looking at the investments that England has in the United States, or the Canadians or Australians, the Dutch, the Germans. And I was like, you know, the media say all these things about Japanese taking over and it (pause) it's going to affect me here, a Japanese American, because the ignorant white person isn't going to (pause) it's going to be like, "Oh you're just one of those Japanese who are trying to take over." So they don't realize the effect, the effect on how people view Asians in this country.

As for the possibility of another mass internment, opinions were mixed. About a third did not believe it could happen again. Some felt the country had learned its lesson and would not repeat the mistakes made with Japanese Americans. References were made to how "times have changed" as indicated by interest in multicultural issues and greater respect for human rights. Others referred to the growing political power of Asian American organizations who would fight against such actions. Still a third response, captured by Greg Okinaka's comments, suggests that the imprisonment of the spirit may be more damaging than that of the flesh:

> I don't think they'd be sending mass people to prison, but if something like a war came up with the Japanese, you would be getting a lot more widespread discrimination. It's more like a mental internment than an actual physical internment, understand?

The rest either conceded internment was possible but unlikely or adamantly agreed that mass incarceration was not only possible but probable if the political situation became volatile enough.

In response to the question, *"Does it mean something different to say you are an American of Irish (any European ethnicity) descent compared to saying you are an American of Chinese or Japanese descent?"* Morrison Hum had this to say:

> Yeah there is a difference. They still look at the Chinese as a foreigner. For an Irish American, they don't see him as a foreigner. I don't know how long it is going to take, but you are still looked upon as a foreigner. I think so.

Diane Okihiro chose to personalize the question by applying it to her Irish American girlfriend and herself. Her response is revealing:

> Like my girlfriend, it's kinda funny because she's of Irish descent, but people would never think that or ask where are you from because they see her as being Caucasian. And if they look at me they would say, "Oh where are you from," because I'm perceived as being Asian first. It's like girl, an Asian girl, and anything that follows after that. For my girlfriend it would be like, she's white, she's of Irish descent but it doesn't really matter. It's like way down the list of whatever.

Here Diane refers to her racial distinctiveness as featuring prominently in her interactions with strangers; she believes it is the first aspect of her identity to register with others. This, in turn, triggers the stereotype that she must be from someplace else since being Asian is not equated with being from the United States. No one ever thinks to ask her girlfriend of Irish ancestry where she is from, however, given her white racial background combined with a high degree of acculturation.

A related stereotype many Asian ethnics encounter is an assumption of Chinese or Japanese language fluency and its corollary, the surprise over their fluency in English. As Terry Winters put it, "I've had this happen all my life when some stranger will come up and start speaking Japanese to me and I don't speak Japanese." Women, in particular, were more likely to recall instances where unsolicited male strangers approached with the intent of "hitting" on them or otherwise engaging them in conversation. Marilyn Tokubo:

> I get offended and then there's times when somebody will come up to me in a bar and say, "Are you Japanese," and start speaking Japanese to me and actually (pause) people do this to me all the time and I don't know why it's me over anybody else. They always seem to zoom in on me and start speaking this, trying to speak Japanese.
> Q: Who approaches you?
> A: Whites. They'll come up and start gibber jabbering in Japanese and I'll just kind of have to laugh it off and this happens a lot and also that they assume that I know how to speak Japanese and they also want to show off their Japanese.

Far from flattering, Marilyn experiences these instances as invasions into her privacy and resents the arrogance these men display in assuming they are welcome to approach her. Popular racialized and gendered stereotypes such as the "Suzie Wong" character portraying Asian women as subservient, acquiescent, sensual, and exotic have encouraged white men in particular to view the Asian woman as an object for their entertainment.[20] Also at play in situations such as these is the element of white male privilege, the sense of entitlement those in the "driver's seat" feel whether consciously or not.

Other language stereotypes abound. Michael Lowe, a manager for a chain electronics store in the Bay Area, deals with irate customers all of the time. After he soothed one woman who called to complain over purchasing a faulty CD player she exclaimed, "Thank God you're an American! I'm tired of dealing with all those ching chong people!" Another respondent, Barry Sato, who spends a large portion of his day on the phone with clients, struggles with the preconceived notions of those he does business with and their subsequent reactions when they meet in person:

> I think a couple of times my jaws hit the ground. Why should my English be any different? . . . Mostly I was shocked. When I met someone who I've talked on the phone with and when they saw me they'll go, "I didn't realize you were Asian." That was the first time. I was shocked. And on the other side when I met them what I really want to say was, "Oh, I couldn't tell you were black over the phone either." But I held my tongue because now let's not have a fight (laugh).

Without the benefit of sight or knowledge of his last name, Barry's client was surprised to learn he had been conducting business with a Japanese American. Barry has since gotten used to this kind of response from his clients. He claims it does not bother him anymore; he just shakes his head in amazement over the regularity with which people cannot believe that he doesn't "sound" Japanese over the phone.

For the most part, the stereotyping Asian ethnics experience is not intended to wound or alienate. Rather, incidents are largely based on ignorance. Even when no ill will is intended, however, hurt is inflicted since, once again, they are reminded that they are viewed not as individuals but as stereotyped members of a group relegated to a foreign status. The frustration comes from trying so hard to be treated as distinct individuals and then confronting thoughtless stereotypes. Tony Lam:

> My closest friend happens to be Caucasian. He says, Tony, you're a good old boy like me, you know. You're just Asian on the outside but you like burgers and so forth and all that. I told him I like Caucasian women, they look pretty good to me, you know, everybody else, I like Asian too . . . so how does he see me? He sees me as an American but sometimes he has to make off-handed comments like, "Aah So," or something like that and I go, "Why do you have to bring that for? I don't go up to you and say you want to go dance country with all the other rednecks. Why can't we just be neutral?"

Yet another way Asian ethnics are reminded of their marginalized status centers around the stares, comments, and even threats they receive from others who look upon them as strangers or intruders in a public place; about half have felt out of place or suddenly conscious of their racial background during a stop somewhere. Most often this occurs when they travel or visit unfamiliar places but it can also happen in their own neighborhoods. I personally experienced an example of this at a supermarket in the city of San Marino, an affluent suburb in southern California where many Chinese immigrants have recently moved. While standing in line to pay for my items two older white women behind me began to complain over how Asians were taking over the area. Neither woman appeared concerned that I, an Asian woman, could hear everything they were saying; they either assumed I could not speak English or did not care in the least.

The experience of walking into a restaurant ("a McDonalds in the middle of nowhere") and having all heads turn to watch them was a familiar story. Sharon Young:

> (T)here are times when you go to a restaurant or you go somewhere like a business or something and you walk in and they're all Caucasians. I don't know if it's unconscious or what, but you feel like they're staring at you or they're looking or they notice. Even coming down my street sometimes which basically is all

white and we've all lived here for years and still when we drive they all kinda stare at you like, "Oh my gosh, they're Asian." Like we used to experience that a lot when we went to the market and we'd go there and get all these stares, people would look at you. And you first think, "Haven't you seen an Asian in your life?" God, just because you have dark hair and different skin, it's like, wake up, you know. It's occasional, but it's still kinda sad because you still feel that.

Feeling uncomfortable while stopping in gas stations, gift shops, and other stores was also frequently mentioned as was receiving poor service. In all of these cases, the message they received was that they were "out of place" or clearly did not belong where they were. In some cases, local residents were merely confused over their presence and viewed them as oddities. In other cases, hostility was unmistakable. Tony Lam:

> I passed this car, these two Caucasians were in the car. They were slow and I just passed them and they notice that I was Asian and drove alongside me. We drove through the entire town side by side and then they tried to hit me. At first they called me names and I rolled my window up. So then he set himself on the window of the passenger side and started to give me the finger and I ignored it and drive down the road. . . . They tried to run me off, hit me, I guess. So I sped up and got to a four corner stop . . . and I look up and I saw the driver there but where is the other fella? And I find out what he was doing. He grabbed a bottle and now he is sitting himself on the window and trying to position himself so that when they got near me he could throw the bottle. I turn my lights on. They thought I was braking and they suddenly brake and threw the bottle and miss and I drove through the lights. I drove through the stop sign taking a risk of I might be hit or arrested by the police.

Similarly, Paul Leong described the unease he felt while working in a rural part of California. While he never experienced anything close to what Tony Lam endured, he maintained an alert stance during his time there:

> When I worked in Sacramento we used to go to different places in the valley, like all white towns and stuff like that, quite a bit.

And you do feel kinda conscious about how they're gonna treat you and that kind of thing, and I think it actually has maybe socially hindered me in some ways. But I also (pause) it's a safety mechanism because you never know what's going to happen. You're out there in the middle of farmland USA and shit. You never know if Joe Bob's gonna come around the corner with a rake and shit. It's never happened yet, but I do feel very sensitive about that.

Women traveling to unfamiliar places typically encountered gender stereotypes that were used to make sense of their presence. Patti Ito: "When I've gone to places like Oklahoma, you know, I kind of feel like they think I'm some sort of Korean bride that some army person brought back." Again, the point is that some special explanation is needed to placate local residents as to why there are "strangers" in their community.

For their psychological as well as physical survival, many Asian ethnics have honed their sensory skills to a finely tuned level. Upon entering an unfamiliar environment, their "antennae" come out looking for any signs of potential trouble to gauge the degree of safety. The price paid for such attentiveness, however, is high. As Paul Leong mentioned earlier, he has socially hindered himself by being on the lookout for trouble so intently. And yet, he feels compelled to do so because he knows in some communities he is not welcome solely because he is not white.

"When I'm around real Chinese people they don't think I'm Chinese." — Not Asian Enough

As if being deemed inauthentically American wasn't enough, Asian ethnics must also contend with not being seen as Chinese or Japanese enough. They face societal expectations to *be ethnic* since others assume they should be closer to their ethnic roots than to their American ones. Carol Wong, a dietitian, speaks about an experience she had while on the job:

I had just moved to New York, maybe four months, and this doctor came up to me and said something to me in Chinese and I turned around and said something like "Are you talking to me?" And he said yeah, and I said, "I don't speak Chinese." This was a Caucasian guy . . . and he starts going into this tirade like, "Are you ashamed of where you came from, da da da da." And I turned around to him and I looked him straight in the face and I said, "How many Americans do you know who go around speaking Chinese? I'm not ashamed of where I come from. I come from Fresno. The place that provides you with those little red boxes of Sunmaid Raisins."

Whereas for later generation white ethnics to identify along ethnic lines is a matter of personal choice, my respondents have not found this to be the case for them; not identifying in ethnic or racial terms is problematic in their interactions with non-Asians. Asian ethnics are not free to practice *symbolic ethnicity* to the degree white ethnics are.[21] Symbolic ethnicity for the latter, as Stephen Steinberg argues, comes out of a crisis of cultural authenticity that has left later generations with only high profile symbols to champion: "People desperately wish to 'feel' ethnic precisely because they have all but lost the prerequisites of 'being' ethnic.[22]" Asian ethnics, on the other hand, are expected to "be ethnic" in spite of similar degrees of acculturation. Others consistently expect them to identify ethnically (as Chinese or Japanese) or racially (as Asian) as well as be knowledgeable about Chinese or Japanese "things," and express dissatisfaction when they are not.

Meanwhile, Asian ethnics get it from the other end as well. That is, Asian ethnics also experience judgment from their foreign-born counterparts who see them as "too American," not knowledgeable enough about Chinese or Japanese ways. While Asian immigrants were not interviewed for this project, other studies have documented the attitudes the foreign born hold toward the native born.[23] Bernard Wong's work on intergenerational relations in New York's Chinatown is particularly noteworthy:

> In dealing with the members of the community, the traditional (foreign-born) elite tend to claim that they are the "real Chinese," as opposed to the second- and third-generation Chinese Americans. A "real" Chinese means one who speaks and writes the Chinese language, interacts with other Chinese in a "humane," "Chinese" way, practices all the Chinese customs, celebrates the important Chinese festivals, and so on.[24]

My respondents are well aware of how they differ from their foreign-born counterparts in both superficial (i.e., style of clothing, accent, how they carry themselves) as well as more meaningful ways (culture, values, beliefs, lifestyles). They are also aware that immigrants see them as less culturally authentic. Kevin Fong:

> Q: How do you identify?
> A: First and foremost I was born Chinese and this goes back to what my brother told me one time. He said, and I totally related with that, "You're born Chinese, but when you're around Chinese people, like when I'm around real Chinese people, they don't think I'm Chinese because I was born here and I'm kind of Americanized. And if I call myself an American, I hang around with American guys, they don't consider me American because I don't look American, I'm Chinese. So I would say that I'm Chinese American first and foremost. I was born Chinese and I'm proud of that but I'm also proud that I'm an American of the United States.

Except for a handful whose personal histories include prolonged time spent in the motherland or who came from a family with an immigrant parent, few respondents feel comfortable identifying with the foreign born. The vast majority see themselves as a breed apart, as clearly being related to but distinct from Asian immigrants.

As a compromise, most have chosen, like Kevin Fong, to adopt a hyphenated identity to honor their American as well as ethnic roots. Victor Ong spoke insightfully about his decision to call himself a Chinese American:

> Usually I say Chinese American because I realize I'm not Chinese. People from China come over here and like, whoa, they're like a foreign species. And I'm not American because just one look and I'm apart. I used to struggle with this question a lot and to make a long story short, Chinese American is a hybrid of its own. It's kind of like Afro-Americans. Boy, they're not African and they're not American and it's just its own species and that's the way it is.

Both Victor's and Kevin's comments aptly summarize the authenticity dilemma confronting Asian ethnics as well as hint at how they begin to address the dilemma, a topic to which I now turn.

"Where are you really from?" — Playing the Ethnic Game and Other Acts of Resistance

Most Asian ethnics have been asked the question, "Where are you from?" at some point in their lives. All have learned that the question really being asked is, "What is your ancestral homeland?," since answering "San Jose" or "Los Angeles" usually fails to satisfy whoever is asking. Such a localized answer typically results in the response, "No. Where are you *really* from?" While some answer straightforwardly, others choose to play an "ethnic game" with their interrogator. This involves mischievously bantering with whomever is asking the question until they give up or refine their query. Dani Murayama's and Greg Okinaka's experiences provide excellent examples:

> (Dani) A lot of times people will come up to me and ask me where I'm from and I'll answer Los Angeles and they'll look at me really strange (laugh). But that's where I'm from and then they'll say, "No, no, no. Where were you born?" And I'll say Los Angeles. And then they'll ask me where my parents were born and I'll tell them the United States. And then they'll ask me where my grandparents were born and I'll tell them the United States (laugh).
>
> (Greg) I get it all the time. I think it's kind of funny because I always say, "I'm from so and so." And then they say, "No. Where are you from?" And then you say, "Well, actually I'm from Oakland." "No. Where are you *from*?" "And then it's like, "Well, I'm from North Dakota, if you want to go there." Then it's like, "No, no, no. . . ." (laugh)

What strikes me about these passages is the insistence on the part of their interrogators to get to the *truth*, to find out where Dani and Greg are *really* from. They were not satisfied with the responses provided because they believed these two had to come from some place other than this country. Dani and Greg, for their parts, were only willing to provide opaque answers as a gesture of defiance.

Tony Lam, who also plays the ethnic game, refuses to give others the satisfaction of pigeon holing him as a foreigner to this country:

> Yeah, I get that all the time. You know what I tell them? I use the tact now. This guy (was) asking me and I could tell he's

really excited (and) he's anticipating the answer. "Will it be Thailand? Will it be Japan?" He's all excited. Maybe he went to the Orient. And I tell him with a perfect look, "San Jose." And all of a sudden he has all this enthusiasm, flustered and goes, "Oh. San Jose." I'm answering honestly where I came from.

Some might think Tony, Dani, and Greg are being unnecessarily sensitive to a seemingly innocuous question. After repeatedly facing this line of questioning, however, they are marking out their own ways of defiance. After all, the answers they provide are truthful given what is being asked. Where are they from? They are from this country as are their parents and, in some cases, their grandparents and great-grandparents.

While a few experience dissonance or guilt over their seeming drift away from cultural traditions, the majority of my respondents are unapologetic about their lifestyles. The sentiment is captured well by Jan Muramoto:

I took three years of Spanish to qualify for college because it was easier, and you know, people say to me all the time, don't you feel guilty? And I say, you know, you can't live your life feeling guilty. It doesn't make me any less of an Asian person because I can't speak the language. It doesn't make me any less of a person because I don't make sushi. There are other things that I teach my children. I mean my parents didn't speak Japanese at home. They spoke English to us. . . . We speak English at home. We live in this country. We speak English.

Jan is clearly defensive over her authenticity as an "Asian person" because she has been challenged on this issue before. However, she is rebelling against a static, essentialized definition, which stipulates that unless she is fluent in Japanese and can make sushi she is not "really Japanese." She prefers a more fluid interpretation of culture since that is how she was brought up to understand it herself.

Respondents like Jan represent a powerful emerging voice within the Asian American community. They are self-consciously aware of how far the proverbial apple has dropped from the tree and how the resulting sapling has adapted to its own unique circumstances and soil conditions. As such, they are actively engaging in the process of cultural production and are embracing the resulting forms and practices.[25]

"They passed on a Chinese-American culture to me, not as much a Chinese culture"—Ethnic Authenticity on Their Own Terms

Despite all of the ways ethnicity has ceased to influence their daily lives, Asian ethnics do consider it to be a salient aspect of their identity. What matters to them, however, has increasingly little to do with cultural traditions as practiced by Chinese and Japanese nationals. Gary Hong:

> My parents don't have a whole lot to pass on because my dad doesn't speak the language. The primary thing they could have passed on to me would be the language because both my grandparents and my parents don't do traditional stuff like lighting incense. We're all Christians so we don't do the Buddhist or Confucius things.
> Q: So what Chinese American things did they pass on?
> A: It's not really cultural, partly social. Being Chinese American, being Asian American, it's a combination of ideological, cultural, social. There is that social part because there is a community there. Just because they don't do traditional things like lighting incense in a temple doesn't mean that it's not a Chinese American community. Chinese American community in the sense that they do things together, they all understand each other, have a common background, look out for each other, do things in the community together. That's what they passed on to me. A recognition, they brought me up in that community, playing sports, doing things with their other friends. In that sense that's what they passed on to me. They passed on a Chinese American culture to me, not as much a Chinese culture.

The attention of respondents like Gary Hong rests squarely on the evolving cultural patterns being generated in this society by Japanese American, Chinese American, and other Asian American groups. The cultural elements they feel are worth retaining are the emergent as well as reinterpreted values and practices they grew up with, which weave together strands of Japanese, Chinese, and American mainstream cultures. Lisa Lowe speaks to this theme when she writes: "The making of Asian American culture includes practices that are partly inherited, partly modified, as well as partly invented."[26] Gary Hong again, reflecting on his third-generation father:

> My dad is uniquely Chinese American in the true sense. He's really Asian American because he grew up in (pause) because his father passed away, he doesn't even speak Chinese. . . . I think there is a direct link there. So he does have a background in Chinese culture because he hung out with all these Chinese people in the Bay Area in that generation in Berkeley. There are a lot of Chinese people around, so he had the culture, he knows some of the stuff. He didn't practice it but he knew it. He hung around Chinese people a lot. He's definitely Chinese but a lot of the things they did as kids were like Happy Days, American stuff. Cars, girls, and baseball. That's kinda cool. So I look at all of them as Chinese American.

Gary makes an important observation in stressing the cultural fusion that took place for his father's generation. Without denying the historical basis of culture, it is essential not to reify it either. Traditional Chinese culture was not simply transferred over to the United States and preserved in the exact same state as when the first Chinese came over. A uniquely Chinese American culture developed in this country and it was within this cultural context that his father grew up. In turn, an ethnic identity fashioned out of both Chinese and American elements was forged and adopted by Gary's father. What Gary's father passed on to him was not Chinese culture as traditionally defined but, rather, what Yancey et al. (1976) refer to as an emergent identity and practices centered around both Chinese and "American stuff," created and shared with coethnics and in some cases other Asian ethnics.

Greg Okinaka, a sansei in his twenties, was particularly insightful about the dynamic character of culture. He describes his philosophy:

> I mean, I think it is very important for the next generation, the younger, the next bunch of people to realize . . . I think there's such a specific Japanese, no not Japanese, well, Asian American (pause) culture that has evolved and that is in the process of evolving (and) that it's more important to learn about that than it is to learn about . . . I mean because the Asia, the Japan that my parents knew when they were my age was a completely

different Japan than I know at my current age. And it's gonna be a different Japan that any other generations learn fifteen or twenty years from now.

Greg is speaking of a "homegrown" culture and identity that reflect the cultural frames of reference influencing his life, and his pride as well as defensiveness around that developing identity are important features. It is more important, in his estimation, to be well versed in the culture that is evolving here in the United States (which is increasingly pan-ethnic in orientation) than in Japan's culture, a value he acquired from his parents and continues to uphold in his own life.

One cultural value that has been modified to reflect the boundary shifts taking place among different Asian ethnic groups includes their preference for ethnic friendships. While clearly not a new cultural value, my respondents have put their own twist on it by expanding the category pan-ethnically to include Asian Americans more generally. Less than a fifth described their friends as consisting exclusively of coethnics, but more than a third have friendship circles consisting primarily of other Asian Americans; the remainder describe their friends as being racially diverse or primarily white.

Those with predominantly Asian American friends claim to share a special bond or sense of kinship with them which they do not necessarily experience with non-Asians. According to Barry Sato, "It was easier to hang out with Asians. Thing is when you talk about things, your experiences and values seem to mesh a little bit more." References were repeatedly made to perceived similarities between themselves and their Asian American friends based on similar upbringing, parental expectations, values, and even experiences with stereotyping and intentional prejudice, discrimination, and marginalization. These shared experiences, as Laura Nee put it, result in comfortable interactions: "There's less explaining because we were brought up pretty much the same." Whereas in the past this sentiment would have extended only to coethnics, today it increasingly applies to other Asian Americans irrespective of ethnicity.

As was the case during their childhood, the activities they engage in with their Asian American friends are not ethnically centered in any traditional sense. As later generation Americans, they are highly acculturated and participate in many of the same activities as other Californians irrespective of race or ethnicity. About a third are members of one or more organized ethnic activities. Especially popular among younger respondents are Asian American sports leagues of which there are myriad to choose from: JAVA (Japanese-American Volleyball Association), Westside Volleyball League, and LA Asian Ski Club to name only a few. Some have also joined college fraternities and sororities and other campus groups geared to Asian American students. For professionals, there are a wide range of business networks and employee associations to choose from where members share both class and ethnic resources (i.e., Asian Professional Exchange (APEX), Asian Business League (ABL), Asian-American Journalist Association, Young Generation Asian Professionals (YGAP), Asian Business Association (ABA), M Society, and Orange County Chinese-American Chamber of Commerce). Vo's (1996) research, for example, on the San Diego branch of the ABA demonstrates how members develop business opportunities and deal with issues such as glass ceilings in the workplace and trade with the Pacific Rim. And, of course, membership in long-standing political interest groups such as the Japanese American Citizens League (JACL) and the Organization of Chinese Americans (OCA) is common, as is church attendance in predominantly Asian congregations.

In this sense, Asian ethnics are carrying on a tradition dating back to an earlier period of racism and social exclusion. Because native-born Asian Americans were barred from participating in mainstream clubs and activities with white children, community leaders took it upon themselves to sponsor their own chapters and clubs to meet their children's needs.[27] Many of these clubs have survived to the present day and, while no longer forced to participate in ethnically specific leagues, many choose to do so out of family tradition or sense of comfort.

Their preferences toward Asian American friends are also extending to their dating practices. Of the forty-eight single men and women we interviewed, only four exclusively date coethnics. The rest date interracially (mostly commonly with whites) as well as interethnically (with other Asian Americans). That they frequently choose white partners is not surprising given their demographic dominance and availability (Sung 1990).

What is surprising, however, is how frequently they date other Asian Americans, their casual attitudes toward doing so, and in some cases, the purposefulness of their choices. Some, in fact, do not consider it interdating since, "after all, we're both Asian." Diane Okihiro, for example, spoke of the interchangeability in her mind between Chinese American and Japanese American men:

> I think most of the guys I've gone out with who are Chinese American, the guy I'm with now, it's not any different. To me it's the same as being with someone who would be Japanese American.

While at an earlier time a Japanese American woman would have encountered stubborn resistance if she dated or married a Chinese American man, today this union hardly raises an eyebrow among contemporary and single Asian ethnics.

I believe the matter of fact attitude my respondents have toward interethnic dating is both the producer and product of an intense boundary shift currently taking place. More and more Asian ethnics, particularly younger ones, are defining themselves pan-ethnically as Asian Americans and identifying along racial lines.[28] They subsequently can have a casual attitude because they believe it is still "within the family," the family of Asian Americans, that is.

This has not come about easily or naturally, however. Pan-ethnic categories are initially created by forces beyond the control of the subsumed groups and the resulting label, in this case Asian American, must first be externally imposed. Ignoring cultural, linguistic, and oftentimes long-standing animosity between different ethnic groups, members of the dominant society have historically invoked their power to categorize others according to criteria that are convenient for them.

Only over time do groups who were forcibly lumped together (usually on the basis of shared language or presumed racial similarities) begin to recognize the commonalities in their experiences and form alliances to protect and promote their collective interests.[29] Eventually, the identity that was originally imposed on them, in this case Asian American, takes on a life and meaning of its own as a new cultural base reflecting their common experiences in the United States is gradually constructed.

Ethnic distinctions matter less and less in the face of an emerging racial consciousness. This does not mean they cease to think of themselves in ethnic-specific terms as Chinese or Japanese American or that the pan-ethnic progression is irreversible or even inevitable. The point to keep in mind is that they are more willing to see themselves as Asian Americans in a larger variety of contexts.

From one perspective, my respondents' dating behavior may be viewed as further proof of the erosion of ethnicity's meaningfulness in their lives. Clearly, younger respondents do not feel constrained by social mores to exclusively date or eventually marry a coethnic. Given how many have chosen to exercise their freedom of choice, their behavior could easily be interpreted as signaling the death knell for ethnicity as fewer and fewer homogeneous couples are formed and eventually sanctioned by marriage.

Viewed from a different perspective, however, their openness to dating other Asian Americans can also be seen as an example of a new and thriving racial salience. Increasingly, the issue is not whether they date coethnics, but whether they date others within the same pan-ethnic and racialized category as themselves.

Conclusion: Who Qualifies as an American?

It would only be a slight exaggeration to say that the quintessential American experience is rooted in the experience of immigration. The ability to recall an earlier time when one's ancestors traveled great and unfamiliar distances to seek a new life, the difficulties they faced, their eventual triumph over adversity, and their contributions toward building a new nation are the stuff from which we have built our cultural mythology—countless American morality tales have been written using this basic template. White ethnics today are united by this collective public memory; the journey across the Atlantic and subsequent pioneer experience are nostalgically recalled as rites of passage toward becoming an American.[30]

Less clear is how the experiences of non-European–origin groups fit into this public memory. The fact that African Americans were forcibly brought over on slave ships or that Native Americans and Mexicans were incorporated into this country against their will, adds a troubling element to an otherwise straightforward picture of assimilation.

Unlike these other groups, Asian America has its roots in voluntary immigration. Like their European counterparts, Chinese and Japanese immigrants freely entered this country in the nineteenth and early twentieth centuries in search of economic opportunity. Where they differed, however, was in the level of exclusion, resistance, and outright rejection they encountered. This is not to deny the rejection experienced by some European groups, most notably Irish, Italians, and Poles, but the extreme "foreignness" of the Chinese and Japanese in terms of a culture, language, and phenotype so different from European and Western norms set them off for a unique degree of persecution and exclusion.

In short, while they did immigrate voluntarily, they were not put into the same category as European immigrants and therefore not worthy or capable of becoming "real" Americans. And so we have the World War II internment of innocent Japanese Americans, racist housing convenants barring rental or sale of property to "Orientals," miscegenation laws prohibiting marriages between whites and "Mongolians," and on and on. And let us not forget the 1790 Naturalization Act, which restricted citizenship eligibility to "free white persons," and which was not fully nullified until 1952.

So what becomes of groups whose experiences do not neatly fit with the collective memory of what it took to become an American? Where does that leave them today? In the case of Asian ethnics, it leaves them feeling like "guests in someone else's house," as Ron Wakabayashi, former director of the Japanese American Citizens League (JACL) puts it, "that we can never put our feet up on the table."[31] Not only do they not fit the romanticized and sentimentalized account of assimilation offered in the melting pot metaphor, their own pioneer roots, unique experiences and contributions in building this country have been and continue to be erased from collective memory. Lowe speaks powerfully to this point in her work on the Asian American experience as she explains how and why Asian Americans continue to be located outside the cultural and racial boundaries of the nation.[32] As Alba argues, what it means to be an American continues to demand European ancestry. Whites continue to feel a sense of "proprietary claim" to being the "real" Americans.[33]

Today, Asian ethnics exercise a great deal of choice regarding the elements of traditional ethnic culture they wish to incorporate or do away with in their personal lives. They befriend whom they please, date and marry whom they please, choose the careers they please, and pursue further knowledge about their cultural heritage if they please. In this sense, ethnicity has indeed become optional in my respondents' personal lives. But in another very real way, being ethnic remains a societal expectation for them despite how far removed they are from their immigrant roots or how much they differ from their foreign-born counterparts.

Notes

This chapter is a modified reprint of "Neither *Real* Americans nor *Real* Asians? Multigeneration Asian Ethnics Navigating the Terrain of Authenticity," published in *Qualitative Sociology* 22(2): 105–25, 1999.

1. Sam Chu Lin, "Radio Tirade," *Asian Week*, April 5, 1996.

2. Lee, *Unraveling the "Model Minority" Stereotype*; H. Chen, *China-town No More* (New York: Cornell University Press, 1992); M. Weiss, "Division and Unity: Social Process in a Chinese-American Community," in *Asian Americans: Psychological Perspectives*, ed. Stanley Sue and Nathanial Wagner (Palo Alto, Calif.: Science and Behavior Books, 1973), 264–73; Bernard Wong, "Elites in Chinatown, New York City," *Urban Anthropology*, 6 (1977): 1–22.

3. Harry Kitano, *Generations and Identity: The Japanese-American* (Needham Heights, Mass.: Ginn, 1992); Espiritu, *Asian-American Panethnicity*; Michael Omi, "Out of the Melting Pot and into the Fire: Race Relations Policy," in *The State of Asian Pacific America: Policy Issues to the Year 2020* (Los Angeles: LEAP Asian Pacific American Public Policy Institute and UCLA Asian-American Studies Center, 1993), 199–214.

4. More recent examples include the 1982 killing of Vincent Chin, a second-generation Chinese American, by two angry white autoworkers who saw him as a "job-stealing Jap" and the harassment of only Asian American campaign donors in response to charges of illegal campaign finance activities on the part of Asian nationals.

5. See in particular Kyeyoung Park, "I Really Do Feel I'm 1.5!" *Amerasia Journal*, 25 (1999): 139–64.

6. Findings from this study can be found in my book, *Forever Foreigners or Honorary Whites?*.

7. Herbert Barringer, Robert W. Gardner, and Michael J. Levin, *Asian and Pacific Islanders in the United States* (New York: Russell Sage Foundation, 1993).

8. John Horton, *The Politics of Diversity: Immigration, Resistance, and Change in Monterey Park, California* (Philadelphia: Temple University Press, 1995); Leland Saito, "Contrasting Patterns of Adaptation: Japanese Americans and Chinese Immigrants in Monterey Park," in *Bearing Dreams, Shaping Visions: Asian Pacific American Perspectives*, ed. L. Revilla, G. Nomura, S. Wong, and S. Hune (Pullman: Washington State University Press, 1993), 33–43.

9. Park, *Race and Culture*.

10. Gordon, *Assimilation in American Life*.

11. Gans, "Symbolic Ethnicity," 1–19; Waters, *Ethnic Options*; A. Bakalian, *Armenian-Americans: From Being to Feeling Armenian* (New Brunswick, N.J.: Transaction Publishers, 1992); Richard Alba, *Ethnic Identity in America: The Transformation of White America* (New Haven, Conn.: Yale University Press, 1990).

12. Alba, *Ethnic Identity in America*, 62.

13. John Higham, *Strangers in the Land* (New Brunswick, N.J.: Rutgers University Press, 1963).

14. See especially Gordon, *Assimilation in American Life* and Park, *Race and Culture*.

15. All names have been changed to protect the anonymity of study participants.

16. Alba, *Ethnic Identity in America*; Waters, 1990.

17. Herbert Blumer, "Race Prejudice as a Sense of Group Position," *Pacific Sociological Review*, 1 (1958): 3–7.

18. See especially Espiritu, *Asian-American Panethnicity* and Lowe, *Immigrant Acts*.

19. Setsuko M. Nishi, "Perceptions and Deceptions: Contemporary Views of Asian-Americans," in *A Look Beyond the Model Minority Image: Critical Issues in Asian America*, ed. Grace Yun (New York: Minority Rights Group, 1989).

20. D. Hamamoto, *Monitored Peril: Asian-Americans and the Politics of TV Representation* (Minneapolis: University of Minnesota Press, 1994); Elaine Kim, "Asian American and American Popular Culture," *Dictionary of Asian American History* (Chicago: University of Chicago Press, 1986).

21. See Gans for an extended discussion of "symbolic ethnicity."

22. Stephen Steinberg, *The Ethnic Myth: Race, Ethnicity and Class in America*, 2d ed. (Boston: Beacon, 1989), 63.

23. Lee, *Unraveling the "Model Minority" Stereotype*; M. Weiss and L. Uba, *Asian Americans: Personality Patterns, Identity, and Mental Health* (New York: Guilford, 1994).

24. Wong, "Elites in Chinatown, New York City," 6.

25. Nagel, "Constructing Ethnicity," 152–76; Yancey, Ericksen and Juliani, "Emergent Ethnicity: A Review and Reformulation," 391–403.

26. Lowe, *Immigrant Acts*, 65.

27. Chan, *Asian Americans: An Interpretive History*.

28. N. Onishi, "New Sense of Race Arises Among Asian-Americans," *New York Times*, May 30, 1996, A1; Shinagawa and Pang, "Asian-American Panethnicity and Intermarriage," 127–32.

29. Omi and Winant, *Racial Formation in the United States*.

30. Alba, *Ethnic Identity in America*; J. Bodnar, *Remaking America: Public Memory, Commemoration, and Patriotism in the Twentieth Century* (Princeton: Princeton University Press, 1992).

31. Michael Moore, "Scapegoats Again," *The Progressive* 52 (1988): 25–28.

32. Lowe, *Immigrant Acts*.

33. Alba, *Ethnic Identity*.

BIBLIOGRAPHY

Abramson, Harold. *Ethnic Diversity in Catholic America*. New York: Wiley, 1973.

Agbayani, Amefil. "Community Impacts of Migration: Recent Ilokano Migration to Hawaii." *Social Process in Hawaii* 33 (1991): 73–90.

Agbayani-Siewert, Pauline, and Linda Revilla. "Filipino Americans." In *Asian Americans: Contemporary Trends and Issues*, ed. Pyong Gap Min. Thousand Oaks, Calif.: Sage, 1995.

Aguino, Valentin R. "The Filipino Community in Los Angeles." Masters' thesis, University of Southern California, 1952.

Alba, Richard. *Ethnic Identity: The Transformation of White America*. New Haven: Yale University Press, 1990.

———. *Italian Americans: Into the Twilight of Ethnicity*. Englewood Cliffs, N.J.: Prentice-Hall, 1985.

Alba, Richard, and Victor Nee. "Rethinking Assimilation Theory for a New Era of Immigration." *International Migration Review* 31 (1997): 826–72.

Alexander, Meena. *The Shock of Arrival: Reflections on the Postcolonial Experience*. Boston: South End Press, 1996.

Allen, Theodore. *The Invention of the White Race*. New York: New York University Press, 1994.

Almirol, Edwin B. "Filipino Voluntary Associations: Balancing Social Pressures and Ethnic Images." *Ethnic Groups* 2 (1978): 65–92.

Alsaybar, Bangele D. "Constructing Deviance: Filipino American Youth Gangs and Party Culture." Ph.D. dissertation, University of California, Los Angeles, Department of Anthropology, forthcoming.

———. "Satanas: Ethnography of a Filipino American Street Brotherhood in Los Angeles." Masters thesis. University of California, Los Angeles, Department of Asian American Studies, 1993.

Anderson, Margaret, and Patricia Hill Collins, eds. *Race, Class, and Gender*. 4th ed. Belmont, Calif.: Wadsworth, 2001.

BIBLIOGRAPHY

Anderson, Perry. "The Origins of the Present Crisis." *New Left Review* 23 (1964): 26–35.

Anthias, Floya, and Nira Yuval-Davis, eds. *Woman–Nation–State*. New York: St. Martin's, 1989.

Applebome, Peter. "Nation's Campuses Confront an Expanding Racial Divide." *New York Times*, October 25, 1995.

Awanohara, Susumu. "Filipino-Americans: High Growth, Low Profile." *Far Eastern Economic Review* 7 (February 1991): 39–40.

Bacon, Jean. *Life Line: Community, Family, and Assimilation among Asian Indian Immigrants*. New York: Oxford University Press, 1996.

Bakalian, A. *Armenian-Americans: From Being to Feeling Armenian*. New Brunswick, N.J.: Transaction, 1992.

Bald, Vivek. "Taxi Meters and Plexiglass Partitions." In *Contours of the Heart: South Asians Map North America*, ed. Sunaina Maira and Rajini Srikanth. New York: Asian American Writers' Workshop, 1996.

Bankston, Carl L. III, and Min Zhou. "Effects of Minority-Language Literacy on the Academic Achievement of Vietnamese Youth in New Orleans." *Sociology of Education* 68 (1995): 1–17.

Barringer, Herbert, Robert W. Gardner, and Michael J. Levin. *Asian and Pacific Islanders in the United States*. New York: Russell Sage Foundation, 1993.

Basch, Linda, Nina Glick-Schiller, and Cristina Szanton-Blanc, eds. *Nations Unbounded: Transnational Projects, Postcolonial Predicaments, and Deterritorialized Nation-States*. Langhorne, Pa.: Gorden and Breach Science, 1994.

Bell, Daniel. "Ethnicity and Social Change." In *Ethnicity: Theory and Experience*, ed. Nathan Glazer and Daniel Moynihan. Cambridge: Harvard University Press, 1975.

Bentley, Carter G. "Ethnicity and Practice." *Comparative Studies in Society and History* 29 (1987): 24–55.

Bhattacharjee, Annanya. "The Habit of Ex-Nomination: Nation, Women, and the Indian Immigrants Bourgeoisie." *Public Culture* 5 (1992): 19–44.

Blumer, Herbert. "Race Prejudice as a Sense of Group Position." *Pacific Sociological Review* 1 (1958): 3–7.

Bodnar, J. *Remaking America: Public Memory, Commemoration, and Patriotism in the Twentieth Century*. Princeton: Princeton University Press, 1992.

Borrero, Grace. "Shedding Some Light on the Dark Boys." Unpublished paper for the University of California, Los Angeles, 1997.

Bozorgmehr, Mehdi. "Internal Ethnicity: Iranians in Los Angeles." *Sociological Perspectives* 4 (1997): 387–408.

240

Brake, Michael. *Comparative Youth Culture*. London: Routledge and Kegan Paul, 1985.

Cabezas, Amado, Larry H. Shinagawa, and Gary Kawaguchi. "New Inquiries into the Socioeconomic Status of Filipino Americans in California." *Amerasia* 13 (1986–1987): 1–21.

Campomanes, Oscar V. "The Institutional Invisibility of American Imperialism, the Philippines, and Filipino Americans." Paper presented at the 1993 annual meeting of the Association of Asian Studies, Los Angeles, 1993.

Carlson, Alvar W. "The Settling of Recent Filipino Immigrants in Midwestern Metropolitan Areas." *Crossroads* 1 (1983): 13–19.

Carrera, John Willshire. *New Voices: Immigrant Students in U.S. Public Schools*. Boston: National Coalition of Advocates for Students, 1988.

Chan, Sucheng. *Asian Americans: An Interpretive History*. Boston: Twayne, 1991.

Chattergy, Virgie, and Belen C. Ongteco. "Educational Needs of Filipino Immigrant Students." *Social Process in Hawaii* 33 (1991): 142–52.

Chatterjee, Partha. *The Nation and Its Fragments*. Princeton: Princeton University Press, 1993.

Chen, H. *Chinatown No More*. Ithaca, N.Y.: Cornell University Press, 1992.

Cheng, Lucie, and Philip Q. Yang. "Asians: The 'Model Minority' Deconstructed." In *Ethnic Los Angeles*, ed. Roger Waldinger and Mehdi Bozorgmehr. New York: Russell Sage Foundation, 1996.

Chung, Ruth. "Reflections on Korean American Journey." In *Struggle for Ethnic Identity: Narratives by Asian American Professionals*, ed. Pyong Gap Min and Rose Kim. Walnut Creek, Calif.: AltaMira, 1999.

Cloward, Richard, and Lloyd Ohlin. *Delinquency and Opportunity: A Theory of Delinquent Gangs*. New York: Free Press, 1960.

———. *Delinquent Boys: The Culture of the Gang*. Glencoe, NY: Free Press, 1960.

Cohen, Stanley. 1972. *Against Criminology*. New Brunswick, N.J.: Transaction, 1992.

———. *Folk Devils and Moral Panics*. London: MacGibbon and Kee, 1972.

———. *Visions of Social Control*. Cambridge, UK: Polity Press, 1985.

Cole, S. G., and M. Cole. *Minorities and American Promise*. New York: Harper, 1954.

Collins, Patricia Hill. *Black Feminist Thought: Knowledge, Consciousness, and the Politics of Empowerment*. New York: Routledge and Chapman, 1990.

Cordova, Fred. *Filipinos: Forgotten Asian Americans, A Pictorial Essay, 1763–1963*. Dubuque, Iowa: Kendall/Hunt, 1983.

Cornell, Stephen, and Douglas Hartman. *Making Identities in a Changing World*. Thousand Oaks, Calif.: Sage, 1998.

Cornell University, Asian American Studies Program. *Directory of Asian American Studies Programs*.

Cruz, Cecile V. "Relocating Myths: An Analysis of Two Filipino Transmigrants." Unpublished paper, University of California, San Diego, 1993.

Daniels, Roger. *Asian America: Chinese and Japanese in the United States since 1850*. Seattle: University of Washington Press, 1988.

Das Dasgupta, Shamita, and Sayantini DasGupta. "Astride the Lion's Back: Gender Relations in the Asian Indian Community." In *Contours of the Heart: South Asians Map North America*, ed. Sunaina Maira and Rajini Srikanth. New York: Asian American Writers' Workshop, 1996.

Das Gupta, Monisha. "What Is Indian About You? A Gendered Transnational Approach to Ethnicity." *Gender and Society* 11 (1995): 572–96.

DasGupta, Sayantini. "Thoughts from a Feminist ABCD." *India Currents* 6 (1993): 26.

DasGupta, Sayantini, and Shamita Das Dasgupta. "Sex, Lies, and Women's Lives: An Intergenerational Dialogue." In *A Patchwork Shawl: Chronicles of South Asian Women in America*, ed. Shamita Das Dasgupta. New York: Routledge, 1998.

Davis, Mike. *City of Quartz*. London: Verso, 1990.

Desperess, Leo. *Ethnicity and Resource Competition in Plural Societies*. The Hague: Mouton, 1976.

di Leonardo, Micaela. *The Varieties of Ethnic Experience: Kinship, Class, and Gender among California Italian Americans*. Ithaca, N.Y.: Cornell University Press, 1984.

District Attorney's Office. *Gangs, Crime, and Violence in Los Angeles*. Los Angeles: District Attorney's Office, 1992.

Diversity Project. *An Interim Report to the Chancellor*. Berkeley: Institute for the Study of Social Change, 1989.

Do, Hien Duc. "The New Outsiders: The Vietnamese Refugee Generation in Higher Education." Ph.D. dissertation, University of California at Santa Barbara, 1995.

Dominguez, Virginia R. "From Neighbor to Stranger: The Dilemma of Caribbean Peoples in the United States." *Occasional Papers*, No. 5. New Haven: Antilles Research Program, Yale University, 1975.

Dublin, Thomas, ed. *Becoming American Becoming Ethnic: College Students Explore Their Roots*. Philadelphia: Temple University Press, 1996.

Dumont, Jean Paul. "The Visayan Male Barkada: Manly Behavior and Male Identity in a Philippine Island." Transcript.

Dunleep, Harriet Orcutt, and Sheth Sanders. "Discrimination at the Top: American-Born Asian and White Men." *Industrial Relations* 31 (1992): 416–32.

Emirbayer, Mustafa, and Ann Mische. "What Is Agency?" *American Journal of Sociology* 103 (1998): 962–1023.

Endo, Russell, and William Wei. "On the Development of Asian American Studies." In *Reflections on Shattered Windows: Promises and Prospects for Asian American Studies*, ed. Gary Okihiro, Shirley Hune, Arthur Hansen, and John Liu. Pullman: Washington State University Press, 1988.

Espin, Oliva M. "'Race,' Racism, and Sexuality in the Life Narratives of Immigrant Women." *Feminism and Psychology* 5 (1995): 223–38.

Espiritu, Yen Le. *Asian American Panethnicity: Bridging Institutions and Identities*. Philadelphia: Temple University Press, 1992.

———. *Asian American Women and Men: Labor, Laws, and Love*. Thousand Oaks, Calif.: Sage, 1997.

———. "The Intersection of Race, Ethnicity and Class: The Multiple Identities of Second-Generation Filipinos." *Identities* 1 (1994): 234–73.

Essed, Philomena. *Understanding Everyday Racism*. Newbury Park, Calif.: Sage, 1991.

Ewen, Elizabeth. *Immigrant Women in the Land of Dollars: Life and Culture on the Lower East Side, 1890–1925*. New York: Monthly Review Press, 1985.

Fernandez-Kelly, Maria Patricia, and Richard Schauffler. "Divided Fates: Immigrant Children in a Restructured U.S. Economy." *International Migration Review* 28 (1994): 662–89.

Foner, Nancy. "The Jamaicans: Race and Ethnicity among Migrants in New York City." In *New Immigrants in New York*, ed. Nancy Foner. New York: Columbia University Press, 1987.

———. "What's New about Transnationalism? New York Immigrants Today and at the Turn of the Century." *Diaspora* 6 (1997): 355–75.

Ford, Donna Y., John L. Harris, Karen S. Webb, and Deneese L. Jones. "Rejection or Confirmation of Racial Identity: A Dilemma for High-Achieving Blacks?" *Journal of Educational Thought* 28 (1994): 7–33.

Fordham, Signithia, and John U. Ogbu. "Black Students' School Success: Coping with the Burden of Acting White." *The Urban Review* 18 (1986): 176–206.

Foucault, Michel. *Discipline and Punish: The Birth of the Prison*. New York: Vintage, 1979.

Frankenberg, Ruth. *White Women, Race Matters: The Social Construction of Whiteness*. Minneapolis: University of Minnesota Press, 1993.

Freeman, James. *Changing Identities: Vietnamese Americans, 1975–1995*. Boston: Allyn & Bacon, 1995.

Gans, Herbert. "Second Generation Decline: Scenarios for the Economic and Ethnic Futures of the Post-1965 American Immigrants." *Ethnic and Racial Studies* 15 (1992): 173–92.

———. "Symbolic Ethnicity: The Future of Ethnic Groups and Cultures in America." *Ethnic and Racial Studies* 2 (1979): 1–20.

———. "The Possibility of a New Racial Hierarchy in the Twenty-First-Century United States." In *The Cultural Territories of Race: Black and White Boundaries*, ed. Michele Lamont. Chicago: University of Chicago Press, 1998.

———. "Toward a Reconciliation of 'Assimilation' and 'Pluralism': The Interplay of Acculturation and Ethnic Retention." *International Migration Review* 31 (1997): 875–92.

Gardner, Robert W., Bryant Robey, and Peter Smith. "Asian Americans: Growth, Change, and Diversity." *Population Bulletin* 40 (1985): 1–44.

Gibson, Margaret. *Accommodation without Assimilation: Sikh Immigrants in an American High School*. Ithaca, N.Y.: Cornell University Press, 1989.

Giddens, Anthony. *The Constitution of Society*. Berkeley: University of California Press, 1984.

Giles, Winona. "Remembering the Portuguese Household in Toronto: Culture, Contradictions, and Resistance." *Women's Studies International Forum* 20 (1997): 387–96.

Ginsburg, Faye. "Dissonance and Harmony: The Symbolic Function of Abortion in Activists' Life Stories." In *Interpreting Women's Lives: Feminist Theory and Personal Narratives*, ed. Personal Narratives Group. Bloomington: Indiana University Press, 1989.

Glaser, Barney, and Anselm Strauss. *The Dictionary of Grounded Theory: Strategies for Qualitative Research*. Chicago: Aldine, 1967.

Glazer, Nathan. "Is Assimilation Dead?" *Annals of the American Political and Social Sciences* 530 (1993): 122–36.

Glick-Schiller, Nina, and Georges Fouron. "'Everywhere We Go, We Are in Danger': Ti Mano and the Emergence of a Haitian Transnational Identity." *American Ethnologist* 17 (1990): 329–47.

Glick-Schiller, Nina, Linda Basch, and Cristina Szanton Blanc. *Toward a Transnational Perspective on Migration: Race, Class, Ethnicity, and Nationalism Reconsidered*. New York: New York Academy of Sciences, 1996.

————. "Transnationalism: A New Analytic Framework for Understanding Migration." *Annals of the New York Academy of Sciences* 645 (1992): 1–24.

Gold, Steven. "Transnationalism and Vocabularies of Motive in International Migration: The Case of Israelis in the United States." *Sociological Perspectives* 40 (1997): 409–27.

Goldberg, David Theo. *Multiculturalism: A Critical Reader*. Cambridge, Mass.: Blackwell, 1994.

————. *Racist Culture*. Cambridge, Mass.: Blackwell, 1994.

Gordon, Milton. *Assimilation in American Life: The Role of Race, Religion, and National Origin*. New York: Oxford University Press, 1964.

Greeley, Andrew. "The Ethnic Miracle." *Public Interest* 45 (1976): 20–36.

————. *Ethnicity in the United States: A Preliminary Reconnaissance*. New York: Wiley, 1974.

————. *Why Can't They Be Like Us? America's White Ethnic Groups*. New York: E. P. Dutton & Company, 1971.

Hagedorn, John. *People and Folks: Gangs, Crime, and the Underclass in a Rustbelt City*. Chicago: Lakeview, 1988.

Hall, Stuart. "Cultural Identity and Cinematic Representation." In *Black British Cultural Studies: A Reader*, ed. Houston Baker Jr., Manthia Diawara, and Ruth Lindeborg. Chicago: University of Chicago Press, 1996.

Hamamoto, D. *Monitored Peril: Asian-Americans and the Politics of TV Representation*. Minneapolis: University of Minnesota Press, 1994.

Hayano, David. "Ethnic Identification and Disidentification: Japanese-American Views of Chinese-Americans." *Ethnic Groups* 3 (1981): 157–71.

Hebdige, Dick. *Subculture*. London: Methuen, 1979.

Higham, John. *Strangers in the Land*. New Brunswick, N.J.: Rutgers University Press, 1963.

Hing, Bill Ong. *Making and Remaking Asian America through Immigration Policy, 1850–1990*. Stanford: Stanford University Press, 1993.

Hirschman, Charles, and Morrison Wong. "Trends in Socioeconomic Achievement among Immigrants and Native-Born Asian Americans." *Sociological Quarterly* 22 (1981): 495–513.

Hirschman, Charles, Philip Kasinitz, and Josh DeWind. *The Handbook of International Migration: The American Experience*. New York: Russell Sage Foundation, 2000.

Hochschild, Arlie. "The Culture of Care: Traditional, Postmodern, Cold-Modern, and Warm-Modern Ideals of Care." *Social Politics* (1995): 331–46.

Hochschild, Jennifer. "American Racial and Ethnic Politics in the 21st Century: A Cautious Look Ahead." *Brookings Review* (1998): 43–46.

Hong, Joanne, and Pyong Gap Min. "Ethnic Attachment among Second-Generation Korean Adolescents." *Amerasia Journal* 25 (1999): 165–80.

Hong, Maria, ed. *Growing Up Asian American: Stories of Childhood, Adolescence and Coming of Age in America, from the 1800s to the 1990s by 32 Asian American Writers.* New York: Avon, 1993.

Horton, John. *The Politics of Diversity: Immigration, Resistance, and Change in Monterey Park, California.* Philadelphia: Temple University Press, 1995.

Huey-Long, John, Song Dombrink, and John Dombrink. "'Good Guys' and Bad Guys: Media, Asians, and the Framing of a Criminal Event." *Amerasia Journal* 22 (1996): 25–45.

Hune, Shirley, and Kenyon S. Chan. "Special Focus: Asian Pacific American Demographic and Educational Trends." In *Minorities in Higher Education*, ed. D. Carter and R. Wilson. Washington, D.C.: American Council on Higher Education, 1997.

Hurh, Won Moo, and Kwang Chung Kim. "Religious Participation of Korean Immigrants in the United States." *Journal of the Scientific Study of Religion* 19 (1990): 19–34.

————. "The 'Success' Image of Asian Americans: Its Validity, and Its Practical and Theoretical Implications." *Ethnic and Racial Studies* 12 (1989): 512–37.

Ignatiev, Noel. *How The Irish Became White.* New York: Routledge, 1995.

Ileto, Reynaldo. *Pasyon and Revolution.* Quezon City, Philippines: Ateneo De Manila University, 1979.

Issacs, Harold. *Idols of the Tribe.* New York: Harper and Row, 1975.

Janlowski, Martin Sanchez. *Islands in the Street: Gangs and American Urban Society.* Berkeley: University of California Press, 1991.

Jensen, Leif, and Yoshimi Chitose. "Today's Second Generation: Evidence from the 1990 U.S. Census." *International Migration Review* 28 (1994): 714–35.

Jo, Moon H. "Korean Merchants in the Black Community: Prejudice among the Victims of Prejudice." *Ethnic and Racial Studies* 15 (1992): 395–411.

Jocano, Landa. *Management by Culture.* Quezon City, Philippines: Punlad, 1990.

Kasinitz, Philip. *Caribbean New York: Black Immigrants and the Politics of Race.* Ithaca, N.Y.: Cornell University Press, 1992.

Katz, Jack. *Seductions of Crime: Moral and Sensual Attractions of Doing Evil.* New York: Basic, 1988.

Kibria, Nazli. "College and Notions of 'Asian American': Second Generation Chinese and Korean Americans Negotiate Race and Identity." *Amerasia Journal* 25 (1999): 29–52.

———. "The Construction of 'Asian American': Reflections on Inter-marriage and Ethnic Identity among Second-Generation Chinese and Korean Americans." *Ethnic and Racial Studies* 20 (1997): 523–44.

———. *Family Tightrope: The Changing Lives of Vietnamese Americans.* Princeton: Princeton University Press, 1993.

———. "Not Asian, Black or White: Reflections on South Asian Racial Identity." *Amerasia Journal* 22 (1996): 77–88.

Kim, Elaine. "Asian American and American Popular Culture." *Dictionary of Asian American History.* Chicago: University of Chicago Press, 1986.

Kim, Elaine, and Eui-Young Yu. *East to America: Korean American Life Stories.* New York: New Press, 1996.

Kim, Sang-Hoon. "Discovering My Ethnic Roots." In *Becoming American, Becoming Ethnic: College Students Explore Their Roots,* ed. Thomas Dublin. Philadelphia: Temple University Press, 1996.

Kitano, Harry. *Generations and Identity: The Japanese-American.* Needham Heights, Mass.: Ginn, 1992.

———. *Japanese Americans: The Evolution of a Subculture.* Englewood Cliffs, N.J.: Prentice Hall, 1976.

Kitano, Harry, and Lynn Kyung Chai. "Korean Interracial Marriage." *Marriage and Family Review* 5 (1982): 35–48.

Kitano, Harry, W. T. Yeung, L. Chai, and H. Hatanaka. "Asian American Interracial Marriage." *Journal of Marriage and the Family* 16 (1989): 696–713.

Laguerre, Michel S. *Diasporic Citizenship: Haitian Americans in Transnational America.* New York: St. Martin's, 1998.

Lee, Sharon M. "Asian Immigration and American Race-Relations: From Exclusion to Acceptance?" *Ethnic and Racial Studies* 12 (1989): 368–90.

Lee, Sharon, and Marilyn Fernandez. "Trends in Asian American Racial/Ethnic Intermarriage: A Comparison of 1980 and 1990 Census Data." *Sociological Perspectives* 41 (1998): 323–42.

Lee, Stacey. *Unraveling the "Model Minority Stereotype": Listening to Asian American Youth.* New York: Teachers College Press, 1996.

Lieberson, Stanley. "Unhyphenated Whites in the United States." *Ethnic and Racial Studies* 8 (1985): 159–80.

Lieberson, Stanley, and Mary C. Waters. *From Many Strands: Ethnic and Racial Groups in Contemporary America.* New York: Russell Sage Foundation, 1988.

Lin, Sam Chu. "Radio Tirade." *Asian Week,* April 5, 1996.

Liu, John, and Lucie Cheng. "Pacific Rim Development and the Duality of Post-1965 Asian Immigration to the United States." In *The*

New Asian Immigration in Los Angeles and Global Restructuring, ed. Paul Ong, Edna Bonacich, and Lucie Cheng. Philadelphia: Temple University Press, 1994.

Liu, John, Paul Ong, and Carolyn Rosenstein. "Dual Chain Migration: Post-1965 Filipino Immigration to the United States." *International Migration Review* 25 (1991): 487–513.

Loeb, Paul R. *Generation at the Crossroads: Apathy and Action on the American Campus*. New Brunswick, N.J.: Rutgers University Press, 1994.

Lopez, Haney. *White by Law: The Legal Construction of Race*. New York: New York University Press, 1996.

Los Angeles Times. "Crime Rates Continue Record Seven-Year Plunge." May 17, 1999.

Lowe, Lisa. "Heterogeneity, Hybridity, Multiplicity: Marking Asian Differences." *Diaspora* (Spring 1991): 24–44.

———. *Immigrant Acts: On Asian American Cultural Politics*. Durham: Duke University Press, 1996.

Lyman, Stanford, and William Douglass. "Ethnicity: Strategies of Collective and Individual Impression Management." *Social Research* 40 (1973): 344–65.

Maharidge, Dale. *The Coming White Minority: California Eruptions and America's Future*. New York: New York Times Books, 1996.

Maira, Sunaina. "Chaste Identities, Ethnic Yearnings: Second Generation Indian Americans in New York." Ph.D. thesis, Graduate School of Education, Harvard University, 1998.

Manning, Nash. *The Cauldron of Ethnicity in the Modern World*. Chicago: University of Chicago Press, 1989.

Maram, Linda E. "Brown Hordes in McIntosh Suits: Filipinos, Taxi Dance Halls, and Performing the Immigrant Body in Los Angeles, 1930s–1940s." In *Generations of Youth: Youth Cultures and History in Twentieth Century America*, ed. Joe Austin and Michael Nevin Williard. New York: New York University Press, 1998.

Massey, Douglas. "The New Immigration and Ethnicity in the United States." *Population and Development Review* 21 (1995): 631–52.

Matza, David. *Becoming Deviant*. Englewood Cliffs, N.J.: Prentice-Hall, 1969.

———. *Delinquency and Drift*. New York: Wiley and Sons, 1964.

McWilliams, Carey. *North From Mexico*. New York: Greenwood, 1968.

Miller, W. B. "Lower Class Culture as a Generating Milieu of Gang Delinquency." *Journal of Social Issues* 14 (1958): 5–19.

Min, Pyong Gap, ed. *Asian Americans: Contemporary Trends and Issues*. Thousand Oaks, Calif.: Sage Publications, 1995.

———. *Caught in the Middle: Korean Merchants in America's Multiethnic Cities*. Berkeley: University of California Press, 1996.

———. *Changes and Conflicts: Korean Immigrant Families in New York.* Boston: Allyn & Bacon, 1998.

———. "A Comparison of Post-1965 and Turn-of-the-Century Immigrants in Intergenerational Mobility and Cultural Transmission." *Journal of American Ethnic History* 18 (1999): 65–94.

———. "Contemporary Immigrants' Advantages over Turn-of-the-Century Immigrants in Intergenerational Cultural Transmission." In *Mass Migration to the United States: Classical and Contemporary Periods,* ed. Pyong Gap Min. Walnut Creek, Calif.: AltaMira, 2002.

———. "Cultural and Economic Boundaries of Korean Ethnicity: A Comparative Analysis."*Ethnic and Racial Studies* 14 (1991): 225–41.

———. "Korean Americans' Language Use." In *New Immigrants in the United States: Readings for Second Language Educators,* ed. Sandra Lee McKay and Sau-Ling Cynthia Wong. New York: Cambridge University Press, 2000.

———. "Korean Immigrants' Marital Patterns and Marital Adjustment." In *Family Ethnicity: Strengths and Diversity,* ed. Hariette McAdoo. Newbury Park, Calif.: Sage, 1993.

———. "The Structure and Social Functions of Korean Immigrant Churches in the United States." *International Migration Review* 26 (1992): 1370–94.

Min, Pyong Gap, and Youna Choi. "Ethnic Attachment among Korean-American High School Students." *Korea Journal of Population and Development* 22 (1993): 167–79.

Min, Pyong Gap, and Rose Kim, eds. "Formation of Ethnic and Racial Identities: Narratives by Young Asian-American Professionals." *Ethnic and Racial Studies* 23 (2000): 735–60.

———. *Struggle for Ethnic Identity: Narratives by Asian American Professionals.* Walnut Creek, Calif.: AltaMira, 1999.

Montero, Darrel. *Vietnamese Americans: Patterns of Resettlement and Socioeconomic Adaptation in the United States.* Boulder, Colo.: Westview, 1979.

Moore, Joan. *Going Down to the Barrio.* Philadelphia: Temple University Press, 1991.

Moore, Michael. "Scapegoats Again." The Progressive 52 (1988): 25–28.

Morales, Royal. "Pilipino Americans: Youth Gang and Delinquency." Unpublished manuscript, n.d.

Mura, David. "Strangers in the Village." In *The Graywolf Annual Five: Multi-Cultural Literacy,* ed. Rick Simonson and Scott Walker. St. Paul, Minn.: Graywolf Press, 1988.

Nagel, Joane. "Constructing Ethnicity: Creating and Recreating Identity and Culture." *Social Problems* 41 (1994): 152–76.

Nahirny, Vladimir, and Joshua Fishman. "American Immigrant Groups: Ethnic Identification and the Problems of Generations." *American Sociological Review* 13 (1965): 323.

Nelson, Candace, and Marta Tienda. 1985. "The Structuring of Hispanic Ethnicity: Historical and Contemporary Perspectives." *Ethnic and Racial Studies* 8 (1985): 49–74.

Nishi, Setsuko M. "Perceptions and Deceptions: Contemporary Views of Asian-Americans." In *A Look Beyond the Model Minority Image: Critical Issues in Asian America*, ed. Grace Yun. New York: Minority Rights Group, 1989.

Novak, Michael. *The Rise of the Unmeltable Ethnics: Politics and Culture in the Seventies*. New York: Macmillan, 1973.

Ogbu, John. "Immigrant and Involuntary Minorities in Comparative Perspective." In *Minority Status and Schooling: A Comparative Study of Immigrant and Involuntary Minorities*, ed. Margaret Gibson and John Ogbu. New York: Garland, 1991.

Ogbu, John, and Maria Eugenia Matute-Bianchi. "Understanding Sociocultural Factors in Education: Knowledge, Identity, and Adjustment." In *Beyond Language: Sociocultural Factors in Schooling, Language, and Minority Students*. Los Angeles: California State Department of Education, 1986.

Okamura, Jonathan Y. "Beyond Adaptationism: Immigrant Filipino Ethnicity in Hawaii." *Social Process in Hawaii* 33 (1991): 56–72.

Olzak, Susan, and Joane Nagel, eds. *Competitive Ethnic Relations*. New York: Academic Press, 1986.

Omatsu, Glenn. "Asian Pacific Americans: In 'Motion' and 'Transition.'" *Amerasia Journal* 18 (1992): 81–88.

———. "The 'Four Prisons' and the Movement of Liberation: Asian American Activism from the 1960s to the 1990s." In *Contemporary Asian America: A Multidisciplinary Reader*, ed. Min Zhou and James Gatewood. New York: New York University Press, 2000.

Omi, Michael. "Out of the Melting Pot and into the Fire: Race Relations Policy." In *The State of Asian Pacific America: Policy Issues to the Year 2020*. Los Angeles: LEAP Asian Pacific American Public Policy Institute and University of California, Los Angeles, Asian-American Studies Center, 1993.

Omi, Michael, and Howard Winant. *Racial Formation in the United States*. New York: Routledge and Kegan Paul, 1986.

———. *Racial Formation in the United States: From the 1960s to the 1990s*. 2d ed. New York: Routledge and Kegan Paul, 1994.

Ong, Paul. *California's Asian Population: Past Trends and Projections for the Year 2000*. Los Angeles: Graduate School of Architecture and Urban Planning and Asian American Studies Center, University of California, Los Angeles, 1989.

Ong, Paul, and Tania Azores. "The Migration and Incorporation of Fil-ipino Nurses." In *The New Asian Immigration in Los Angeles and Global Restructuring*, ed. Paul Ong, Edna Bonacich, and Lucie Cheng. Philadelphia: Temple University Press, 1994.

Ong, Paul, Edna Bonacich, and Lucie Cheng. *The New Asian Immigra-tion in Los Angeles and Global Restructuring*. Philadelphia: Temple University Press, 1994.

Onishi, N. "New Sense of Race Rises among Asian-Americans." *New York Times*, May 30, 1996, A1.

Park, Kyeyoung. "I Really Do Feel I'm 1.5!" *Amerasia Journal* 25 (1999): 139–64.

Park, Robert E. *Race and Culture*. Glencoe, Ill.: Free Press, 1950.

Park, Robert E., and Ernest W. Burgess. *Introduction to the Science of So-ciety*. 2d ed. Chicago: University of Chicago Press, 1924.

Parrenas, Rhacel. "'White Trash' Meets the 'Little Monkeys': The Taxi Dance Hall as a Site of Interracial and Gender Alliances between White Working Class Women and Filipino Immigrant Men in the 1920s and 1930s." *Amerasia Journal* 24 (1998): 115–34.

Perlmann, Joel, and Roger Waldinger. "Second Generation Decline? Immigrant Children Past and Present—A Reconsideration." *Inter-national Migration Review* 31 (1997): 893–922.

Penaranda, Oscar, Serafin Syquia, and Sam Tagatac. "An Introduction to Filipino American Literature." In *Aiiieeeee! An Anthology of Asian American Writers*, ed. Frank Chin, Jeffery Paul Chan, Law-son Fusao Inada, and Shawn Hsu Wong. Washington D.C.: Howard University Press, 1974.

Personal Narratives Group. "Origins." In *Interpreting Women's Lives*, ed. Personal Narratives Group. Bloomington: Indiana University Press, 1989.

———. "Truths." In *Interpreting Women's Lives*, ed. Personal Narratives Group. Bloomington: Indiana University Press, 1989.

Pomeroy, William J. "The Philippines: A Case History of Neocolonial-ism." In *Remaking Asia: Essays on the American Uses of Power*, ed. Mark Deden. New York: Pantheon, 1974.

Portes, Alejandro. *The New Second Generation*. New York: Russell Sage Foundation, 1996.

Portes, Alejandro, and Robert Bach. *Latin Journey: Cuban and Mexican Immigrants in the United States*. Berkeley: University of California Press, 1985.

Portes, Alejandro, and Dag McLeod. "What Shall I Call Myself? His-panic Identity Formation in the Second Generation." *Ethnic and Racial Studies* 19 (1996): 523–46.

Portes, Alejandro, and Ruben G. Rumbaut. *Immigrant America: A Por-trait*. Berkeley: University of California Press, 1990.

BIBLIOGRAPHY

———. *Immigrant America: A Portrait.* 2d ed. Berkeley: University of California Press, 1996.

Portes, Alejandro, and Min Zhou. "The New Second Generation: Segmented Assimilation and Its Variants among Post-1965 Immigrant Youth." *Annals of the American Academy of Political and Social Science* 530 (November 1993): 74–98.

Portes, Alejandro, and Richard Schauffler. "Language and the Second Generation Bilingualism Yesterday and Today." *International Migration Review* 28 (1994): 640–61.

Pyke, Karen. "'The Normal American Family' as an Interpretive Structure of Family Life among Children of Korean and Vietnamese Immigrants." Paper presented at the annual meeting of the American Sociological Association. San Francisco, 1998.

Radhakrishnan, R. "Is the Ethnic 'Authentic' in the Diaspora?" In *The State of Asian America: Activism and Resistance in the 1990s,* ed. Karin Aguilar-San Juan. Boston: South End Press, 1994.

Rayaprol, Aparna. *Negotiating Identities: Women in the Indian Diaspora.* New Delhi: Oxford University Press, 1997.

Reimers, David M. *Still the Golden Door: The Third World Comes to America.* New York: Columbia University Press, 1985.

Reitz, Jeffrey. *The Survival of Ethnic Groups.* Toronto: McGraw-Hill, 1980.

Roediger, David. *The Wages of Whiteness.* London: Verso, 1991.

Rosaldo, Renato. "Ideology, Place, and People without Culture." *Cultural Anthropology* 3 (1988): 77–87.

Rose, Peter. "Asian Americans: From Pariahs to Paragons." In *Clamor at the Gates: The New American Immigration,* ed. Nathan Glazer. San Francisco: IGS, 1985.

Rosenblum, Karen. *The Meaning of Difference: American Constructions of Race, Sex, Social Class and Sexual Orientation.* New York: McGraw-Hill, 1996.

Rosenthal, Erich. "Acculturation without Assimilation." *American Journal of Sociology* 55:2 (1960): 275–88.

Rubin, Lillian. *Just Friends: The Role of Friendship in Our Lives.* New York: Harper & Row, 1985.

Rubin-Dorsky, Jeffrey, and Shelley Fisher Fishkin, eds. *People of the Book: Thirty Scholars Reflect on their Jewish Identity.* Madison: University of Wisconsin Press, 1996.

Rumbaut, Rubén. "The Agony of Exile: A Study of the Migration and Adaptation of Indochinese Refugee Adults and Children." In *Refugee Children: Theory, Research, and Services,* ed. Frederick Ahearn Jr. and Jean Athey. Baltimore: Johns Hopkins University Press, 1991.

———. "The Crucible Within: Ethnic Identity, Self-Esteem, and Segmented Assimilation among Children of Immigrants." *International Migration Review* 28 (1994): 748–94.

Rumbaut, Rubén, and Wayne Cornelius, eds. *California's Immigrant Children: Theory, Research, and Implications for Educational Policy.* San Diego: Center for U.S.–Mexican Studies, California State University, 1995.

Rumbaut, Rubén, and Kenji Ima. *The Adaptation of South Asian Refugee Youth: A Comparative Study, Final Report to the U.S. Department of Health and Human Services.* Office of Refugee Resettlement, 1988.

Rushdie, Salman. *Imaginary Homelands.* London: Penguin, 1991.

Saito, Leland. "Contrasting Patterns of Adaptation: Japanese Americans and Chinese Immigrants in Monterey Park." In *Bearing Dreams, Shaping Visions: Asian Pacific American Perspectives*, ed. L. Revilla, G. Nomura, S. Wong, and S. Hune. Pullman: Washington State University Press, 1993.

———. *Race and Politics: Asian Americans, Latinos, and Whites in a Los Angeles Suburb.* Urbana: University of Illinois Press, 1998.

Sandhu, G. S. "Indian-Americans Are Industrious, Resourceful, and Prudent." *India Worldwide*, January 31, 1995.

San Juan, E., Jr. "Mapping the Boundaries: The Filipino Writer in the U.S.A." *Journal of Ethnic Studies* 19 (1991): 117–31.

———. *Racial Formations/Critical Transformations: Articulations of Power in Ethnic and Racial Studies in the United States.* Atlantic Highlands, N.J.: Humanities Press, 1992.

Shankar, Lavina Dhingra, and Rajini Srikanth, eds. *A Part, Yet Apart: South Asians in Asian America.* Philadelphia: Temple University Press, 1998.

Shinagawa, Larry Hajime, and Gin Yong Pang. "Asian American Panethnicity and Intermarriage." *Amerasia Journal* 22 (1996): 127–52.

Sidel, Ruth. *Battling Bias: The Struggle for Identity and Community on College Campuses.* New York: Penguin, 1994.

Simon, Rita. "Old Minorities, New Immigrants: Aspirations, Hopes, and Fears." *Annals of the American Political and Social Science* 530 (1993): 61–73.

Smith, Timothy. "Religion and Ethnicity in America." *American Historical Review* 83 (1978): 1155–85.

Stanfield, John H., II. "Espistemological Considerations." In *Race and Ethnicity Methods*, ed. John H. Stanfield II and Rutledge M. Dennis. Newbury Park, Calif.: Sage, 1993.

Steinberg, Stephen. *The Ethnic Myth: Race, Ethnicity, and Class in America.* New York: Atheneum, 1988.

———. *The Ethnic Myth: Race, Ethnicity, and Class in America.* 2d ed. Boston: Beacon, 1989.

Stevens, Gillian. "Nativity, Intermarriage and Mother Tongue Shift." *American Sociological Review* 50 (1985): 74–83.

Stonequist, Everett. *Marginal Man.* New York: Scribner's, 1961.

Strauss, Anselm, and Juliet Corbin. *Basics of Qualitative Research: Grounded Theory Procedures and Techniques.* Newbury Park, Calif.: Sage, 1990.

Suárez-Orozco, Carola, and Marcelo M. Suárez-Orozco. *Transformations: Immigration, Family Life, and Achievement Motivation among Latino Adolescents.* Stanford: Stanford University Press, 1995.

Sung, B. L. *Chinese American Intermarriage.* New York: Center for Migration Studies, 1990.

Takagi, Dana. "Post-Civil Rights Politics and Asian-American Identity: Admissions and Higher Education." In *Race*, ed. Steven Gregory and Roger Sanjek. New Brunswick, N.J.: Rutgers University Press, 1994.

——. *The Retreat from Race: Asian American Admissions and Racial Politics.* New Brunswick, N.J.: Rutgers University Press, 1992.

Takaki, Ronald. *Strangers from a Different Shore: A History of Asian Americans.* Boston: Little, Brown and Company, 1989.

——. *Strangers from a Different Shore: A History of Asian Americans.* 2d ed. New York: Penguin, 1994.

Tang, Joyce. "The Career Attainment of Caucasian and Asian Engineers." *Sociological Quarterly* 34 (1993): 467–96.

——. "The Model Minority Thesis Revisited: Evidence from the Science and Engineering Field." *Journal of Applied Behavioral Science* 33 (1997): 291–315.

Taylor, Ronald. "The Black Ethnicity and Persistence of Ethnogenesis." *American Journal of Sociology* 84 (1979): 1401–24.

Thai, Hung. "Splitting Thins in Half Is White: Conceptions of Family and Friendship, and the Formation of Ethnic Identity among Second-Generation Vietnamese Americans." *Amerasia Journal* 25 (1999): 53–88.

Tuan, Mia. *Forever Foreigners or Honorary Whites? The Asian Ethnic Experience Today.* New Brunswick, N.J.: Rutgers University Press, 1999.

U.S. Bureau of the Census. "Selected Population Characteristics of the Population by Race: March 1997. [www.bls.census.gov/cps/pub/1997/int_race.htm].

U.S. Commission of Civil Rights. *Civil Rights Issues Facing Asian Americans in the 1990s.* Washington, D.C.: U.S. Government Printing Office, 1992.

Vallangca, Roberto V. *Pinoy: The First Wave.* San Francisco: Strawberry Press, 1977.

van den Berghe, Pierre. *The Ethnic Phenomenon.* New York: Elsevier, 1981.

Vigil, James Diego. *Barrio Gangs.* Austin: University of Texas Press, 1988.

Vo, Linda. "Asian Immigrants, Asian-Americans, and the Politics of Ethnic Mobilization in San Diego." *Amerasia Journal* 22:2 (1996): 89–108.

Warner, Stephen. "The Place of the Congregation in the American Religious Configuration." In *The Congregation in American Life*. Vol. 2, ed. J. P. Wind and J. W. Lewis. Chicago: University of Chicago Press, 1994.

Warner, W. Lloyd, and Leo Srole. *The Social Systems of American Ethnic Groups*. New Haven: Yale University Press, 1945.

Waters, Mary. *Black Identities: West Indian Immigrant Dreams and American Realities*. New York: Russell Sage Foundation, 1999.

——. *Ethnic Options: Choosing Identities in America*. Berkeley: University of California Press, 1990.

——. "Ethnic and Racial Identities of Second-Generation Black Immigrants in New York City." *International Migration Review* 28 (1994): 795–820.

Wei, William. *The Asian American Movement*. Philadelphia: Temple University Press, 1993.

Weiss, M. "Division and Unity: Social Process in a Chinese-American Community." In *Asian Americans: Psychological Perspectives*, ed. Stanley Sue and Nathanial Wagner. Palo Alto, Calif.: Science and Behavior Books, 1973.

Weiss, M., and L. Uba. *Asian Americans: Personality Patterns, Identity, and Mental Health*. New York: Guilford, 1994.

Weitzer, Ronald. "Racial Prejudice among Korean Merchants in African American Neighborhoods." *Sociological Quarterly* 38 (1997): 587–606.

Williams, Brackette. "A Class Act: Anthropology and the Race to Nation Across Ethnic Terrain." *Annual Review of Anthropology* 18 (1989): 401–44.

Williams, Patricia. *The Alchemy of Race and Rights: Diary of a Law Professor*. Cambridge: Harvard University Press, 1991.

Wilson, Kenneth, and W. Allen Martin. "Ethnic Enclaves: A Comparison of the Cuban and Black Economies in Miami." *American Journal of Sociology* 88 (1982): 135–60.

Wilson, Williams J. *The Declining Significance of Race: Blacks and Changing American Institutions*. Chicago: University of Chicago Press, 1978.

——. *The Truly Disadvantaged: The Inner City, the Underclass, and Public Policy*. Chicago: University of Chicago Press, 1987.

Witzel, Michael Karl, and Kent Bash. *Cruisin': Car Culture in America*. Osceola, Wis.: Motorbooks International, 1997.

Wolf, Diane. "Family Secrets: Transnational Struggles among Children of Filipino Immigrants." *Sociological Perspectives* 40 (1997): 457–82.

Wong, Bernard. 1977. "Elites in Chinatown, New York City." *Urban Anthropology* 6 (1977): 1–22.

Wong, Morrison G. "The Cost of Being Chinese, Japanese, and Filipino in the United States, 1960, 1970, 1976." *Pacific Sociological Review* 25 (1982): 59–78.

———. "A Look at Intermarriage among Chinese in the United States in 1980." *Sociological Perspectives* 32 (1989): 87–107.

Wong, Sauline Cynthia. *Reading Asian American Literature: From Necessity to Extravagance*. Princeton: Princeton University Press, 1993.

Woo, Deborah. "The 'Overrepresentation' of Asian Americans: Red Herrings and Yellow Perils." In *Race and Ethnic Conflict*, ed. Fred Pincus and Howard Ehrlich. Boulder, Colo.: Westview, 1994.

Wulff, Helena. "Introducing Youth Culture in Its Own Right: The State of the Art and New Possibilities." In *Youth Cultures: A Cross-Cultural Perspective*, ed. Vered Amit-Talai and Helena Wulff. London: Routledge, 1995.

Yancy, William, Eugene Ericksen, and Richard Juliani. "Emergent Ethnicity: A Review and Reformulation." *American Sociological Review* 76 (1976): 391–403.

Yinger, Milton. *Ethnicity: Source of Strength? Source of Conflict?* Albany: SUNY Press, 1994.

Yu, Elena. "Filipino Migration and Community Organizations in the U.S." *California Sociologist* 3 (1980): 76–102.

Zhou, Min. *Chinatown: The Socioeconomic Potential of an Urban Enclave*. Philadelphia: Temple University Press, 1992.

———. "Growing Up American: The Challenge Confronting Immigrant Children and Children of Immigrants." *Annual Review of Sociology* 23 (1997): 63–95.

———. "Segmented Assimilation: Issues, Controversies, and Recent Research on the New Second Generation." *International Migration Review* 31 (1997): 975–1008.

Zhou, Min, and Carl Bankston III. *Growing Up American: How Vietnamese Children Adapt to Life in the United States*. New York: Russell Sage Foundation, 1998.

———. "Social Capital and the Adaptation of the Second Generation: The Case of Vietnamese Youth in New Orleans." *International Migration Review* 28 (1994): 795–820.

Zhou, Min, and Yoshinori Kamo. "An Analysis of Earnings Patterns for Chinese, Japanese, and Non-Hispanic Whites in the United States." *Sociological Quarterly* 35 (1994): 581–602.

NAME INDEX

SUBJECT INDEX

ABOUT THE CONTRIBUTORS

Bangele (Nonoy) D. Alsaybar is a Ph.D. candidate in anthropology at the University of California, Los Angeles, where he also earned an M.A. in Asian American studies. His interest in Filipino American gangs and youth culture stems from his experience as a gang outreach worker for SIPA (Search to Involve Filipino Americans), a community-based organization in Los Angeles. Through the Asian American Studies Center, he is part of a team currently researching violence among Asian American youths in Los Angeles. He has an ongoing interest in the study of folk religion and millennialism both in the Philippines and in North America.

Yen Le Espiritu is professor of ethnic studies at the University of California, San Diego. Her most recent book is *Asian American Women and Men: Labor, Laws, and Love* (Thousand Oaks, Calif.: Sage, 1997), which received the American Sociological Association, Asia/Asian American Section Book Award in 1999. She has a forthcoming book on the transnational and gendered lives of Filipino Americans. Her newest research project (in collaboration with Diane Wolf, University of California-Davis) explores the socioemotional lives of second-generation Vietnamese and Filipino Americans.

Joann Hong is an associate professor and librarian at Long Island University Library, C. W. Post Campus in Brookville, New York. She conducts library workshops for undergraduate students and is committed to several LIU-Korean University joint programs. As a catalog librarian, she contributes bibliographic records to WorldCat (the OCLC Online Union Catalog), an important research database for library users.

Nazli Kibria is associate professor of sociology at Boston University, where she teaches courses on race and ethnicity, family, and childhood. Her publications include *Family Tightrope: the Changing Lives of Vietnamese Americans* (1993). She is also the author of a forthcoming book, *Becoming Asian American: Identities of Second-Generation Chinese and Korean Americans.*

Rose Kim is a doctoral student in Sociology at the Graduate Center of the City University of New York and a Graduate Teaching Fellow at Queens College. Before entering graduate school, she worked for a year as an intern at the Los Angeles Times and, for six years, as a newspaper reporter at Newsday, the eighth largest daily newspaper in the country. During her internship at the Los Angeles Times, she belonged to a team of reporters and editors who covered the Los Angeles riots and were awarded the Pulitzer Prize for Spot News Reporting in 1992.

Pyong Gap Min is professor of sociology at Queens College and the Graduate Center of the City University of New York. He is the author of three books, including *Caught in the Middle: Korean Communities in New York and Los Angeles* (1996), the winner of two national book awards, and *Changes and Conflicts: Korean Immigrant Families in New York* (1998). He is the editor of *Asian Americans: Contemporary Trends and Issues* (1995), *Mass Migration to the United States: Classical and Contemporary Periods* (2002), and a coeditor of *Struggle for Ethnic Identity: Narratives by Asian American Professionals* (1999) and *Religions in Asian America: Building Faith Communities* (2001).

Sharmila Rudrappa is an assistant professor in Asian American studies and sociology at the University of Texas-Austin. She is working on a book on social work in a South Asian shelter for battered women, and an Indian American cultural center in Chicago. Her research interests concern race, the nation-state, and citizenship.

Hung Cam Thai is a Ph.D. candidate in the Sociology Department at the University of California, Berkeley. His research interests concern family and intimate relations among immigrants, transnational and global processes, comparative diasporic communities, and the relationships between individuals in countries of destination and countries of origin. He is currently spending a year as a scholar-in-residence at Pomona College in Claremont, California, where he is also a lecturer in sociology and Asian American studies. His dissertation examines social processes involved in the marriage arrangements between women in Vietnam and Vietnamese men who live in Western countries.

Mia Tuan received her B.A. in sociology from UC Berkeley and M.A./Ph.D. in sociology from UCLA. She is currently assistant professor of sociology at the University of Oregon in Eugene. Her research interests include racial and ethnic identity, immigrant adaptation, and racial reconciliation/mediation work. She is the author of *Forever Foreigners or Honorary Whites? The Asian Ethnic Experience Today* (1999). She is currently conducting a qualitative study (along with Jiannbin Shiao) of Asian adoptees raised by white families (funded by the Russell Sage Foundation).